HUMAN RIGHTS

HUMAN RIGHTS

FIFTY YEARS OF INDIA'S INDEPENDENCE

By

K.P. SAKSENA

GYAN

Published by

GYAN

Gyan Publishing House
5, Ansari Road
Daryaganj, New Delhi-110002
Phone: 011-47034999, 9811692060
E-mail: books@gyanbooks.com

Distribution Network
gyanbooks.com
India, USA, Canada, UK, Australia, France

ISBN: 978-81-212-0605-1 (HB)

Reprint in India, 2024
First Published, 1999

Printed at: Gyan Press, Delhi.

Human Rights: Fifty Years of India's Independence
Author: K.P. Saksena

CONTENTS

IV

V

Appendices

Preface

Commemoration of fifty years of India's independence has been a very special event. It was but natural that festivals, cultural programmes, conferences, seminars, etc. highlighting India's achievements were held in India and abroad. Many of us concerned with human rights issues thought it appropriate to do a stock-taking of the last fifty years in the context of realisation and protection of human rights. What progress have we made and where have we failed? What are the unfinished tasks and what was needed to carry on the movement towards the goal?

Hence, the Institute for World Congress on Human Rights (IWCOHR), in collaboration with India International Centre (IIC), organised in commemoration of fiftieth anniversary of India's independence, a two-day national seminar on "Human Rights in India" on 21-22nd November, 1997 at IIC. Participants included some eminent human rights activists, educationists, exponents and jurists with wide experience on human rights problems. This book has resulted from that national seminar.

The first chapter is an introduction to the theme and subthemes discussed in the volume. In the chapter that follows, Mr. K.C. Pant, presents overall observations on the state of human rights in India, its genesis and the reasons behind the lack of progress. He stresses that our priority concern should be removal of illiteracy and that to improve the state of human rights in India we should first generate awareness of these rights among the people, secondly to develop the inclination to assert their rights and thirdly to provide them access to the means of enforcement.

Mr. Justice M.N. Venkatachaliah brings to focus some of "the inherent weaknesses in our psyche and the lack of political culture". He contends that "the biggest and the most sinister violation of human rights in this country stems from the cynical and derisive attitude of those in authority to the issues of survival of this nation as a civilised country". Another inherent weakness, he points out, is that "we have yet to develop the spirit of liberty within us, as part of our political faith". He contends that although we have the "constitution guaranteeing fundamental rights and democratic system of government but we lack the spirit; no constitution can work without the spirit of constitutionalism". He strongly advocates the removal of illiteracy and points out "the beneficial effect of primary education on a variety of social issues" and that "the role and participation of the civil society in this great national endeavour is of utmost importance."

The next six chapters (4-9) are devoted to various facets of the rights of the child. Mr. Justice Ranganath Mishra shares his experiences and reflections on the state of human rights in India with special reference to the rights of the child. He contends that "what we lack is social perception and human rights culture", everyone is asking for his/her rights while ignoring their basic obligations to the society. He points out that the child is not in a position to make demands, he cannot form trade union, it is therefore obligatory on every adult to do his/her part to provide at least minimum facilities to every child for a healthy growth.

Dr. R.M. Pal presents a critical evaluation of the efforts so far made both by governmental agencies and NGOs to eradicate child labour and calls for "a significant change in the mindset" and "for a creative positive movement for implementing the overall social welfare programme". In the chapter that follows, Dr. Joseph Gathia elucidates facts and figures to indicate the sordid state of India's children and makes constructive suggestions to bring about progressive change to conform with existing laws and principles.

The next chapter (Chapter 7) provides a critique of recent Supreme Court judgements on child labour.

Ms. Pritam Arora discusses why basic rights to the child are denied in India and contends that "the problem of children cannot be resolved in isolation" as they are "directly related to overall socio-economic programmes".

Dr. Regina Mulay Parakh discusses the role of the media and how it can help promote and protect rights of the child.

The next two chapters (10-11) take up the question of human rights and law enforcement with a special reference to the rights of the under-trials and prisoners. Mr. Justice Rajinder Sachar focuses attention on the wide gap between laws and their implementation. He draws particular attention to our laws regarding the rights of the undertrials and how undertrials along with those convicted, are denied basic human rights. He specifically notes "this absurdity and anomaly in a law which permits a convicted person and sentenced to less than 2 years to contest elections even from jail and vote in an election if one is on bail even those sentenced for 10 years or less. Such a system, he argues, has led to criminalisation of politics. Another absurdity, he points out, is that undertrials in prisons not yet proved guilty are denied the right to vote while those under Preventive Detention Act are allowed to vote by postal-ballot."

Mr. Sankar Sen (in Chapter 11) provides an insight to Indian prisons and lack of adequate facilities for prisoner including medical facilities. He points out how transportation of prisoners to court and back have become a perenial problem and prisoners are very often not produced in the court because no transport and security personnels are available.

The next two chapters (12-13) take up the role and functioning of the National Human Rights Commission (NHRC). As we know establishment of NHRC was a very significant attempt in the context of realisation and protection of human rights in the post-independent India. Mr. G.S. Bhargava recapitulates the attitude of the Government of India and a section of the population concerned with human rights and their promotion in the run up to the constitution of the Commission in October 1993. He discusses the circumstances that necessitated the establishment of NHRC and analyses its functioning during the last four years and the impact it has made in taking corrective action and remedial measures in case of violation of human rights and the limitations it has experienced in performing its task.

In the chapter that follows Dr. Y.P. Chhibbar concentrates on PUCL experience and assessment of working with NHRC. He draws specific attention to certain limitations inherent in the primary act that established NHRC and calls for necessary changes.

The last section of this volume (Chapters 14-19) attempts an overall assessment of the state of human rights in India. Mr. Justice V.M. Tarkunde in his keynote address argues that for the majority of the people in India the national movement for independence was a "negative movement", since it aimed at, and succeeded in much desired removal of foreign rule. Although India did become a free country, he argues, "but its people did not attain political or socio-economic freedom". Mr. Justice Tarkunde also gives his reflection on freedom which, he regards, is essentially an individual value. Since it is the individual and not the society or a nation which has consciousness and who either suffers from bondage or feels exultation in freedom. He gives an assessment of what has been done and need to be done in regard to civil liberties, political, economic, socio-cultural rights and the progress or lack of it during the last 50 years. In conclusion he expresses "cautious optimism" and that a great deal can be done by grass-root organisations with the help of the people who are gradually getting conscious of the fact that they must work voluntarily for the improvement of their conditions of life, without depending solely on the machinery of the State.

Mrs. Shanti Sadiq Ali provides a historical perspective of abortive attempts which India made to bring in socio-economic uplift of the nation and to usher in a truly democratic system of government. She also examines how and why these attempts did not succeed to reach the desired goals which Mahatma Gandhi and Jawaharlal Nehru envisioned.

Prof. N.R. Madhava Menon concentrates on the state of economic and social rights and also reflects on so-called "liberalisation" and economic reforms carried out in recent years and their economic, social and cultural impact.

Prof. V.S. Mani provides an overall survey of the efforts made to improve various facets of human rights in India including the rights of the vulnerable section of society such as women and the children, SCs and STs and disabled persons.

All these chapters are revised version of the text of the discourses or the papers presented at the seminar. They cover various facets of human rights. However, we deemed it desirable to include some more details and analytical information on human rights education and also on liberalisation and economic reforms initiated in India in the context of escalating globalisation. Thus two chapters have been added for this volume, one relating to "human rights education and role of institutions of higher education" and the other on "globalisation" and its likely impact on human rights in India.

We hope that this volume will help contribute wider awareness of human rights issues in our country and also help strengthen better understanding, advocacy and policy-making in regard to human rights problems confronting us, at the turn of the century.

In preparation of this volume, we have had the benefit of support and cooperation of many individuals and organisations and I am indebted to them, although it is difficult to name them all.

We wish to place on record our appreciation and gratitude to the contributors who despite having pressing engagements agreed to join us at the seminar and made invaluable contribution to the seminar-deliberations and to this volume.

We also wish to extend our gratitude and appreciation to Mr. Justice M.N. Venkatachaliah, Chairperson, National Human Rights Commission (NHRC) whose support and encouragement have been a source of inspiration to us and NHRC's financial assistance towards the overall expenses of the seminar was a great help.

As convenor of the seminar and as editor of this volume, I am also personally grateful to the members of the Board of Trustees of the Institute for their support and guidance and to the members of the editorial board —Mr. R.P. Sinha, Mrs. Malti Singh, Prof. V.S. Mani and Mr. J.C. Batra.

Thanks are also due to Dr. R.S. Saini, Dr. Kanan Gahrana, Ms. Una Gupta for providing assistance in the organisational work of the seminar and in the preparation of this volume, to Mr. Susheel Kumar for painstakingly typing several drafts of various chapters and assisting me in putting the text in final shape.

October 1998 **—KPS**

NOTES ON CONTRIBUTORS

K.C. Pant	—	Former Union Cabinet Minister and former Vice-Chairman, UN Commission on Human Rights.
M.N. Venkatachaliah	—	Former Chief Justice of India, presently Chairperson, National Human Rights Commission (NHRC), New Delhi.
Rajindar Sachar	—	Former Chief Justice of Delhi High Court, former Member of UN Sub-Commission on the Prevention of Discrimination and the Protection of Minorities and former President, People's Union for Civil Liberties (PUCL), is senior advocate, Supreme Court of India, a human rights activist and exponent.
Sankar Sen	—	Director General (Investigation), NHRC, New Delhi.
Ranganath Mishra	—	Former Chief Justice of India and former Chairperson of NHRC, New Delhi.
R.M. Pal	—	Retd. Principal, Delhi University, human rights activist, exponent and author, Editor, *PUCL Bulletin*.
Joseph Gathia	—	Policy Analyst and Director, Centre of Concern for Child Labour, New Delhi.
Pritam Arora	—	Retd. Principal, is General Secretary, All India Mahila Congress.
Regina Mulay Parakh	—	Research Scientist at the Centre for International Politics, Organisation and Disarmament, School of International Studies, JNU, New Delhi.

G.S. BHARGAVA — Eminent journalist and author. Former resident editor of *Indian Express* and Principal Information officer to the Government of India (1978-80).

Y.P. CHHIBBAR — Former Reader, Delhi University, now General Secretary, PUCL, New Delhi.

V.M. TARKUNDE — Senior advocate, Supreme Court of India, eminent human rights activist, exponent and author. He resigned his justiceship at the Bombay High Court in 1969 along with Jai Prakash Narain, founder Citizens for Democracy and People's Union for Civil Liberties and Democratic Rights, later known as PUCL.

SHANTI SADIQ ALI — Member, UN Committee on Elimination of Racial Discrimination (CERD).

N.R. MADHAVA MENON — Director, National Law School of India University, Bangalore.

V.S. MANI — Professor of International Law, author of several books, is Director, Centre for Human Rights Teaching & Research (HURITER), JNU, New Delhi, is also Life Member of Board of Trustees of Institute for World Congress on Human Rights (IWCHOR), New Delhi.

K.P. SAKSENA — Former Professor and Honorary Director, HURITER, JNU, is Secretary General, IWCOHR, New Delhi.

Introduction

K.P. Saksena

Fifty years is a very small span in a nation's history. Nevertheless, this span for India, as a sovereign, socialist, secular democratic republic, was a very significant one. Fifty years back, after two centuries of colonial rule, India emerged as an independent nation for the first time in modern history and began its "tryst with destiny".

What path have we traversed over the period? What promises we made then and where do we stand today?

There has, of course, been significant progress in the fields of agriculture, industry, science and technology. But then, the important question is: how all this progress measures in the context of availability of minimum conditions essential for the development of innate characteristics, which nature has bestowed every Indian with as a human being irrespective of one's race, religion, caste, creed, colour, gender or social origin, birth or any other status? In other words, what has been the state of human rights enshrined in our Constitution and international instruments?

I

A mere glance at the situation shows that India remains a country of stark contrasts. While over the period, despite linguistic, religious and regional diversities and abortive secessionist activities, the concept of one nation has been strengthened from one corner to the other, a feeling of being an Indian and of belonging to this country is much more pronounced today than it was fifty years ago. On the other hand, old caste and clan conflicts and intraregional differences have been sharpened, creating a messy situation. Again, despite hot and cold winds, blowing from both inside and outside the country, India, unlike most of the other Afro-Asian countries, has adhered to a democratic system of government. On the other hand, while we have maintained is a semblance of a democratic system of government and rule of law. The practice of our legal and political system leaves much to be desired. Corruption, nexus between politicians and criminals, gang–rivalry and violence are widely rampant. Indeed, corruption and criminalisation of politics, spread from top to bottom of the administration are, in a way, subversion of democracy and gross violation of human rights. If money, favour and privilege are the factors that make Indian democratic system work, then it is not a democracy. At least, it runs the danger of being no longer able to call itself a democracy.

There is another dimension to the failure of the democratic processes. What we have evolved during the last fifty years, is not a democracy of the people, by the people and for the people. People's participation in the government is minimal. They are remembered only at the time of election, when an electorate of some 600 million elect, at the national level, some 545 members to Lok Sabha and a few hundred members to respective state–level legislatures.

At the national level, the ratio comes down to just one elected representative for every 1.1 million people . However, the constituencies are so unevenly drawn as to defy any just principle of representation. Most of the constituencies have electorate of 1 million to 1.4 million. But there are constituencies as small as Sheohar (Bihar) with an electorate of just 0.109 million (1.09 lakh) and as large as, for instance, Mumbai (North-East) with an electorate of more than 2 million (20 lakh). Delhi State elects 7 members to the Lok Sabha, but constituencies of New Delhi and Chandni Chowk, constituting small compact areas, have an electorate of little more than 0.3 million (3 lakh), while that of Outer Delhi and East Delhi, more than 10 times the size of the other two constituencies, spread to sprawling areas, have an electorate of more than 2 million (20 lakh). Thus, the ratio between the voters and the legislators is much larger than in any other democratic system of government. Compared to this, Britain, with an electorate of just 35 million sends 650 members to the House of Commons.

At state level also, the situation is not very different. For example,

Uttar Pradesh, with a population of some 120 million and an electorate of 85 million, elects just 425 members to the State Legislature.

Thus, in India, it is not possible to have any close interface between the citizens and the elected legislators. Once the elections are over, the electorate are conveniently forgotten by the politicians. India has yet to develop viable institutions for local self-governance. Most of the statutory bodies such as municipal corporations and district boards, in various states, get frequently superseded and run by administrators of the state governments. At village level, state government officials, such as Tehsildars and Block Development Officers (BDOS) manage the affairs and corruption is widely rampant.

Recently, the Panchayat System Act (1993) has been a laudable attempt to revive the traditional democratic system at local (village) level. In operation, however, India—a country of continental size continues to remain a centralised system largely ruled from Delhi or by respective state capitals.

The stark contrast is pervasive in every walk of life. India's GNP per capita income has increased fourfold but average income comes down to less than one dollar a day; and income distribution between the rich and the poor has widened from 1:30 in 1950 to 1:61 today.

Thus, for small percentage of people, life is as comfortable, indeed, luxurious, as for affluent people living in any other part of the world. On the other hand, approximately 400 million people live in extreme poverty.

Between 1951 to 1995, food-grain production increased fourfold and occurrence of famines have almost been eliminated, yet 40 per cent of the people do not get enough food. This includes some 60 million children, under 4 years of age, who remain undernourished.

The guidelines setforth in the form of Directive Principles of State Policy regarding the removal of poverty and illiteracy still remains a distant dream. As noted above, approximately 400 million people or nearly 40 per cent of the total population live on the margin of poverty—enduring unemployment or underemployment, hunger, disease and shelterlessness.

Against this background, one may well visualise the situation in the context of "right to life"—a primordial right which constitutes the raison d'etre of all other rights. Twenty-nine per cent of the people in rural areas do not have access to even safe drinking water. In most of the towns and cities, including Delhi and Mumbai, the water taps frequently go dry during most of the summer season. Again, while all developed nations and some of the developing countries like Thailand, South Korea enjoy 24 hours water supply, India lags far behind. Metropolitan cities like Mumbai, Chennai and Delhi get water for just 4-5 hours a day[1]. There are no sanitation facilities for 71 per cent of the people[2]. This is partly why diarrhoeal diseases which are transmitted by human faecal contamination of soil, food and water are so widespread. Some 8 lakh people die of diarrhoea and those who die of tuberculosis (TB) number 5 lakh. What aggravates their plight is lack of medical facilities and the necessary sources needed to provide health care. At an average, there is one doctor for 2,500 patients and one nurse for 3,300 patients[3]. Thus, millions of people are caught in a vicious circle of poverty, malnutrition and disease.

II

A more sordid reality is that among the victims children are the worst sufferers.

Information and varying statistics are, of course, available. But we all know, statistics provide a very limited picture and may lead to measures which could be counter-productive. For instance, statistics regarding number of child labour in India which so far have failed to give exact figures, might incite international protests and government legislation to abolish child labour. Indeed such legislation exists but do such legislations help the situation in the context of overall welfare of the child and the family he/she belongs to? What should be of concern is not the existence of exploitation of child and child labour but the factors that perpetuate its existence.

There is more to the situation. Millions of children around the country live under pathetically difficult circumstances—as orphans and street children, as juvenile delinquents, as child workers or youth trapped in bondage, prostitution, sexual abuse and other forms of exploitations. For nearly 30 per cent of the children there is no shelter from sun or the wind, rain and cold. They suffer from hidden hunger—what is referred in the UN jargon, as "invisible malnutrition".

The (UNICEF) reports indicate that malnutrition touches the life of approximately one quarter of the developing countries and some 40 per cent of them are in India. Malnutrition quietly steals away their energy and gently restrains their growth. It also gradually lowers their resistance and in both causes and consequences, it is inextricably interlocked with the illness and infections which both, sharpen and are resharpened by malnutrition itself.

The UNICEF reports indicate that no statistics can express what it is to see even one child die in such a way, to see a mother sitting, hours after anxious hours, leaning her child's body against her own; to see the child turn on limbs which are unnaturally still, stiller than in sleep. The child yawns and one sees the living pink at the roof of the child's mouth in shocking contrast to already dead–looking greyness of the skin, the colours of its life and death; to see the uncomprehending panic in eyes which are still the clear and lucid eyes of a child and then to know in one endless moment that life has gone. Some forty thousand children die, in developing countries, like this everyday and nearly half of them (i.e., 20,000) in India.

Let us turn to another aspect of sharp contrast. While we have institutions providing best of education in every discipline of knowledge, and a large number of foreign universities have opened their educational facilities right in India for those who can afford to pay the price; but nearly half of the population still remains illiterate. That is equivalent to the sum total of populations of Canada, Mexico and the United States of America. Some 63 million children have never been able to go to even primary school. More than 40 per cent of the children, who join primary school, do not reach grade five; 68 per cent do not go to secondary school level.

The directives contained in our Constitution urging all states to provide, by 1960, free and compulsory education for all children until they complete the age of 14 and the Supreme Court verdict that primary education is a fundamental right, have so far been disregarded with impunity by all successive governments.

It is often said that poor parents, perhaps illiterate themselves, are not interested in educating their children. The same excuse was cited by the colonial authorities; Lucknow District Gazette (1940), for instance, claimed that the mass of the lower classes was ignorant, superstitious and unambitious and do not care for education. This perception still continues in several quarters. In an analysis of the factors responsible for India's failure to achieve universal elementary education. *The Times of India*, August 15, 1997 cited one factor responsible as "Illiterate and semi-literate parents see no reason to send children to school".

This claim was authentically refuted by the recent survey[4] carried out by a group of researchers based at Delhi School of Economics and the Indian Social Institute. The survey covered all the schooling facilities in a randomly selected sample of 188 villages in Bihar, Madhya Pradesh, Uttar Pradesh and Rajasthan. About 1,225 parents were interviewed, 98 per cent of them felt that primary education should be made compulsory for all children; as many as 89 per cent expressed similar views in regard to their daughters. Only a small minority felt that it was not important for girls to be educated. The argument advanced was, the same traditional view, that a girl was not going to take a job and that her proper place was at home, doing domestic work and learning the skill of running a household.

Another myth exploded was children of poor families were unable to go to school because they were working children. It is estimated that some 80 million children go to work to supplement the family income. The survey disclosed that even the working children have seven and a half hours per day to go to school, provided that school hours are so staggered as to accommodate their free time.

The real reason for failure of India's primary education is poor educational system and crumbling schools. The survey cited that the percentage of government primary schools with specified facilities was vastly lacking. In Bihar, 25 per cent of the 65000 odd primary schools have no proper buildings. Some 63 per cent of school premises have leaking roofs, 89 per cent do not have functioning toilets, 58 per cent do not have drinking water facilities, 27 per cent do not have any black-boards and 52 per cent have no playgrounds.

The other reason was that there were many students but very few teachers and that teachers were hardly trained and very poorly paid.

What has been synoptically sketched above is discussed in some details in the chapters that follow, contributed by some eminent human rights activists, exponents and jurists. The attempt is to examine various aspects of state of human rights in India, the progress, or lack of it, made during the last fifty years and the measures necessary to improve upon the existing situation.

"Rights of the child" has received specific attention for obvious reasons. The future of a nation depends on the quality of socio-economic environment and education that we provide to the children. Indeed, the nation owes to the child the best it can give.

The other two themes that have been specifically examined are: "human rights and the law enforcement with a special reference to the rights of the prisoners behind prison-walls" and the "National Human Rights Commission (NHRC) : its significance and an assessment of its functioning".

Rights of persons behind prison-walls are least known to the public. People in general are not concerned about prisoners, their rights and treatment meeted out to them in prisons which provide fertile ground for persistent and all pervasive violation of human rights. The reason is the invisibility surrounding these violations. Prisoners are a forgotten lot, except those who are accused of sensational crimes and make newspapers headlines. People generally avoid mention of their relations and friends who are in prison to escape social embarrassment. People in general are not concerned about prisoners and their treatment in prisons. This attitude stems from the feeling that prisoners are the undesirable elements of society and must expiate the wrong they have done.

At the end of 1995, there were some 2,26,000 persons behind prison walls. Of them as may as 1,63,000 persons were non-convicted remandees or undertrials. Many of them have been in jail without a trial for almost twenty years. The worst part is that though during the last fifty years some reforms have been carried out, the Indian Police Act (1869) and Indian Prison Act (1894), both instituted during the British colonial regime, still govern the overall police structure and management of prisons.

In 1996, the Supreme Court of India specifically directed that the cases of undertrials in jails for more than two years under Section 302 of IPC, be decided within three months. More than a year has passed, but most of the undertrials are still languishing—right here in the Capital's Tihar Jail. Hence, we felt that this aspect of human rights be highlighted.

Further, since the adoption of the Constitution after independence, perhaps the most significant step taken to protect human rights was the institution of a high power NHRC in 1993. When the NHRC came into being, persons concerned with human rights issues were skeptical about the functioning and the extent to which it could help improve the human rights situation in our country. As such, some chapters are devoted to NHRC: an assessment of its four years of functioning and the direction it has taken to meet the growing expectations of the people.

REFERENCES

1. Figures ciled here are taken from *Asian Development Bank Report*, 1997.
2. World Bank Report, 1997.
3. *Ibid.*
4. The survey's findings which will be soon issued as a part of the "Public Report on Basic Education" (PROBE) was previewed in the weekly journal *India Today*, October 13, 1997, pp. 69-73.

I

1

Fifty Years of Independence : Some Observations*

K.C. Pant

We tend to take for granted the democratic rights and freedom of the individual, political rights and so on that prevail in our country, but the fact is that, historically speaking, this country has not always had these rights and freedom. Further, other countries in Asia have not followed the same path after independence, so their citizens in many cases do not enjoy these rights. Thus, it is not as though this was a God given direction to India to adopt these rights.

The fact is that the leaders of our freedom struggle were committed to the values of individual liberty and democracy. They recognised the key role of tolerance in our plural system. From Gandhiji, they got the inspiration for Sarvodaya and Sarvodaya is an important concept because while freedoms may have been enjoyed by certain sections of the population over the centuries, the fact that these freedoms should extend to all. It is a relatively new concept in history and therefore Sarvodaya concept is much wider than merely being economic or social. It impinges on the extension of the freedoms and obligations which human rights as well as duties which Gandhiji stressed upon.

* Excerpted from the transcript of the Chairman's observations (Hon'ble K.C. Pant) at the inaugural session of the national seminar on "Human Rights in India" (21-22 November, 1997) convened in observance of fifty years of India's Independence.

Now Gandhiji's freedom struggle, cannot be viewed in isolation. If you look at the totality of his life, it was a struggle against injustice in all forms—political, economic and social; and what he did in South Africa had a logical continuation in India and therefore this is the background against which the leaders of India, after her independence, chose the system which was to be established in our country. The fact that India became independent through a process which ultimately led to the liberation of a large number of countries in the world and colonial era came to an end. India's policies contributed also to the ending of apartheid; these two systems had legitimised the denial of human rights in a most fundamental sense. Therefore, India's freedom struggle apart from winning freedom for India had an impact on the promotion of human rights throughout the world and these ideals and values of the freedom struggle ultimately were enshrined in our Constitution.

Let us turn to another aspect. There is a guarantee of equality before law but equality of law is meaningful only to those who can legally enforce their rights and that brings us to the hard realities prevailing in the country. There are many vulnerable groups who are not even aware of these legal rights, are exposed to exploitation, to oppression etc. As such, the first requirement is that they should be made aware of their rights. Great stress needs to be laid on the role of education and the incorporation in it of the concept of human rights which the individual enjoys under our Constitution. So once that awareness is there then it will be easier for these people—children and the grown-ups, to do their part in society, with the full knowledge that they can lean upon the legal provisions of the Constitution and can get relief. Then, the other aspect is that even if they are aware of these rights, are they able to exercise these rights?

Certain tribal groups have been helped by NGOs and these NGOs have had to struggle right from the local courts up to the Supreme Court to get them their rights But the whole process has to be gone through and these legal processes are lengthy and expensive and so everybody cannot have recourse to them.

Then there is the role of the executive. It is seen that the executive, is very often unresponsive, particularly at the local level, so where does the complainant turn to seek relief. In our country there used to be social sanctions for various actions of which society did not approve. Today, the social sanctions have to be revived with respect to those human rights which we want society to enforce.

Child labour, for instance. Gradually there is a greater realisation that child marriage is against the law and therefore one should be careful, but we know very well that even now in many areas child marriage is still quite common. We also know about other atrocities concerning the girl child. The social sanctions have to be forged by people who are aware and people who can have some influence on the thinking of our leaders. This is a difficult question—legal aspect and the other one, and while there is no easy solution, this lies at the root of a solution.

Over a period of time, we have to have a caring society, a sensitive society and a society which does not pay lip service only to human rights but sees to it that they are available to all classes/castes and sections of our society.

Fifty years have gone by, after independence. The fact that democracy has struck roots and is accepted and recognised; that when a government loses power then the transfer of power has not posed any problem in this country. Again, this is something which we take for granted but I submit to you that it is a very very important ingredient in the mental make up of our polity, our political parties. They accept it. They accept the verdict of the people without question and this is a very big achievement.

Agriculture, industry, science and technology, have made progress. Longevity is better than it used to be but we have poverty which still is wide spread. We have illiteracy. Malnourishment and environmental degradation, which ultimately affects everybody. So the problems are there and yet we claim to be making progress.

Now there are some areas which are of special concern to human rights activists. Custodial deaths is one of them. The Supreme Court had to intervene and there has been, some progress in this respect, but the question of undertrials, which is engaging the attention of everyone, can be sorted out much more easily if the executive is a little more active in the matter. During the British Raj, District Magistrates and other senior officials used to make rounds of the police stations. They would ask for all the undertrials to be produced before them and took on the spot decisions about releasing some of them. Something as simple as that should be done and once that is done a big blot on our system can be removed.

We have failed to ensure elementary education to all children between the age of 6 to 14, as provided for in our Constitution, and for that lapse, we have paid a heavy price, in terms of, apart from other aspects, population growth, infant mortality and other social indices. There cannot be any two opinions in that regard that we must concentrate on this area.

As regards our food production, the rate of growth has been more than that of population and we have stocks of foodgrains and we have even exported some. But the absence of purchasing power is a factor which has to be taken into account while assessing the availability of food-stuffs against the requirements in the country. Lack of food is one major problem for the poor people and certainly for the child who is malnourished; his entire life is affected because that is the period of growth for his mind and body.

The general question of people living below the povertyline, who are the most vulnerable, is really at the heart of our problem. That has to be a national priority because if we aim at equality and humaneness, the measure of our success must be the extent to which we tackle the problem of poverty and provide the means to meet the basic needs of a large section of our population. Now the government has a very heavy responsibility but in a democratic society, public awareness, activism, you may say, and alertness perhaps, are the most effective guarantors of human rights. Now I know that there are many public spirited individuals and NGOs who have done excellent work in this area. Public interest litigation has opened a significant avenue; there is lot of work which is being done.

There is another dimension to the situation. Everyone knows that there is need for greater transparency in the functioning of our institutions. That is now also almost accepted by all and if there is continued vigilance, transparency will come. There is inbuilt resistance to the concept of transparency in our system and if we have to overcome the resistance, there has to be a strong public demand for transparency, otherwise it will not come because there is a natural sort of inbuilt resistance. In this area, the role of the Press in mobilising the people to action is obvious. Steadily, the role of the NGOs is becoming more effective and that has made people in India, more or less, among the more sensitive observers of the world scene in the field of human rights.

UN Human Rights Commission is an important forum but the element of politics does enter into such forums whether it is the Human Rights Commission or the United Nations General Assembly, political factors do enter into their decisions and that is something which we should keep at the back of our minds while even accepting the very useful work that these institutions are doing.

Today the world is becoming much smaller. All countries are becoming each other's neighbours and in this changing situation, the universality of human rights is no longer a theoretical concept. People in one country are aware of what is happening in other countries. Now the concept of sovereignty is being questioned. It is not that the concept of sovereign is going to go away or the nation state is going to vanish, but these concepts/ideas have their own momentum and they have their own limitations and so in that sense, today universality has a much more concrete and real meaning.

Science and technology has made it possible, for the first time in history, for every single citizen to be provided with his basic needs. Today it is possible; only there is maldistribution. So something which is possible can be aimed at but today it is a distant dream. While we should do what can to proceed faster in the field of human rights, we should remind the developed countries that they still pay far too much attention to civil and political rights, and that they do not pay the same kind of attention to economic and social rights. While we must accept the responsibility to see that we protect and promote the human rights of our citizens—that is our responsibility—we must express a sense of disappointment at the failure of the developed countries to recognise that a just economic order is necessary if human rights are to be made a reality for large sections of the global population. One can talk about it, but if the world economic order continues to be iniquitous, it does not underpin this concept of human rights. The fact that there is no just world economic order; makes it much more difficult for the developing countries to ensure human rights even within their boundaries.

Similarly, there is a question of global environment. Today, if the strategy for protection of the global environment—whether it is warming, ozone, bio-diversity or anything else—if the strategy is such that the vital interests of the needy in the developing countries are affected, to that extent we really are doing something that militates against extension of human rights of these people. For instance, the question of child labour is very often coming up in international forums. We have number of people abroad who are interested in this, many of them are sincere people and seriously concerned. Their concern and any help from them in tackling this problem is welcome. But when child labour is used as an excuse to curb the exports to India then it is obvious that the focal point of interest is not human rights, it is commerce.

So we have to be aware of these things so that even while we work for the elimination of child labour in our country, we do not fall prey to such elements in the international world, who are using this only as an economic tool against us.

Similarly, there is a question of biodiversity. Today this is one of the most important areas—the conservation of biological diversity and continued access of flora and fauna to our people who are traditionally using them. For instance, in medicine, in rural medicine, whether it is the Ayurvedic or the Unani physicians—all of them are using local medicinal plants; and today efforts are on in developed countries to support MNCs which want to have patent rights over such plants. If that is done in a manner which deprives the traditional users of this bio-diversity of their rights of what they have preserved over the centuries, then you can see what a direct impact it will have on their lives and how it will affect them in the years to come. So, there are many dimensions to human rights problems.

We all look up to the NHRC to provide leadership in this field; its basic integrity is something which all of us have confidence in.

2

Human Rights in India : The Balance Sheet—A Perspective*

Justice M.N. Venkatachaliah

In 1993, Vienna Declaration reiterated that all human rights are interdependent, collective, indivisible and universal; but somehow there is today a growing sense of cynicism about the universality of the principles. The crudities and inequalities of the international economic order, we find today, is one of the contributing factors. Human Development Report says that just ten dollar billionaires—just ten of them—own as much as the combined income of one thousand seven hundred million people in the developing countries. If anything at all over the last thirty years, the chasm has widened.

It is said, in personal terms, that a man is treated exactly the way he allows himself to be treated; in the case of a nation, it will be treated just the way it allows itself to be treated. We are increasingly becoming a society obsessed by the new wave of unbridled consumerism. Some such things are overtaking us. We have all the symptoms of the civilisational diseases of the Western world; but without its penchant for hardwork, orderliness and good governance.

We have only a half per cent of the share of world's trade, with almost 18 per cent of the world population. United States has about five per cent

* Excerpted from the transcript of the inaugural address at the inaugural session of the national seminar on "Human Rights in India" (21-22nd November, 1997) in observance of fifty years of India's Independence.

of the world population but consumes, 40 per cent of the world's natural resources. Japan has about 2.5 per cent of the world's population and it has about 18 per cent of the share of world's trade.

There is more to the situation. We have 38 per cent of our demographic breakdown in the form of children below the age of 14. We have over 350 million children. We have the problem of educating them, taking care of their health, their well-being, both physical and mental. That is a tremendous task. The terrible truth is that almost one-third of our children below the age of 16 have to work. There is child prostitution—thousands of young girls below the age of 15 are sold every year to the flesh trade and millions of children work in hazardous industries.

The biggest and most sinister violation of human rights in this country is the cynical and derisive attitude of those in authority to the issues of survival of this nation as a civilised country. It is this scornful impatience, this derisive cynicism to values, that we see all around, which constitute some of the most embarrassing realities of our predicament today.

In the past this great land made perhaps the most profound contributions to philosophy and to great issues of man's spiritual quest. Its contribution to aesthetics, art, dance, drama, music, architecture and sculpture are breath-taking. But then why do we wallow in this kind of squalor, insensitivity, and pervasive inequality today? Over hundred years ago Swami Vivekananda attributed our precipitous downfall to what he identified as our five national sins. He counted two amongst them as the neglect of masses and the neglect of women. How true! These now are perhaps the most critical issues in today's governance. But the politics of backwardness is again typically Indian. Political leaders excepting, of course honourable exceptions, have now found it convenient to don the role of brokers or agents for the anger of the people. They have nothing to offer them, they have no jobs for them, no education to give, but have found it convenient and profitable to exploit their anger and discontent.

But all this is not to belittle the great blessings of independence. Fifty years ago the country became independent. We had just 10 per cent of the literacy and life expectancy at birth was just 27 years. Today it is 74 for females in Kerala. Kerala has shown that just by one expedient, viz. the education of the girl child, society can transform itself. Infant mortality whose statistical national average is at 70 is only 16 for 1000 births. This compares favourably with the most advanced countries in South Asia.

Kerala achieved this by the literacy route. The literacy is 92 per cent for women and 98 per cent for men in Kerala. Tamil Nadu and Andhra Pradesh adopted the non-literacy route also to the Malthusian problem and they have achieved remarkable results. Tamil Nadu's performance in population control is also significant.

There are some other remarkable achievements. We have almost reached a figure of 195-200 million tonnes of food production. Till 1970, we were importing food.

Modern mind is said to be the product of the seventeenth century science. But we should note that the century was followed by the eighteenth century which was the most skeptical period in the history of the world. There was something in the scientific attitude which turned the human mind ethic-neutral and to claim that moral values were not objective resulting in a process of dehumanisation. The twentieth century became the bloodiest century in consequence. The two world wars had devastating effect on human tranquillity. Men of vision thought there should be some philosophy to serve as a foundation for human behaviour, either individual or collective, everywhere. That is how a universal Bill of Rights recognising an international standard for human behaviour in society and polity came to be recognised in the form of a Universal Declaration of Human Rights, to give every human being by virtue alone of his birth in the human family, irrespective of one's situational differences of caste, creed, race and language, certain irreducible minimal rights. These rights were not conferred by the Universal Declaration. These great rights of man were self-evident and were always recognised as universal and inalienable and not as 'conferred' rights.

In the 1940s, after the turmoils of the two world wars, the world's conscience having been devastated by the gruesome experience of the horrors of the wars, the international community needed these standards as ethical touchstone for the domestic laws of the country. Human Rights are self-extinguishing rights, in the sense that the Universal Declaration of Human Rights and the content of human rights under the covenants are ultimately intended to find their echo in corpus-juris either as fundamental constitutional rights or as enforceable statutory rights.

Now we have, in India, a beautiful Constitution; part three embodies everything that the human rights declarations and international human rights covenants and conventions prescribe. The Supreme Court, by a process of a constructive interpretation, has breathed, into each one of these articles of part three of our Constitution vital life-breath. But the problem is, if you borrow some of the loftiest ideas and expressions from all other Constitutions of the world, pick-up the finest sentiments and the loftiest ideas in their most profound expressions and put them in the form of a book and adopt and give yourselves that document, then what have given to yourself perhaps, is just a book. You have not given yourself a Constitution, unless that is backed by a will to live by the great values of the document and develop a political tradition of a liberal democracy. If we do not have the spirit of liberty within us as part of our political faith, we perhaps delude ourselves that some book can give that to us. No Constitution can work without the spirit of constitutionalism. Some such delusion has possessed us today. We have started blaming the Constitution for our own wickedness. Each one of us, in one's own way, is collaborating in our own defeat both individually and as a nation. We defile the Constitution everyday. Every policeman who illegally detains a man in a police station and shows cynical and derisive disregard to constitutional values is destroying the Constitution bit by bit. What he does is not only something which is illegal, but he is perhaps unaware that he is defiling the Constitution itself. The poignant thing is that he draws his own powers ultimately from the Constitution itself but disowns the obligations and limitations that go with the possession of the powers. The purpose of all public law is to discipline and civilise public power and to make it run within the pale of law. This is the essence of the rule of law and if you talk to any government official wielding wide powers over his fellow-men, he has his own philosophy justifying how the Constitution is too ideological to be useful and pragmatic in the day to day administration. Nobody seems to give a thought to the fact that everyday, everywhere there is some kind of defilement of our fundamental faith and of fundamental law. How do we go about it? First is awareness of these rights among the people, then the inclination to assert and then third is the access to the means of their enforcement. These are some of the most fundamental things which are being continuously articulated by the Supreme Court of India over the last quarter of a century.

Nobody claims that democracy is the most ideal form of political organisation of man; nobody claims that it is even a good enough system; nobody says that it is the most ideal-system but mankind has realised, after painful experiences, that it is perhaps the least hostile amongst all other systems tried so far.

In discussing the problems of human rights in India, today, we have no Western inspirations. Each country has had its own embarrassing record of human rights. It, therefore, ill behoves us to call into question each other's record. Indeed, the history of British legal system bears testimony to these embarrassing inquisitorial methods, of its almost tyrannical system of criminal justice in the past. American track-record of the past is also no better. Some 150 yeas ago, the US Supreme Court (Dred Scott vs. Sanford) found nothing wrong with the slavery. Chief Justice Taney, in delivering the judgment, argued that Negros of slave descent could not be treated as citizens. Even after the slavery was abolished, the US Supreme Court was faced with cases of racial discrimination and segregation. The judges found that if equally comfortable seats were provided in the Railways for both black and white Americans, there was nothing wrong with such separate treatment as long as it was equal though separate. Little did they pause to think that what was separate could never be equal. But the American conscience was hurt and later in 1954 in the Brown case, the Supreme Court in its historic judgment declared segregation as illegal. The point to note is that no country can boast of an ideal role in the area of Human Rights and no country's performance has been particularly idyllic. The censorial and denunciatory attitude of the Western powers against the developing countries do not recognise that the cause is more important than its champions and that great universality of the entire human rights regime suffers by rendering them contentious and controversial by some countries, by reason of their power of wealth, constituting themselves the universal arbiters of human rights.

Let us turn to some other specific issues. It is relevant to note that the percentage of convicted prisoners in this country is amongst the lowest in the world; for a country of 960 million, we have hardly 65,000 convicted prisoners. On the other hand, out of the prison population of about 2,35,000; 75 per cent are "undertrials". The protracted trials result in the undertrial being in prisons for long years. Some of them languish in prison for petty offences, for gambling in the streets, for ticketless travel, etc., for sheer lack of sureties for their bail bonds. Indian society today is not the great Indian society of Mahatma Gandhi's dreams. We have never been able to build that great Indian society. It is just a conglomeration of conflicting groups and interests which are quite often at war against each other. It is, therefore, that it has not developed itself into a caring society.

There are certain things, which if adopted and implemented with some circumspection, the delays in criminal trials could be reduced. In England, you have part-time lawyers working as part-time judges, as recorders/assistant recorders. They work for a specific number of days a year and dispose of hundreds of criminal matters, leaving the more serious cases to the regular magistrates. In India, cases remain pending, not so much because of their intrinsic complexity, but simply because magistrates are overworked and do not have time to reach them. The system of honorary judicial magistrates can be an answer to the problem of docket-logging. There must be some thinking on the alternatives to custodial punishment, whether in the form called community service sentences of what are now being tried out in some countries or in some other way. The system of 'plea bargaining' is another idea worth trying in cases not involving heinous crimes.

The other thing worth discussing is primary education. This is the most burning issue. The country has realised the great beneficial effect of primary education on a variety of social issues. The inverse ratio between literacy on the one hand and fertility, infant mortality, post-natal maternal mortality, malnutrition of children, industrial productivity are now well recognised and well documented. The role and participation of the civil society in this great national endeavour is of utmost importance. It is high time we come out with practical suggestions in the policy-formulation and actual work of the NGOs in primary education.

The other important issue is the significance and performance of the National Human Rights Commission (NHRC). National Institutions must have two important attributes. They must be independent and be composed of men of highest integrity and independence. In addition the technology of management must be adequate to meet the challenges.

In the complaint redressal system of Commission, in the beginning, there used to be 65 complaints, a month, in the first six months. This year, the figure is likely to cross 50,000 mark. The Commission realises the importance of interaction with all well meaning persons of society and the NGOs to draw upon the great pool of talent available in the civil society. Systems are being worked out to enlist such services and support.

It is equally important that the NHRC should be subject to social audit and periodic seminars be held on its role and efficacy. These will ensure the achievement of the great objects and purposes of its founding.

II

3

Rights of the Child*

Justice Ranganath Misra

International Convention to which India became a party in 1992 and the 54 clauses which are there, indicate what are the rights of the child. To what extent these rights have been implemented and are implementable in this country is more important. We have more laws in this country than anywhere else in the world and what is wanting is its implementation. We have to understand the law in its true spirit and put into the life's process. We have almost failed in that respect; law remains in the book.

We have a provision, Article 51(A), in the Constitution, called: fundamental duties; its insertion was the result of the Swaran Singh Committee Report, recommending amendment of the Constitution which, in the black period of emergency, came as the 42nd amendment of the Constitution; a part of it was of Mrs. Gandhi's attempt to rewrite the Constitution of her liking. However, the other part was excellent elaboration of fundamental duties.

In the first 25 years (1950-75), we created a right-oriented society—everybody asking for his/her rights/institutional rights and nobody thought of any duty. At school level, in the civics book, the first lesson is that rights and duties are supplementary and complementary to each other, two sides of the same coin. When we wrote our Constitution, our Constitution

* Excerpted from the transcript of the keynote address, on "Rights of the Child" at the national seminar (See n. page 25).

fathers forgot that there must have been also duties enumerated in the Constitution.

1998 marks the 50th anniversary of the Universal Declaration of Human Rights. The Declaration is nothing less than a monument to humankind, for the first time ever human rights of all human beings irrespective of colour, gender, race, religion, nationality, descent were recognised and elaborated. In the years that lapsed since the adoption of the inspiring document, scores of international instruments, some of them having international mechanism for the monitoring observance of human rights have been adopted. The declaration has been the guideline of many international and national legislation and judicial decisions. Yet we are still far away from realisation of what the declaration has setforth as a "common standard of achievements for all peoples and all nations". More than 50 per cent of the peoples do not know about the famous declaration neither they have derived any benefit. How do we account for this sordid state of affairs?

Do we hold the governments who bear the responsibility of assuring human rights for all? Or is it that institutions, both at global and national level, of exploitation and domination of which Harold Laski warned against on the adoption of the declaration? This brings us to a related issue, the so-called globalisation. Many western scholars have referred to globalisation and universalisation of human rights as twin development each supporting the other as the most significant phenomenon of our times. Is it that globalisation is conducive to realisation of human rights or it represents institutionalisation of domination and exploitation.

When universal declaration was adopted the world was still not free from eurocentricism. Indeed, many scholars and global leaders have argued that universal declaration is a victory for western civilisation and that the genesis of human rights is inherent in western philosophical tradition. Many people in Asia and Africa are persued to believe that because of western aggressive attitude.

How do we trace the genesis of concept of human rights? How the concept is perceived in Indian tradition and way of life?

They were not even discussed in the lawyers chamber. They were not part of a court's proceedings. Rights remained in the Constitution as if they were a sacred thing to be worshipped/prayed. Nothing happened. They never came in to the living process of the nation. Therefore, we continued to have the same culture of fundamental rights to be worked out, implemented without any duties being assigned.

Society is not a repository of some special process from Heaven that everything will be available to be shared; what is available to be shared is what is given to us and it is a pool and if we have the right to take, we have also the duty to give and then take; otherwise what is to be taken, nothing is left there to be taken, not to be shared. So, therefore, duties first, rights thereafter had been the philosophy in this nation. In India, we have always believed, give you share, then demand whatever is your right, but we never bothered about it.

When we are thinking of the rights of the child, it has got to be understood that we have to do our part to the community to make it rich and only when the community is rich, we can think of sharing out of it. If we do not pay our taxes, the finance minister is not having a direct pipeline with the creator of limitless funds; that he will ask for funds, send a requisition and the other side will open and money will flow in. It is our money and it is a trust, government is a trustee, the finance minister is a trustee and the State exchequer is the fund in which our contributions have to flow in that, is the expectation. So, therefore, unless we have the pool of the duties, how the rights will flow and how the rights of the child will be implemented without our putting into the pool our duties? So, therefore, unless we turn our conscience, into a situation where all of us will be prepared to give and not demand, no rights whether it is of the child, of the men or women can be worked out.

The first consideration while looking at the rights of the child is that these 54 articles be implemented effectively to ensure that each one of us has performed ones duties to the community in accordance with the expectations. The standard of living, the level of a society will depend upon its members contributing honestly to the national pool or the social pool. A societal adjustment is possible only when the pool is full and therefore, the first premise to deal with a subject like rights of the child would be to start with the obligations, the duties to put in enough into a common pool where child would be really benefited out of it.

The difference between the child and other living in a community is that child is not able to demand, has no capacity to form a union, is probably incapable of speaking and therefore public opinion in regard to the rights of the child, is not supposed to be claimed by the child itself. It is necessary to be done by those who are responsible for taking care of the child and therefore whether we are able to implement the child's right, depend upon our outlook, to understand the demand of the child. The child has no right to demand in the sense he has not the capacity to demand but the child has accepted rights as given in the convention. So this is the first premise to impress upon that all of us must become duty conscious and work out the fundamental duties which have been prescribed.

Some day we have to give a link between the part IV A and part III of the Constitution. It was unfortunate that "Fundamental Duhs" instead of becoming part III A, this became part IV A. Part 4 is Directive Principles of State Policy and the Constitution makers who amended the Constitution at least should have thought of it that it has nothing to do with part IV A, it has directly linkage with part III. Therefore, it should have been part III A and then thereafter one more line should have been there, which would have provided the linkage.

Text of part IV A should have been in part III, implying that if we ask for a right, we should first pledge that I have done my duty to entitle me to the right. It is that link which is wanting in society. Today everybody thinks that it is right that should claim priority even at the cost of society. We are living in a community of this type. That is why no one has bothered to think of the neglected section of society including the rights of the child.

In such a backdrop, one has to consider the conventions of the rights of the child, its status and how it is being implemented? What we have done after the international convention was accepted by India in 1992? These are the questions really seriously to be looked into. We have already been party to this convention for 5 years. Government announced sometime back that 6 per cent of the GDP will go to children's education and the Human Resource Ministry came forward with big articles, messages, press releases, etc.; what is being given annually for education against the declared policy of 6 per cent is precious little, just 3 per cent.

Education, on the judgement of the Supreme Court, became fundamental right about 4/5 years back. The first judgement came four years back, then came a repetitive judgement. There have been four decisions of the Supreme Court saying that education in terms of Article 24 and Article 45 of the Constitution is a fundamental right.

Article 141 of the Constitution says that decision of the Supreme

Court is a law of the land, if that is a law of the land, then what is the meaning of Government saying that we are going to amend the Constitution, making it a fundamental right. It has been made a fundamental right. They have interpreted the existing law and said that this already is an existing fundamental right. If it is an existing fundamental right instead of proceeding to implement it forthright, immediately, what is the idea of saying we are now trying to take steps to make it a fundamental right, by incorporating an amendment in the Constitution; two years have been lost in finding out in what way it can be implemented. Why the Government is not abiding by the Supreme Court's decision?

They are already in contempt, and no NGO is thinking of putting a petition of contempt in the Supreme Court saying that four years back it was declared a fundamental right, where is the implementation? There have been lot of public litigations on the issues which are really not in public interest, why not this fundamental issue? Making an amendment is not the implementation, on account of the fact that Supreme Court did not direct that make an amendment in the Constitution to make it fundamental right. Supreme Court said that the existing law makes it a fundamental right. Article 21—right to life interpretated, Article 24 was given its meaning, Article 45 in proper perspective was adjusted and putting all of them together, the Supreme Court came to the conclusion that right to education is a fundamental right.

Our Constitution-makers wanted all children up to the age of 14 to be educated and to become literate and wanted every child to go up to matriculation; they wanted this to happen in ten years (1950-60). Thirty-seven years more have rolled by. Many things have happened and many things have been done but nobody bothered about this and in next year the golden jubilee of the Constitution will be over. We will be getting into the next century. And if that has not been done in spite of the fact that the Supreme Court reiterated that it is a fundamental right then it is very difficult to say that the right to education will be implemented or is being implemented. We require many more schools if we want children to go for education than what we have today.

Article 24 indicated, children will not work particularly in hazardous occupations. Article 45 wanted that they should read up to the age of 14. These have to be read together. The Supreme Court, quite sometime back, looking into the Article 37 declared that the Directive Principles of State

Policy are not justiciable. Article 45 also occurs in part IV and not justiciable yet, they said that right to education is a fundamental right.

Therefore, it is our obligation and NGOs must come forward with the demand; we are a trustee of the society for children because children have no capacity to demand their rights. All of us, in the community, who are grown up, are trustee for looking after the interests of the children. Unless we do our part, we are failing in our trust. It is time to rise to the occasion. We are not discharging our duties as trustees of the society. NGOs have taken a self-appointed role to look after the interest of the community and children are the most neglected section of the society.

As NGO, our first obligation to take the responsibility, in an effective way and approach and activate the proper machinery so that rights of the children are protected.

India has become a party to various international conventions, including the Convention on Rights of the Child. It is, therefore, necessary to ensure the greater guarantee for these human rights to be operative, whether it is general human rights, children human rights or specific human rights. It is the culture of human rights that must be prevalent in society.

In England, criminal law is very well worked out. It is on account of the fact that criminal law in England is operative. The laws are enforced very quickly and properly. And the common man takes interest in enforcement of law. In India, when an accident takes place people avoid that scene of occurrence because they might be called upon to become a witness. We lack civic sense. In England, if a man sees the accident has happened, he will try to recount what he saw, get his statement recorded and would volunteer to come to the court to support what he saw. This is the difference between a 'conscious' society and a society which avoids this obligation. This is the reason why 90 per cent of cases in India fail to earn a conviction on account of the fact that evidence is lacking. The doctor who comes into the role of a witness does not appear, ultimately 10 years are there, he retires and goes away, his address is not known. So on account of the fact that our social perception, our civic sense and our contribution to social well being, are not there, all this is happening.

For last 10 years, we have been campaigning against child labour in carpet industry. We also accepted the position that carpet-making is a hazardous industry. From the economic point of view, the family has to live, there must be an adjustment among the social requirement, the family requirement and the child's requirement so we would think of adjusting rights and duties in some way. In 1984-85, the first judgement from the Supreme Court relating to carpet industry, this was the consideration—four hours of work, one hour of rest, one hour of food, two hours of study. That is how six or seven hours work for the child was considered. Similarly, in Sivakasi area, the Court took the view that we should have a compromise—children will not go to the hazardous section because that is the minimal area of difficult situation and they will be only concerned with packing. A group insurance of Rs. 50,000 was made compulsory for everyone who went into the factory to work; and the premium was to be paid by the employer and not out of the children's wages, children would be given 75 per cent of the remuneration of the minimum wages fixed at a particular point and then food and other things and couple of hours of education.

But now in these 10 years, the attitude has again changed. The Court does not want children to work. The Court wants that children must take to study up to the age of 14; they should really be fully engaged and engrossed in education.

The type of education we provide for children is not "man-building" education. It neither gives any strength, nor build-up character. It does not help to promote good conduct. Therefore, this type of education has to change and ultimately the education must be developed in such a way so as to bring into existence good citizenship, their own perceptional things, which are in tune with the concept of the UN Charter. They are in tune with the Declaration of Human Rights. The Declaration of Human Rights is a philosophy, and not a contract. It only declares what your rights are, they have standardised the human rights whether you are in Africa, in India, in Europe, in a developing country or in a industrially developed country, everywhere, everyman is having the same rights standardised. That is why in the preamble of the Declaration it is said that it has standardised the rights and it falls upon each one of you to be an agent of agency of standardisation, an agency to bring it together to implementation. It calls upon every individual to support human rights to make them viable, visible in everybody's life and conduct.

It is on account of the fact that all these years, we have not been really vibrant that human rights have remained a distant dream. Human rights must be observed by us, in such a way, that they would be seen in our day-to-day conduct and until we have been able to bring in that level where there is assurance of human rights being observed.

As of now, violation of human rights is widely rampant. Violation of human rights is in the homes, the streets, the public offices, the educational institutions.

Some universities have started working on human rights. The Cochin University has started human rights. Universal Education is available so that the transformation takes place. Ours is a country, where education was given not through books, but through conduct. We must not spend our time on the wrong direction, every moment must be utilised to sensitize the entire nation and in fact the entire homosepian race because human rights cannot exist in one country, it has got to be internationally accepted and transformed from the written language into human conduct and then only when we find it manifested in human conduct in the daily way of living, then only can we think that an assurance has come and human rights remain ensured tó be performed.

Promotion and protection of human rights is the only way by which the human society can be saved in an effective way. We are degenerating and degenerating very fast and unless there is first stoppage of this degenerating process and then an attempt for elevation thereafter, we might lose our status of being homosepians and a group above animal life.

4

Wrongs and Rights of the Child

R.M. Pal

If one goes by newspaper reports about (1) activities of a large number of very articulate NGOs working for eradication of child labour, (2) by the loud noise made by government agencies (like governmental programme to end child labour by 2000 AD, the constitution of a National Authority for Elimination of Child Labour, and a National Child Labour Project), and (3) by Supreme Court judgements of 1993 and 1996, it would appear that the evil of child labour is about to be eradicated. It is in this context that we may note what the NHRC states in its annual report 1995-96: "The question which the commission asks itself is whether the stated objective of ending child labour in hazardous industries will indeed be achieved by the year 2000 on the basis of the present approach and whether and how the country will be prepared to deal with the much vaster problem of child labour in other occupations as well–the estimate of these so working varying from 50 million to a number much higher" (p 29).

The solution of "the much vaster problem" depends not on "determination to enforce the laws of the country is respect of child labour, most notably the Child Labour Prohibition and Regulation Act 1986" as stated by the NHRC in the above report (p. 30), but by adopting "a different approach to that of Government.... the implementation of which is most important (and that is) that the problem of child labour will persist... until the reality of free and compulsory education for all up to the completion of the age of 14 years is realised" (p. 30).

The fact remains that there has not been any realisation either on the part of government or on that of NGOs that there is correlation between widespread and increasing child labour, and literacy, that depriving the child of free primary education is one of the worst forms of human rights violations, and that all big talks/claims about eradication of child labour without introducing universal primary education amounts to putting the cart before the horse.

At this point, a point made by the NHRC is worthy of criticism–it has perhaps been made unintentionally. The report states: "The Commission, which has monitored the situation in Ferozabad carefully, both through visits and through regular meetings–involving Central, State and district level officers in addition to UNICEF–is of the view that success is possible in that district. But the Commission is not yet convinced that the goal will be achieved. The elimination of child labour, even in a circumscribed area and in a single hazardous industry, requires, above all, persistence, dedication and sustained leadership, both official and non-governmental, that has been proven over a period of time. And it requires far greater evidence than has been revealed so far of a determination to enforce the laws of the country, in respect of child labour, ... (and) there have been conspicuously few prosecutions and lamentably fewer convictions". Emphasis should be laid on the point that no amount of dedication, persistence, and sustained leadership, and prosecutions and convictions can eliminate child labour, as the Commission itself admits while recommending implementation of free and compulsory primary education. Surely, the Commission is now convinced that the focus must be changed–the focus must be on primary education. Our NGOs and government must accept this fact–even though after fifty years.

Our activists are no doubt very serious about eradication of child labour. Many of them, well known in our country and more widely known abroad (some of them are treated as "heroes" in western countries) think that child labour can be eradicated through sanctions imposed by foreign governments/business houses. Such an approach will certainly bring "name and fame" to our activists. But will it eradicate the evil? In a recent research conducted by a human rights intellectual/activist, Ms. Katarina Tomasevski of Denmark (Between Sanctions and Elections–Aid Donors and their Human Rights Performance, 1997) reviews the human rights policies of donor governments and their practices. The main thesis of the study is that sanctions cannot benefit human rights; on the contrary, sanctions undermine human rights protection by their reliance on external policing and sanctioning. As we know, some of our activists rely heavily on policing from business houses and governments from abroad to bring an end to child labour. Is it necessary to add that they are on the wrong track? And, what could be the motive behind soliciting such policing? It is left to the readers to come to their own conclusion.

II

India is a party to the Rights of the Child 1989 Covenant. Let us therefore have a quick look at the scenario relating to the child.

The Girl Child: The condition of the girl child, relating to human rights violations, has been determined by our religions and their approach to women in general. The three major religions of India–Hinduism, Islam, and Christianity–treat women as inferior to men, often on the authority of divine scriptures and sanctions. According to all socio-religious traditions, women are required to find their fulfilment in motherhood and domesticity. Their duty is to render service to the husband, his family and to the children. In fact, some of the scriptures have warned that if women enter public life there will be utter chaos and disaster. We are warned that the society will break up if men and women forget the sacredness of marriage. The foundation of society would be shaken, we are warned day in and day out, not only by men but also by women (and such women's number is not insignificant and most of them are well educated) if women expressed dissatisfaction at the treatment accorded to them. (One is reminded of the almost total opposition to the Hindu Code Bill by women parliamentarians in the fifties). How do we reconcile this outlook with the *Universal Declaration of Human Rights*? What is most disheartening is the effort of a significant section of our intellectuals to rationalise the irrational. They–both ancient and modern–have fabricated many fables about the exalted position of women in our society to convince us and the world portraying them as goddesses. They remain silent on the codes of Manu which have advised men to treat women as their property and slaves, brush aside the issue with the plea that our society is governed not by the codes of Manu, but by the Constitution. Then, there are others, including highly educated and sophisticated women, who maintain that we must not raise the question of quality between a man and a woman because that disturbs the natural balance, whatever that may mean.

The depressing position of the girl child is to be viewed in the light of the place a woman occupies in our society.

Crimes against woman and the girl child have been on the rise. Furthermore according to available data, there has been considerable decline in sex ratio–fewer females than males. The 1991 Census figures indicate that the all-India sex ratio is 929 females per 1000 males (the ratio has been declining consistently since the last several census). In some areas it is more dismal. For example, in Gujarat it is as low as 901, in Haryana it is 874 and in some districts it is as low as 832.

The UN Report for Human Development, 1996, has drawn our attention to very insignificant efforts made by India to improve the condition of women's lot as compared to nations which got independence much later than India. That there is a definite gender bias in our country hardly needs any research. But why is it so?—that needs research.

Why is it, for example, that 25 per cent of the girls die before they attain the age of 15? If it is malnutrition, then why in the case of girls only? Why is it, again, that in some parts of the country parents resort to most inhuman and cruel methods to kill girl babies? According to a study by the Indian Council of Child Welfare, in Madurai district of Tamil Nadu alone about 6000 baby girls were killed in the past decade, either by giving poisonous milk or by other means. This criminal practise is prevalent in about 600 villages in the district. One hospital records in Mumbai has revealed that out of 8000 foetuses aborted, 7099 were of females–cruel gift of amniocentesis. Have NGOs, research institutes devoted to women's studies, the NHRC, and the National Commission for Women ever tried to find out the reasons behind such crimes and violations of human rights? There are a number of sophisticated women's organisations in Delhi who are working overtime by cultivating the political rulers for reservation for women in legislatures. Which is, of course, a legitimate demand. But I have never heard any of the women leaders refer to the increasing violations of human rights of children and women; nor or do they think compulsory primary education is at all necessary!

Female illiteracy, according to the 1991 census, is about 60 per cent of the total women population. UP, Bihar, Rajasthan and Madhya

Pradesh, apart from having highest number of illiterate women, have the highest birth rate and death rate of women, and also the highest infant mortality rate.

Our do-gooders point to dowry and other economic factors responsible for the depressing and tragic situation. Not many, not even those women leaders who have been fighting for reservation, refer to our religious scriptures that have given rise to gender bias. For example, according to one scriptural sanction, "Let the bridegroom ask the bride to join him in a sacred ritual with the prayer, 'let our union beget sons only'...", there was also the tradition of *Putreshti Yagna* praying for *putra* (birth of a son), and so on. We do not hear women's organisations demand the burial of the ugly relics of our past. Obviously, they are afraid of lie-hunting.

I have specifically referred to the girl child, in the context of human rights violations, for no development of any kind can take place without educating the girl child. Furthermore, eradication of girl child labour will remain a distant goal, without implementing universal primary education. As is well known, in some of the hazardous industries (like the Sivakasi Industries) vast majority of child labour are girls.

III

The painful fact in regard to the social welfare programme of compulsory primary education is that the picture (except in Kerala) is grim all over. In this field India is not only behind countries like China, Indonesia, Kenya, Myanmar, Philippines, Zimbabwe and Zambia–we are far behind even the poorest of the poor, sub–Saharan Africa.

Any one with sensitivity will realise that the tragedy, all the greater because a wholly avoidable one, that has befallen our country is the non-implementation of the programme of universal primary education and not putting this social welfare programme first on the list of priorities. For this the rulers of our country during the period from 1947 till the mid-sixties are squarely to blame. They wanted to make India and not the Indians rich, for that they relied on heavy industries. They wanted to make India a strong nation–without making the people strong. They wanted to have the atom bomb, and they succeeded–but did not make any effort to create a new man and a new woman who only could make India great.

The fact that we can make India great is provided by the example of Kerala. All children in the age group of 10 to 14 years are literate in

Kerala. So that Kerala has life expectancies–71 years for males and 74 for females. The fertility rate in Kerala is 1.8, one of the lowest in the world. The infant mortality rate there is 17 and 16 per thousand for boys and girls respectively. And, all these despite Kerala's low income levels. In spite of its per capita income being lower than that of India as a whole, Keralites are not poor. Latest figures indicate that a few other states are going to catch up Kerala soon.

The Kerala example must summarily dismiss lack of funds as the main reason for failure in the primary education sector. If we have the money for everything else–like atomic energy, heavy industries, defence–we must have the money for compulsory primary education implementation which only can make us proud, can eliminate child labour, in short, this social welfare programme can usher in freedom and welfare of the people, social welfare programme can usher in freedom and welfare of the people, social change, better health and quality of life, eradication of evils like female infanticide, doing away with abysmal poverty and economic disparity, can put a stop in the alarming rise in population, eradicate social evils like discrimination based on caste and sex, and above all will eradicate the evil of child labour. (Let us remember, India contributes the largest share in the child labour force–it is all the more tragic, as mentioned earlier, that almost 90 per cent of child workers employed in the notorious match factories in Sivakasi in Tamil Nadu are girls).

Let us also remember that the vast majority of child workers belong to the depressed sections of our population and the Muslim minority. Which means that vast majority of children belonging to these sections have never gone to school.

IV

Dalit children (SCs/STs) have been deprived of their basic right of education for centuries. In fact, they have not been even recognised as person. How can we call ourselves a great nation and great people if we continue to treat a section of our people as non-person?

Let us be frank and forthright. The Dalits, together with other deprived sections like women, the children, and the minorities, have not been enabled, during the last fifty years, to reap the rewards of independence. Basically, the struggle for implementation of the social welfare programme of compulsory primary education is a struggle for human rights and human dignity. If the Dalits succeed in their struggle, as they must, it will prove a blessing for the entire nation–not merely any group or community. If this programme is not implemented, Dalits and other deprived sections like the Muslims (who constitute a sizeable section of our population) will continue to be alienated from the mainstream, and the very concept of integration, assimilation, patriotism –in short pride in being an Indian, pride in being involved in nation-building–will be undercut. Making the dominating section of our population respond to the national need is a veritable challenge because the dominant section continues to assume innate superiority that its members being clever, intelligent, educated, cultured and refined deserve what they have. They want the others to shelter under their dominance and seek sustenance at their mercy. This mind-set (conditioned by the divinely ordained hierarchical system of our society) is one of the most important reasons for non-implementation of the all-important social welfare programme.

Values and respect for other fellow human beings cannot be legislated. But human rights groups including the NHRC and social activists-intellectuals have the mandate to put the issues in proper perspective both before the government and the society. The NHRC can, if it can summon up the will, contribute considerably to change the mind-set referred to above. We know that it is a difficult and daunting task–all the more because this mind-set has not been a product of accident; it was injected in by some of the most sophisticated scholars and "wise men". It is precisely because of this that pioneers like Gautama Buddha, Raja Rammohun Roy, Ishwar Chandra Vidyasagar, Mahatma Phule found it hard to have a dialogue with such "scholars" and law givers. With the result that the soil has not yet been made ready to receive the seeds of values of human rights. It is one of the tasks of the NHRC in corporation with perceptive activists and NGOs to prepare the soil. If we cannot prepare the soil, universal compulsory primary education will remain a very distant goal.

Let us recognise the one most important fact in this context: "The traditionally elitist tendencies of the ruling cultural and religious traditions in India may have added to the political problem. Both Hinduism and Islam have, in different ways, had considerable inclination towards religious elitism, with reliance respectively on Brahmin priests and on powerful Mullahs, and while there have been many protest movements against each (the medieval poet Kabir fought against both simultaneously), the elitist hold is quite strong in both these religions. ...Buddhist countries have had much higher levels of basic literacy than societies dominated by Hinduism or Islam. In India both ancient and modern biases shape our policies reflecting prejudices of class divisions as well as of traditional cultures. The difficulty in getting even left-wing parties (who call themselves progressive) interested in combating inequalities in education relates to the general social atmosphere in India, including the nature of the leadership of the different parties which takes some major disparities as simply 'given' and not particularly worth battling against in view of other–perceived to be more–'pressing'–challenges" (*India: Economic Development and Social Opportunities*, OUP, 1995, by Jean Dreze and Amartya Sen). (West Bengal which has been ruled by left parties for over two decades is still one of the most backward states culturally and educationally.) It may be added that this has been one of the major reasons why the provisions of Article 45 of our Constitution have not been implemented.

V

It is in the context of what has been submitted above that we may take note of some of the measures that have been taken by different agencies, specially the Supreme Court and the Central Government. The December, 1996 Supreme Court judgement on child labour, while ordering the setting up of a corpus fund to be known as Child Labour Rehabilitation-cum-Welfare Fund with a Rs. 25000 contribution by the employer of a child in a hazardous industry, and giving a number of other rulings to end child labour, directs the government to ensure compulsory primary education for all children, and express the sentiment, "we have the fond hope that the closing years of the 20th century would see us keeping the promise made to our children by our Constitution about half a century ago". The judgement is, no doubt, full of noble sentiments. A careful reading of it, however, would indicate that the judges, with all respect for them and the Court, are totally on the wrong track. This is certainly not the way to go about implementing a social welfare programme, which is a responsibility of the State. The Court does not say anything, except expressing pious hope, as to legal consequences the State must suffer if "the promise made to our children about half-a-century ago" is not kept. Professor Saxena in a detailed analysis of the judgement has pointed out all the lacunae.

It may be recalled that pious sentiments were expressed by Supreme Court judges in an earlier judgement (February 1993) while giving a ruling that primary education be considered a fundamental right. It quotes: "Does not the passage of 44 years, more than 4 times the period stipulated under Article 45 convert the obligation created by the Article into an enforceable right? In this context we feel constrained to say that the allocation of available funds to different sectors of education in India discloses an inversion of priorities indicated by the Constitution. ... Be that as it may, we must say that at least now the State should honour the command of Article 45. It must be made a reality—at least now". Again, the Court is silent on what happens if the State does not perform its duty.

So far as the government is concerned, since the 1993 judgement the only "significant" step taken is the appointment of a Committee by the Centre which recommended early this year that primary education be made a fundamental right and a fundamental duty. The Minister concerned at the Centre has announced that a Bill to this effect is ready and will be placed before the Parliament soon (The government have conveniently forgotten the 1993 Supreme Court judgement which made this subject a fundamental right). What are the implications of the proposed Bill? Is it a fundamental duty on the part of parents? Does it mean that if a child does not go to school, his/her parents are to be prosecuted? Fair enough. But what about the fundamental right aspect? Will the State be prosecuted for violations of fundamental rights? Is or is not the State a criminal for not implementing the provision of Article 45 of the Constitution? Is it fair on the part of the State to take shelter under the Directive Principle provision which makes it non-justiciable? These are simple questions, and the answers are known to all. It can only be said with regard to the proposed Bill that there is a limit to hypocrisy and finding out convenient escape routes.

A few words about noises made by the government and its agencies. There have been a lot of advertisements on the Doordarshan about adult education, value-based education (whatever that may mean), midday meal and so on. These are no doubt very essential, but they are no substitute for compulsory primary education. Incidentally, have we ever seen any advertisement on the need for compulsory primary education!

In this regard it will be useful to quote from an article in the weekly *Mainstream*, April19, 1997: "A number of attempts have been made to camouflage our utter callousness on this issue. Not the least among these is the bogey of adult literacy. The question begging an intelligent answer is that if every year millions of uneducated children become adults, then the burden on adult literacy is going to increase. In which case how is the adult literacy campaign in any way going to reduce the number of illiterate people in the country?... In the absence of formal education, isn't it laughable to discuss the issue of non-formal education? If non-formal education is such a good alternative to the current system, why don't we put our own children through it? Let not the Indian middle class feel they are insulated from the problems arising out of deprivation. After all, to put it crudely, illiteracy leads to population growth which inexorably puts a burden on the entire infrastructure, that very infrastructure which is primarily enjoyed by the haves" (Sangeeta Mall, *Illiteracy–Worst Form of Human Rights Violation*).

On the government level, former Prime Minister Gujral's speech on 15 August, '97 was refreshing when he exhorted the values of education and put gender equality, women, the girl child and universal compulsory primary education first on the list of his priorities. Unfortunately, soon after he must have been warned by the bureaucrats that he had made a mistake: On 7 September, on literacy day, at a function organised by the Ministry of Human Resource Development, he announced: "Let us make it a rule that no child doing his 10+2 will get his certificate till he produces a certificate that he has made five people literate". It is bound to be interpreted as an escape route from his earlier announcement about implementing universal primary education. Apart from the fact that such a rule cannot be implemented and cannot have legal sanction, it will defeat the very purpose of promoting literacy. It must be emphasised that no scheme is a substitute for compulsory primary education, the successful implementation of which is a duty on the part of the State; and if this legal duty is not performed, the State must be held guilty and punished. Children up to the age of fourteen must attend regular school–with the entire infrastructure that a school is required to have, and regularly taught by full-time teachers. Children belonging to disadvantaged sections may be helped by 10+2 students and other social activists after school hours, but certainly not at the cost of regular schooling.

Why can't the government and the bureaucrats, including the Planning Commission and its "progressive and socialist" Vice-Chairman, understand the simple fact that as soon as all children up to the age of fourteen go to school and receive education there, illiteracy will be removed within a short span of time. As I said earlier, it has been removed in Kerala, and a few other states are approaching the goal. They have done so through regular schooling, and not through any other "literacy drive".

Another perceptible comment regarding non-implementation, made in the above mentioned *Mainstream* article is: "There is another equally important reason why literacy does not find a place in the planning exercise". (The unwritten policy of the Planning Commission is that implementation of compulsory primary education will be possible only when poverty is eliminated. Another instance of putting the cart before the horse.) It is because it suits the Indian middle class to keep the fifty per cent of the population unlettered. We think people would have notions above their situation if they aspire to schooling. Although we profess a false sympathy with the plight of the downtrodden, deep down we thank our stars that in these heathen days, with this talk of equality, there are still some 'sensible' people left who will do our bidding unquestioningly! If they too become educated, they may not be so servile and, worse, demand their rights, in which case the poor Indian middle class will be crushed even further. This is the attitude that is, unfortunately, widely prevalent even amongst people who should know better". Very harsh comments and observations, but the NHRC and NGOs need to give thought to this aspect.

There are not many takers for compulsory primary education. A discuss with Gandhians and humanists gives the impression that they too do not give, as much importance to this as it deserves. A few years ago, one of the most important Gandhian intellectual and activist, Dr. J.P. Naik (the virtual author of the Education Commission Report) wrote in a report brought out under the auspices of Citizens for Democracy and Jayaprakash Narayan, that compulsory primary education cannot be implemented by the State because of widespread poverty!

VI

If we want a significant change in the mind-set we need to have a movement to be led by creative thinkers–a positive movement for implementing the social welfare programme, and not merely of a negative movement of child labour eradication. Such a movement can grow only in an atmosphere of creative thinking. Furthermore, without such a movement our society cannot be rendered purposive and placed on the road to progress. And if we want India to occupy her rightful place in the country of nations, we need to raise our voice of reason and do the first thing first.

5
Right to Education

Joseph Gathia

A former UN Secretary General once said, "The way society treats its children reflects not only its qualities of compassion and protective caring but also its justice, its commitment to the future and its urge to enhance the human condition for coming generation."

The founding fathers of the Constitution of India specifically included clauses regarding the child welfare. Article 15(3) of the Constitution is example of this. To give special treatment to children, Article 24, guarantees another important fundamental right to the child below 14 years of protection against exploitations.

Article 45 directs the State to provide for universal free and compulsory education up to the age of 14. Similarly Article 39 in particular suggests the State to direct its politics towards giving opportunities to children to develop in a healthy manner so that childhood is protected. But despite these constitutional provisions India adopted the National Policy on Children only in 1974—almost 27 years after independence.

After adopting the Constitution we did not pay as much attention as we ought to have paid to the welfare of children. The present scenario speaks of pseudo-concern of the State for welfare and rights of the helpless children. With India's ratification of the Convention on the Rights of the Child (CRC) in 1992 new concept of monitoring in term of children's rights has emerged. In Rights of the Child CRC any signatory country has to keep measurable records of the four sets of basic rights. These are:

The right to survival which includes the right to life, the highest attainable standard of health, nutrition and adequate standards of living. It also includes the right to a name nationality.

The right to protection which includes freedom from all forms of exploitation, abuse, inhuman or degrading treatment and neglect including the right to special protection in situations of emergency and armed conflicts.

The right to development which includes the right to education-support for the early childhood development and care, social security and right to leisure recreation and cultural activities. The right to participation which includes respect for the views of the child, freedom of expression, access to appropriate information, freedom of thought, conscience and religion.

Demographic Profile

The population of India is young with nearly 37 per cent consisting children below 15: thus two out of every five person are below 15 years. The total child population in India is roughly 290 million out of 846 million as per the Census report, 1991. Every year some 13 million infants are added to the population. Children below 6 years comprise 21 per cent of the population.

Urban–Rural Ratio

An estimated 77 per cent of India's children live in rural areas. According to one projection about 99.4 million children–nearly two-fifths of the total Indian child population live in conditions adverse to survival. Of them 48.5 million, or nearly half, are less than 6 years old. An estimate of April, 1977 indicates that as many as 126 million children may be living below the poverty line.

It is reported that there were an estimated 7.8 million fewer girls than boys were in 1991. The female-to-male ratio works out to 0.959.

Most of recent data from the Census of India, 1991 indicate that there were 150 million children between 0 and 6 years of age. Some of the characteristics of this population group are given below:

- 73 million out of the 150 million children were girls, and 77 million were boys.
- 78 per cent of children resided in "rural" areas.

- Two states, Uttar Pradesh and Bihar accounted for 30 per cent of India's children in the age of 0 to 6 years.
- There were 27 million (or 18 per cent) children in the age group of 0 to 6 years who belonged to Scheduled Castes. Another 13.6 million (or 9 per cent) of children belonged to Scheduled Tribes.

Right to Survival

The Infant Mortality Rate (IMR) is one of the most sensitive indicators of overall social welfare in a given population. Though overall IMR ranges from 80 to 110 per live 1000 births still forty per cent of all deaths in India occur among children below five years of age. Of these deaths about half are children less than a year old. In the lowest are group (0-12 months), fifty per cent of deaths are due to preventable diseases such as dysentery, diarrhoea, respiratory diseases and gastro-intestinal disorders.

It is reported that there were an estimated 7.8 million fewer girls than boys in 1991. The female to male ratio is 959. In the population of children 0 to 6 years of age, district level data from the Census Report of India (1991) reveal shockingly low female to mâle ratios in several districts. Female infanticide is reported to be a cause for such adverse sex ratios in districts. While in other the female foetus is selectively aborted. In Bombay in 1984, some 40,000 female foetuses were aborted.

Another area of achievements is life expectancy at birth which has increased from 23.63 for male and 23.96 for female at birth in 1901 to 54.1 and 54.7 respectively in 1980. This could be attributed to an extensive network of over 2000 Community Health Centres, 22000 Primary Health Centres and 1,31,000 Village Level sub-Centres. India launched Child Survival and Save Motherhood (CSSM) Programme in August, 1992 which is directed at achieving 9 of the 17 goals of National Health Policy (1983) which are related to maternal and child health. This intervention for reducing morbidity and mortality include among others newborn care, immunisation, oral rehydration therapy, treatment of pneumonia, vitamin A prophylaxes, TT immunisation, prevention and treatment of anaemia, promotion of institutions for maternal care, treatment of maternal complications, management of obstetric emergencies and promotion of birth spacing. In 1996 India successfully completed world's largest immunisation programme covering almost 30 million children.

Perhaps the most crucial challenge to the health of children is in the age group of 0-6 years which is roughly 21 per cent of the population.

Water and sanitation

Water-borne and water-related diseases are the leading killers of infant and children in our country. About 163 million children (0-14 years) in rural India do not have access to safe drinking water, and are thus exposed to infection, which can prove fatal. In 1,13,000 villages the drinking water supply is either more than 1.6 km. away or is substandard and is responsible for diseases like cholera and guinea worm or problems related to a mineral content too high for health.

In another 24,000 villages, the water supply from wells, streams, tanks, and rivers is adequate in quality but open to the risk of pollution. There are at least 1,85,000 villages where the supply of water is both inadequate and unprotected. It is estimated (per 1981 Census) that about 8.7 per cent of deaths in the first year of life, 19.1 per cent of deaths in the 1-4 age groups and 15.2 per cent of deaths in the 5-15 age groups are due to diarrhoea.

Nutrition

Government of India's National Nutrition Policy (1993) draws attention to the serious problems of malnutrition among children in the country. For example :

- Newly 43.8 per cent of children suffer from moderate degrees of PEM (Protein Energy Malnutrition) and 8.7 per cent suffer from extreme form of malnutrition.
- Roughly 56 per cent of pre-school children suffer from iron deficiency.
- Close to 2.2 million children are afflicted with cretinism and about 6.6 million are mentally retarded and suffer from various degrees of motor handicaps.
- Iodine deficiency alone accounts for an estimated 90,000 still births and neo-natal deaths every year.

Government of India has taken several steps to address the problem of malnutrition. The ICDC was launched in 1975 and today it is world's largest nutrition programme encompassing 16.2 million children in the age group of 0 to 6 years and 3.2 million pregnant women. The authorities also claim that through 400,000 fair price shops food is sold to the poor at lower than market prices. But all these have failed to improve the nutritional status of over 43 per cent of India's children. Thus, on the very basic rights of the child, the right to survival, the scenario is not encouraging.

Only one out of every ten Indian children is lucky enough to receive food that conforms to the nutrition grade as defined by international standard. High rate of anaemia among women of child bearing age and young children, widespread iodine deficiency and infant feeding and weaning practices all cause or contribute to nutrition related health concerns.

Anaemia in young children is associated with impaired cognitive performances, motor development and scholastic achievement. A combination of increased intake of food rich in iron, fortification of staple foods with iron and diet supplementation can improve the situation.

The Right to Development

The CRC Article 6 says that "State Parties shall ensure to the maximum extent possible the survival and development of child" the UNICEF document in this context refers to two types of development emergencies that need equal attention: "Loud" emergencies which include natural disorder and armed conflicts which kill children, and "Silent" emergencies resulting endemic poverty and widespread deprivation. Prof. John Xanneth Gaifraith while delivering a lecture in Nov. 92 in New Delhi remarked "an educated populous is the first requirement for economic progress... In this world there is no literate population that is poor, no illiterate population that is other than poor".

In pre-independent India at the beginning of the 20th century Gokhle tried to bring a Bill for Compulsory education in the then Bombay Presidency.

Basic Education

A Directive Principle of the Constitution of India (Article 45) lays down that the State shall endeavour to provide free and compulsory education for all children until they complete 14 years of age. This was to have been achieved within a decade but has not been realised so far. Out of a total of 5,75,926 villages in the country, it is estimated that about 48,566 are not served by any school at all.

Approximately 4.5 million children are being offered any kind of pre-primary programme or the other. This forms barely 5 per cent of the population in the 3-6 years age group and are mainly from the better off sections of society. "India's primary education glass is two-thirds full and one-third empty," says latest World Bank Report on Primary Education. India now has 67 million children aged 6-10 who are primary school literate but 28 to 32 million primary education age children who are not. Another important part of the primary education is the great diversity in performance.

There are some positive achievements in the education sector. They are :

- More than 80 per cent children of 6-year-old are enrolled in the school.
- Enrollment by girls increased by 20 per cent between 1986 and 1993.

Negative side

- About 35 per cent of children enrolled drop-out before completing the primary school.
- About 15-20 per cent of children enrolled do not attend school regularly.

Enrollment data and age specific literacy rate suggests that India has made much progress in expanding access to education in 1993 about 100 million children were enrolled in primary school, up from 85 million in 1987. But school attendance is often irregular and primary school drop-out rates are high. About 32 million of the 105 million children age 6-10 were out of school in six states—Andhra Pradesh, Bihar, Madhya Pradesh, Rajasthan, Uttar Pradesh and West Bengal.

Reaching full enrollment of the age group 6-10 remain a major challenge in all states of India and a distant goal in some. Some states like Kerala and Tamil Nadu now have capacity to enroll all children of age group 6-10.

India has ambitious plan of education for all by 2004 AD and it has committed itself at the 1990 World Conference on Education for All that it will ensure necessary resources indicating that the allocation to education will increase from 3 per cent of GDP to 6 per cent by the end of Ninth Plan in 2002. Despite several lacuna in current state of primary education one could say that India has increased its investment in education from

1.2 per cent of its GDP in 1951-52 to 3.9 per cent of GDP in 1996. For a poor country like India it is no less an achievement. However, the challenge lies in the fact that India will be having the largest number of illiterates in the world by the turn of the century and this is a question mark on our future planning.

One needs to keep in mind that to accommodate all children 6-10 years of age in primary schools by 2007 AD (the final year of the Tenth Plan) we would require 1.3 million classrooms and 740,000 new teachers. The total cost would be around Rs. 40,000 crore. These mind-boggling figures are not to discourage ourselves but to adapt pragmatic policies and financial allocations.

The first step in this direction will be to make primary education compulsory. Some NGOs like Child Labour Action Network started campaigning for such a step way back in 1989 and more recently during the general elections in 1996. The UNICEF has been very active in this field. Some progress is being noticed in the field. One that almost all political parties have pledged their support for universalisation of primary education and secondly the Ministry of Human Resource Development constituted a high power committee on universalisation of primary education. But recently some disturbing news has also come that the plan to make primary education compulsory may be shelved off due to cost factor. This is an area of future action for rights activists.

The Courts in India have played very constructive role in creating enabling environment through its various judgements. In Mohini Jam vs. State of Karnataka (AIR 1992 SC 7673) the primary education has become a fundamental right. In Unnikrishnan vs-AP. (AIR 1993 I SCC 645) the Court reiterated that the right to primary education was a fundamental right. The NHRC also took up the issue of right to education and its chairman wrote letters to all state governments in this context. All this indicates that slowly the importance of basic education is being realised in the quarters where it matters.

The Right to Protection

The Constitution of India as well as the CRC especially refers to the protection of children from economic exploitation and from performing any work that is likely to be hazardous (Article 32 of UN CRC and Article 24 of Constitution of India). The Constitution specifically prohibits the employment of children under 14 years in hazardous occupations. This division of hazardous and non-hazardous has been a cause of problems both at the administration level as well as activist's level. It has led to a distinction being made between 'child labour', and the 'exploitation of child labour'.

It is well known that India has the largest number of child labour ranging from 23 million government figures to 44 million hurled by the NGOs. The Census of 1991 has estimated that there are 11.4 million full time child labour (boys 7.4 million and girls 4.0 million). In marginal child labour category the Census has computed 10.74 million.

The many manifestation of child labour can be broken down into seven main types: domestic services, forced and bonded labour, commercial sexual exploitation, industrial and plantation work, street work, work for the family and girl's work.

The Ministry of Labour and International Labour Organisation's (ILO) International Programme for Elimination of Child Labour (IPEC) has taken up several schemes covering about 380,000 mostly in hazardous industries covering glass industry of Ferozabad, carpet industry in Mirzapur-Bhadoi area, match and fireworks in Sivakasi, gem polishing in Surat and Jaipur, slate pencil making in Makrapur and Mandsaur, brassware industry in Moradabad and lock- making industry in Aligarh. Out of ten geographical areas selected by the Ministry of Labour for intervention four are in Uttar Pradesh. This does indicates that in the North India more children are employed in hazardous occupations than in the South India.

The Government of India has adopted three pronged approach in the matter of child labour legislation, rehabilitation and protection and public awareness. The UNICEF has suggested 6 steps for ending child labour. They are :

1. Immediate elimination of hazardous and exploitative child labour.
2. Provision for free and compulsory primary education.
3. Wider legal protection.
4. Birth registration of all children.
5. Data collection and monitoring.
6. Codes of conduct and procurement policies.

The UNICEF strategies lay heavy stress on corporate sector behaviour. Whatever one may say, one thing is clear that the problem of child labour requires multiple strategies to tackle it.

These strategies must aim at: release of children immediately from most damaging situations such as bonded labour and child prostitution; rehabilitation of those children who are released from work through provision of adequate services and facilities, especially education and protect working children who cannot be immediately red cased.

But most important of all is ensuring that new generation of children are not driven into hazardous forms of work and for this universalisation of primary education is an important step.

Policies for the progressive eradication of child work must be linked to structural change in the education system, requiring:

* increased government spending on education, especially primary schooling.
* provision of school books and essential materials for children.
* greater attention to adequate space, furniture and other physical facilities in schools.
* provision of improved training for teachers which enables them to introduce innovations, including more interactive teaching methods.
* greater flexibility in curriculum, promotion requirements and non-repetition.
* promotion of family participation in school processes.
* introduction of subsidies, scholarships and other mechanism to substitute children's incomes and to make schooling affordable for very low-income families.
* abolition of inefficient form of education (such as night school).
* transformation of schools into learning centres founded on principles of children as citizens. Quantitative indicators of good performance should be established by governments and monitored carefully overtime. Among the most important are:

- public spending on education.
- investments per student at each level of education, especially the primary level.
- proportion of investment in infrastructure and essential facilities.
- investments in textbooks and teaching aids.

In addition, goals and strategies need to be developed for the short, medium and longer term for the different groups of children and adolescents:

* those who work and attend school.
* those who work and do not attend school.
* those who don't do anything (neither work nor study).
* those who have never attended school.
* those who dropped out and are overaged.

Children in Difficult Circumstances

India has several million children living under especially difficult circumstances. These include, for instance, an estimated 500,000 street children in seven cities Bangalore, Mumbai, Calcutta, Delhi, Hyderabad, Kanpur and Chennai. The majority of these children are over eight years of age, have never attended school, and have parents who have low paid unskilled jobs. Destitute and orphaned children are another group about which very little is known. Similarly, there is very little information available about children of prostitutes, construction workers, fisherfolk children in institutions, disabled children and children affected by riots and disasters: all of whom fall under the category of "children in especially difficult circumstances". There is also reportedly sale of such children and girl trafficking across regional and even national borders.

Policy makers have long ignored the special needs of such children. The convention makes a strong case of special consideration to protect the rights of these children.

Handicapped Children

Four major disabilities affect at least three million children in the country. Estimates list two million mentally retarded, 8,00,000 blind, 5,00,000 orthopaedically handicapped and 2,00,000 deaf children.

There is severe lack of facilities for education, training and rehabilitation on handicapped children. Existing services cater to only 4 per cent of physically handicapped, 2 per cent of the blind, 2 per cent of the deaf and barely 0.2 per cent of the known mentally retarded child population.

Prevailing social attitudes towards mentally and physically handicapped children is perhaps single largest reason for our neglect.

Destitute Children

According to the Census figures there are around 151,000 child beggars — 120,000 in rural areas and 30,000 in the towns. Of those listed,

West Bengal has 25 per cent of the national total. Uttar Pradesh, Andhra Pradesh, Maharashtra, Karnataka and Orissa have the next largest incidence of child beggary. However, the officials themselves agree that these figures are underestimated.

The actual number of children in India pushed into beggary is, certainly higher than what the data says. Police records indicate that nearly a third of beggar children have one or both parents living: The parents themselves use their children for begging. Other children may be victims of cruel exploitation in beggar colonies, where kidnapped children are maimed and mutilated and forced to beg. Their earning go to the so-called beggar barons.

Another category of most exploited children are girls who are victims of commercial sexual exploitation. It is impossible to provide accurate statistics on the number of children in prostitution. As per one estimate there are about 400,000 to 5000,000 children who are victim of sex trade. (*India Today,* 1991). While there are no official statistics from Government of India, a study conducted on prostitution in the 6 metro cities in India, by the Central Social Welfare Board, estimated that 39.4 per cent of these prostitutes entered the profession when they were minor.

Commercial sexual exploitation of children is defined as when purpose is exchange for money or in kind favours among the child, the customer, intermediary or agent and others who earn profit from the trade. The three major forms of commercial sexual exploitation are: Child prostitution, trafficking role of children within the country or across borders of the countries for sexual purpose and child pornography.

The National Commission of Women (NCW) has now taken up the issue in right earnest. In a national convention held at Goa the NCW chairperson emphatically declared that eradication of this evil practice will be a priority for the next 10 years. The Delhi State Commission for Women has also taken up the issue and Mrs. Kamala Mankekar wants the capital region to be screened to identify the problem.

In India too, like some other developing countries religion, caste traditions and culture continue to be the basis for much of the exploitation of girls. The child prostitution exists in different forms in rural areas in India; for example, among Rajnets of Rajasthan, Devdasis of Andhra Pradesh, Maharashtra and Karnataka, Jogins of Andhra Pradesh and Banjaras and Bedias of Madhya Pradesh. "A common factor in all these practices is that initiation into prostitution demanded by puberty at the latest? Organised rural prostitution is therefore inherently child prostitution," says UNICEF document.

Right to Participation

The convention states "State Parties shall assure to the child who is capable of forming his or her own views freely in all matters affecting the child, the views of the child being given due weight in accordance with the age and maturity of the child. (Article 12 of CRC).

On this count very little work has been done in India. In fact, not only the Government has virtually neglected this aspect of children's rights; the NGOs have also not paid much attention towards this. Perhaps resource mobilisation for this is the reason. The UNICEF did support some children's gathering. In the schools also we have paid only lip service to the right to participation by the children.

But the most significant neglect, which we face, is of juvenile delinquents. The data are few. To quote some:

- 23,201 were children between the age of 7 and 12 years, 64 per cent were in the age group of 12 to 16 years, and 16 per cent were girls in the age group of 16 to 18 years.
- 38 per cent were illiterate and 36 per cent had completed primary schooling.
- 79 per cent were living with parents, another 19 per cent with guardians, and only 11 per cent were homeless.
- 84 per cent were new delinquents and 16 per cent were old delinquents.
- 60 per cent belonged to families who were earning less than Rs. 500 a month.

Little information, however, is available on the more crucial aspect of treatment meted out to these children. Legal representation of poor children is rare, and very few facilities exist for detention of poor children separately from adults. Much less is known about the availability and effectiveness of rehabilitation facilities. Recently the chairman of NHRC Mr. Justice M.N. Venkatachaliah has taken initiative in this direction. It would not be out of context to mention here that some actions taken by the NHRC of late has given a feeling of fresh breeze in an otherwise stale environment on the children's rights front.

Again, children in India, and girls in particular, have reportedly little say in the matter of marriage. There are still several thousands of child marriages reported throughout the country. In 1981, for instance, 43 per cent of the girls in the age group of 15 to 19 years were married. Although this proportion varied from 7 per cent in Goa, Daman and Diu to 64 per cent in Rajasthan, early marriage are seldom viewed as a violation of a child's freedom to enjoy childhood.

Concluding remarks

From the above account it is clear that so far children in India have been treated only with an object of welfare and not as investment in future. In a country of India's size and diversity there cannot be single set of priorities for the nation as a whole. The state must end tokenism, as it has little visible impact on the situation and much less enduring benefit. It hardly touches the fringe of the problem and in nowhere near solving the problem.

The NGOs have a vital role to play. The first priority must be to generate the political will to do this. The real change in the lives of children will come about only when social attitude and ethics progressively change to conform with laws and principles. Empowering the communities and strengthening the democratic institutions are best safeguards against violation of any human rights. Last but not least today's scenario reminds us Jawaharlal Nehru's words:

> "...the ambition of the
> greatest man of our generation
> has been to wipe every tear from every eye.
> That may be beyond us,
> but as long as there are tears
> and suffering, so long our task will not be over....."

6

Recent Supreme Court Judgements on Child Labour: A Critique

K.P. Saksena

Enactment of laws and judicial decisions concerning human rights have their significance since they identify basic norms and standards for observance and protection of human rights but by themselves they hardly make a difference on ground realities.

Let us take the case of child labour; going by the Indian legislations and various judicial decisions, one finds that child labour in factories, was abolished, by Section 67 of the Factory Act (1948) ; in agriculture, by Section 24 of the Plantation Labour Act (1951); in areas of merchant shipping, by Section 109 of Merchant Shipping Act (1951); in other areas of commercial-industrial activity, by Mines Act (1952), Motor Transport Workers Act (1961), Apprentices Act of 1961, Section 24 of Bidi Cigar Workers Conditions of Employment Act (1966) and by Child Labour (Prohibition and Regulation) Act (1986). Further legislative enactments were made to abolish child labour in shops and commercial establishments by various state governments. Thus, one would conclude that child labour does not exist in India. But the reality is that child labour is widely rampant; it has, indeed, increasingly spread its fangs far and wide; by various estimates number of child labour ranges from 40 million to more than 100 million.

There is more to the legislative measures. During the last 75 years, ILO had adopted 18 Conventions and 16 recommendations on child labour. Most of them have been accepted by the Government of India. India has also acceded (December 1992) to the UN Convention of the Rights of the Child of 1989.

There has been no shortage of studies, reports, pledges and rhetorics, either. Over the period, our national leaders have, time and again, promised to abolish child labour and to provide every child the best the nation has to give. Various ministries, specifically the Labour Ministry, have, over the period, instituted surveys and expert committees.

As regards judicial decisions, there have been several decisions from the apex court. The latest one, which is the focus of this brief write-up, is in the case of M.C. Mehta vs. State of Tamil Nadu and Others, in the context of employment of children in hazardous firework factories in Sivakasi (Tamil Nadu). As the situation in Sivakasi appeared to be a case of gross violation of the laws against employment of child labour, a public spirited lawyer, M.C. Mehta filed a petition, in 1986, invoking Supreme Court's power under Article 32 of the Constitution.

The judgement makes an interesting reading, it held "poverty as the basic reason compelling parents of a child to get it employed" and that "unless family is assured of income aliunde, problem of child labour would not get solved".[1] Under the heading "what to do", the judgement concluded that the least we ought to do is to see the fulfilment of legislative "intendment" behind the enactment of the Child Labour (Prohibition and Regulation) Act 1986. Taking guidance therefrom, the judges were of the view that offending employer must be asked to pay compensation for every child employed in contravention of the provisions of the Act, a sum of Rs. 20,000. This sum can be deposited in a fund to be known as child labour rehabilitation-cum-welfare fund and that income of corpus of the fund be utilised only for concerned child. Having decided what to do, the Supreme Court expressed "the fond hope that the closing years of the 20th century would see us keeping the promise made to our children by our Constitution about a half century ago". It further expressed the hope that beginning the 21st century, child labour would not only be abolished but such conditions would be made available as every child could enjoy "heaven of freedom" which poet Rabindranath Tagore had visualised in *Gitanjali*.[2]

With such pious expressions coming from the highest Court, could we say that judges are any different from our political leaders.

The Court was confused regarding the exact number of cases of child labour and it therefore asked the Central Government and the State Governments to carry out a survey within six months. Till the writing of this note (in August 1997), no progress has yet been made in that regard.

Another disturbing part of the judgement is that its spirit, as judges themselves have noted, was governed by the Child Labour (Prohibition & Regulation) Act of 1986. It is intriguing to note that the Act is contradictory in as much as it attempts to prohibit and at the same time regulate child labour. Secondly, the Act bans the employment in number of hazardous activities in factories but permits them to undertake the same activities at home. Thus, for instance, the child involved in electro-plating, a very hazardous process in manufacturing brass products and locks, is allowed to do so at home. This has resulted in production processes shifting from factories to residences. Indeed, there are a number of loopholes in the 1986 Act which has made it completely ineffective instrument for the removal of children working in industry. For instance, it is impracticable and unrealistic to draw a distinction between hazardous and non-hazardous processes in a particular industry.

In providing "relief", the Court has again relied on the Child Labour Act, 1986 (Section 14) which lays down that all those who have hired child labour in hazardous work should undergo imprisonment and pay a fine of up to Rs. 20,000 (minimum being Rs. 10,000). The Court has come out with the suggestion, as noted earlier, that the sum of Rs. 20,000 could be deposited in a fund to be known as Child Labour Rehabilitation-cum-Welfare Fund and further that the guilty employer should give employment to one of the adult members of the child's family. In those cases where it could not be possible to provide job to an adult of the child's family in the workplace where child was employed, appropriate government (of the State concerned or of the Centre), should make arrangements for providing a job to the adult or else deposit in the aforesaid fund a sum of Rs. 5,000 for each child employed in a factory or mine or in any other hazardous employment. This corpus of the fund amounting to Rs. 25,000 should be placed in some fixed deposit scheme and which would yield monthly income of Rs. 250 approximately.

Is this amount enough to sustain a family? Is it not that even this meagre money instead of getting utilised for child's education would open yet another door for misappropriation of the money by those who administer the fund meant for "social welfare" and "removal of poverty".

The Court held the view that extreme poverty and lack of adequate income is the root cause; if that is so, how child labour problem can be tackled without first removing the factors responsible for this social evil?

Indeed, child labour problem in the country cannot be sought in legal corridors alone, as its genesis and prevalence lies in socio-economic factors.

Why do children go to work? Of course, because they are poor. Poor parents need their children's income or services. Large number of working children have illiterate parents—who may realise the worth of education but cannot cope up with the immediate loss of child's wages. In certain rural or urban areas, school is an empty-structure without a teacher or it is located too far away. Sometimes children are bored in school and drop-out preferring earning some money. There is more to the situation. It is not uncommon of a working child to have unemployed parents. Children easily get employment in preference to adults because they are more compliant. There is another aspect of the situation. There are more girls than boys among the child labourers. This is so because the girl child is eventually going to be the property of her (future) marital home. Girl child is kept by a parent until she is married and leaves. So the thinking is common, why waste precious resources on educating her when the benefit of her education will belong to her husband's family.

Deeply entrenched patriarchal biases, poverty, lack of schools, boring curriculum all combine to push children into work.

Both the Act of 1986 and the Court has expressed concern of children working in hazardous activities. How about the millions of those children working in household or in tea-stalls or in food-shops, as coolies, vendors of newspapers, etc.

A review of the developments of the last fifty years shows that the problem of child labour, in India, has been overstudied, overlegislated and overdiscussed but was underacted upon. We have never been able to formulate an overall action plan to eradicate child labour with a time-bound programme schedule.

Today India is facing various complicated problems, the cancerous problem of child labour is one of them. The government should give top priority to eradicate thins social problem which is directly related to poverty. This is our problem and we owe it ourselves and to the future generations, to eliminate this malady from our society. Let us not ignore the fact that almost all the third world countries–caught in "debt-trap." They are no longer master of their own destiny. Role of external factors have increased, in pervasiveness and potency over the domestic factors. Thus, efforts at local, state and national levels are essential but the problem of poverty which is the root cause have to be tackled at global level. This, in turn, demands that the present lopsided economic world (dis)order should be replaced by equitable management of world economy.

The first step should be to generate wider public awareness against the problem, and to mobilise the support of the business corporates and active participation of trade unions. There is need to focus on liberation of women and family-based approaches to tackle child labour problem, preventive measures for child labour and correction of gender imbalance.

What is most essential is that central, state and local self-government institutions should assign high priority to the elimination of child labour. The key strategy is the provision of free and compulsory schooling of every child up to the age of 14 years through improved access to quality education and friendly school environment.

REFERENCES

1. M.C. Mehta V. state of Tamil Nadu & Ors., JT 1996 (ii) S.C. 685. para 28.
2. *Ibid.*, para 35.

7

Children's Rights in India

Pritam Arora

After having safely come up with the support system of the mother, the child kicks inside the body and establishes the right to independently move about in the space provided by the nature. But ever since it announces its arrival with a loud cry into this wide, wild world it falls into a circle of a family, a society and a nation to be brought up into the set parameters of the system it has born into and needs protection from elders to survive and grow up till it acquires the strength to fend for itself independently and becomes I, you, me, he or she with a specific identity of its own.

The socio-economic condition of a society reflects in the living condition of its children and their survival depends on the thinking of the conscious keepers of that particular class or group, thus foetus destruction, abortions, dowry-deaths, etc. are the banes of higher strata. Poverty, malnutrition, hunger and illiteracy are prevailing in the lower rungs and they comprise people below the poverty line, the disadvantaged sections and it is here that the basic rights to the child are mostly denied, these are the sections which form a large majority in the world. The planners, educators, administrators and the rulers are concerned not for themselves but for the welfare of the deprived humanity.

Basic rights to the child are denied not because of any perverse social system or lack of bonds of love and affection from those who have brought them into this world, but due to hunger, poverty, malnutrition and large scale unemployment. Majority of these unwanted children are born out of sexual needs of the parents who lack any scientific knowledge of family planning and as soon as they survive beyond the age of 5-10 years they are sold out as commodity, to supplement family income, to provide resources to adults, to bring more such hapless creatures into this world and the cycle goes on.

Children are victims of droughts, famine, disease, salc of organs, etc. They are economically exploited by putting them into dangerous jobs on a minimal salary. Deprived of the care-free innocence of childhood and brought up in the atmosphere of fear, beaten and sexually exploited, they are sold to unscrupulous vagabonds to be turned into beggars, camel riders, domestic servants and hazardous jobs like stone quarrying, fire works units, match factories, carpet weaving, diamond cutting, etc.

In spite of the resolve of the governments of the world and voluntary organisations, the things have not changed and conventions of United Nations have only created a little awareness.

Problems of children cannot be viewed in isolation, it is directly related to their parents, taking family as a unit-otherwise nations singly or collectively will continue to pass resolutions. It is necessary to divert sexual urges of the poverty stricken, unemployed and undernourished masses by providing sources to relax, better living conditions, better employment opportunities, so that they channelise their energies into better pass-time and become a responsible citizen of the world. By first educating the parents, the education to the child will automatically follow. It is necessary to stop sexual exploitation, to stop using children to perpetuate the crimes of the adult world, to stop them from purchasing materials produced by children for which adults need to be warned.

Minor girls are brought to cities for sex-abuse and prostitution. Thus the innocent children born out of the sexual urges of the poor end up in satisfying the sexual urges of the rich. Who is more guilty and who is less guilty–those who sell them, those who purchase them or those who have a ready market to exploit them?

When the needs of the food, housing and clothing are met, the habits to gamble, drink and sexualise are formed as a diversion for the rich and these very people throw up cheques here and there for charity and don a mask of nobility and gentlemanliness.

Poverty and affluence are both responsible for all the crimes in the world and in this process we create hundreds of criminals and underworld dons. Out of the milk of humanity, from innocence, is born urge to kill and from truth is born the urge to deceive, to indulge in corruption, bribery, murders, smuggling and drug cartels. At this stage money becomes the only religion whatsoever track, the children grown up in such surroundings are introduced into organised crimes, human sensibilities become ineffectual, after years of marginalisation, dignity of the self vanishes. At this stage teaching them what is right and what is wrong does not provoke them to act in the ways of the civilised society.

It is necessary for the Governments to take steps into reducing infant mortality, ban sex-determination tests, provide immunisation system, safe drinking water, cheap and nutritious food and schools and hospitals on a priority basis as a part of this welfare schemes by reducing the expenditures in higher brackets and enforcing strict family planning laws.

Right to Education

Formative years of a child's life are first 10 years and are affected by:

1. Family atmosphere
2. Parental care
3. Ideas implanted in the primary schools

Thus right to education is a theme of increasing importance and an integral part of the concept of society building process. It is not a preparation for life but very much a part of life.

In 1835 Lord Macaulay created the educational system in India because East India Company found it too expensive to bring lower division clerks from Britain. Thus a bureaucracy was born in India which suited the needs of colonisers; Indian by birth but British in taste. During the freedom movement Gandhiji, Tagore and Dr. Zakir Hussain innovated schemes to take education to masses. In 1960's Kothari Commission and Ishwar Bhai Patel Commission suggested that destiny of India is being shaped in its classrooms and advocated universalization of primary education but majority still remains illiterate, uncared for and unkept, bonded labourers and living in dirty conditions, exploited as child labourers, because in spite of the holy schemes of the Governments, the socio-economic realities have kept us out of this dream.

Out of every 20 people in the world 3 are Indians and out of which 2 are illiterate. Out of every 10 illiterates in the world 5 are Indians and out of every 10 illiterates in India 7 are girls.

Even if you make primary education compulsory and free between 6-14 years you cannot convince the parents to send the child to school and forgo the age of the earnings that they start bringing before the age of 14. Though percentage of literates in India is increasing, it is a paradox that the number of illiterates is also increasing. During the post-independence period there has been spectacular increase in elementary education. In fact the elementary education system in India is one of the largest in the world. In fact, as per 1986 survey 94.5 per cent of rural population had primary schools within walking distance of 1 km, upper primary schools within 3 km. there is notable development in the field of education as per National Education Policy 1968, in the universalization common structure of education throughout the country, introduction of 10+2+3 system with science and maths compulsory in school curriculum. Most of the states have free education up to the secondary level for all and up to graduation level for girls.

Education is a unique investment for the present and future of our nation and expenditure on education should be raised from 6 per cent to 10 per cent of GNP.

Every child has the right to secure and fulfilling life, free from fear and ignorance. It is necessary that every child born in this country is provided at least elementary education of satisfactory quality with full participation of girl child and marginal and disadvantaged groups living in rural backward and far flung tribal habitats.

UN General Assembly in 1989 adopted the convention on the rights of the child; this convention came into force from 1990. As per the convention parents have joint responsibility for raising their children and the State has an obligation to support them in this.

Government of India introduced midday meals scheme for the primary school children on 15th August 1995. It was stated that 1¾ crore children will be having midday meals at 1.00 p.m. everywhere in the country in 5 lakh villages and this is going to be a permanent programme, there was also proposal to bring flexibility in the system and to do away with the failure system in the primary stage and all avenues should be open for further education and facilities be created for the poor and deserving children. Jawaharlal Nehru once said, "The modern world moves on the wheels of the written word, if one does not know the word he will be crushed under the wheel" when India became free about 14 per cent population was literate—and only 1 child out of 3 was enrolled in primary school. This low level was again aggravated by acute regional and gender disparities. In 1951 we had 18.33 per cent literacy and in 1991 52.1 per cent.

On 8th Sept. 1997 K.R. Narayanan, President of India stated that economic development of the country would remain a distant dream unless we eradicate illiteracy and he called for a reappraisal of national policies programme and performance in the field of primacy education. He stressed that since 350 million people in this country are still illiterate shows that somewhere there was a lack of political will.

Even the UN Secretary General in his message stressed the need for political will to meet the challenges of illiteracy and the same is true to facilitate access of every child to education during the formative years of his/her life for free and compulsory education between the years of 6-14 and thereafter facilities to develop.

8

Role of Media

Regina Mulay Parakh

Human rights, deal with the wholistic development of a human being, in harmony with other human beings in society. The concept of human rights is necessarily evolving in nature, keeping pace with the socio-economic changes in the society. Hence, the basic rights of an individual are "those conditions of social rights without which no man can seek, in general, to be himself at his best".[1] These rights are based on elementary human needs as imperatives. Some of these needs are elemental for sheer physical survival and health, others are elemental for psychic survival and health. Accordingly, human beings must be protected from violation, injustice and degradation of these rights.

The all pervasive nature of human rights, have been further classified and codified under various heads as: women's rights, political rights, rights of the child, etc. The present study seeks to evaluate the role of the media in creating awareness, and communicating the rights of the child.

Human rights in general, and the rights of the child in particular, are predominantly western concepts, evolved in the ethos of western, developed social culture. The socio-economic-political environment of the West is in stark contrast to the developing and underdeveloped world. On one hand we have stable economy, abundance of food and shelter, medical aid, educational facilities and social security. There are means for enforcement of the rights and remedies to control the damages done due to violation and abuse of the same. On the other side of the coin there is poverty, hunger, malnutrition, lack of shelter, unstable economy and equally unstable governments. Here the very survival of human life and dignity are at stake. With majority of the population living below poverty line, with ever growing line of children correlating to the serpentine que for food, shelter, work and the endless struggle for mere existence—the rights of the child take a new dimension.

The questions that arise out of such a diagonically opposite scenario for the propagators of Human Rights and for those to whom it is targetted are: is the right of the child to education greater than right to life? Is right to no work for child more important than right to two square meals a day? The child of the third world struggles for existence as against his counterpart of the West.

India, with its enormous population and diverse culture is perhaps the best example of the conflict among various human rights here and in the West.

The Right of the Child

India became a party to the International Convention on the Rights of the Child in 1992. There is no doubt that all the rights must be applicable to the child, as they are necessary for the development of a human being. The convention on the rights of the child is an all compassing document, laying down rules and regulation for the development of the child.

It is perhaps redundant to delve into the intricacies, legalities of the rights of the child. Better to highlight some of the problematic rights in context of the children of India.

The children of India, as most of the children of the Third World, are exploited lot. Their exploitation starts from home, where the eldest child has to look after his/her younger siblings, in order to enable their parents to work, thereby, sacrificing its basic rights to play, to get education, etc. Child labour is rampant with the young ones shouldering the burden of keeping the kitchen fire lit, and everyone fed in the family.

In recent years child labour in the Third World has become an international concern. The convention on the rights of the child in Article 32 states:

> "... the right of the child to be protected from economic exploitation from performing any work that is likely to be hazardous or to

> interfere with the child's education, or to be harmful to the child's health or physical, mental, spiritual, moral or social development."[2]

The exploitative child labour is an evil of the society which cannot be wished away in a blink, as they are deeply rooted in the problem of poverty, illiteracy and overpopulation. It has been reported by the Human Rights Watch that India has about 15 million children in conditions of slavery. Children are engaged in various hazardous industries like fire works, matches, carpet making, glass bangle-making, diamond cutting, etc. In reality child labour exists more in unorganized sector than the organized sector.

Recently, the ban on the child labour in cracker factories at Sivakasi in India, withdrawal of children from carpet, bidi and bangle factories is one step forward in a positive direction. However, it has now created a large section of unemployed children, with nowhere to go. There have been little or no efforts done to sustain these children, either by giving educational facilities or by alternate jobs to them or their parents. Most of these children worked not out of choice but for survival.

Another sector, where there is gross violation of the rights of the child are: child trafficking, child prostitution, sexual abuse and drug peddling. There is sharp rise in crime against children and crime by children. New and innovative methods are being used to exploit children in forms of child beggars, car cleaners, etc.

The question that comes to the fore is how well are we, beyond the four walls of classrooms, conference halls and intellectual discussions, and people outside are aware about the rights of the child. This problem of 'the child' is not just an intellectual property right, but a social disorder needing immediate rectification. It is the people and society at large that needs to be educated. It is here that the media comes in.

Mass Media and Rights of the Child

The media today is faced with the daunting task of informing people, educating them and creating awareness about human rights, and specifically the children's right. It has now become clear that information and communication are central for any action taken nationally or internationally. 'Communication and access to information should be a right in itself. The right of the people to be informed and to express themselves freely is need of today. It is a pity that final declaration of the world conference includes one paragraph on this: paragraph 39 reads:

"Underlining the importance of objective, responsible and impartial information about human rights and humanitarian issues, the world conference on Human Rights encourages the increased involvement of the media, for whom freedom and protection should be guaranteed within the framework of national law."[3]

It is peculiar that the conference stressed on the 'informatics role of the media, and ignored its role as an educator and communicator'.

In today's information centric world, the media in India has to play more dominant role than it is doing today. It has to highlight the rights of the child and educate people on child abuse.

Here again is a dichotomous situation, should one bring to fore the negative social aspect of child abuse, sexual exploitation, torture and deprivation from education or just project a positive image of do-gooders and the scant positive steps taken. The media is embroiled in the eternal question of should it or should it not project a correct picture.

It is well known that the mass media—has a great impact on its audience. Till now this advantage of the media has not been explored in favour of educating people. The track record of newspaper, radio and television has been dismal. Apart from sporadic reporting of cases of child abuse, not much has been done.

A revolution in communication—the radio, the TV, the international satellite network or even Internet—has meant that the national and international community can no longer claim ignorance on the abuse of the rights of the child. Everyday, the global community sees, children dead due to war, drought or sheer poverty. The toll taken by dreadful diseases of children go unnoticed. The occupational hazard of the media is that they are attracted only to atrocities and sufferings which are of spectacular nature. The day-to-day mundane issues hence go unnoticed.

This critical appraisal of the media is not aimed to show where we are lacking, but being home to the emergency of the social crisis faced by children of India and the third world.

Media can be of help by adopting following programme for building up awareness on the rights of the child:

(1) A systematic publication of article in newspapers, stories for children on child exploitation, exhibitions, etc., should be written.

(2) Long and short programmes on radio and television about the rights of the child and its violations.

(3) Sponsoring of short snippets on national and international network.

(4) Use of SAVE programmes to create awareness within the SAARC region.

(5) NGO's with the help of films and video cassettes should educate the people at village level.

(6) A concerted effort through the mass media should be taken up to propagate need for child education, their rights and steps taken to protect the same.

It is not, that nothing is being done to protect the rights of the child, but a lot needs to be done. Unless the exploited and the exploiters are made aware of their rights, how they are violated and what cost is to be paid for that exploitation, not much can be achieved.

The media and the academic, both need to reevaluate their contributions to the cause of HRT. and the Rights of the Child. In fact there is a need to create a new set of rights which are based on our social realities, needs and rights.

REFERENCES

1. Harold J. Laski, *A Grammar of Politics*, 4th ed., London, 1960, p. 91.
2. First Call for Children : Convention on the Rights of the Child, Article 32, New York, 1990, p. 32.
3. Roberto Savio, "Raising Awareness", in *Human Rights the New Consensus*, UN, 1994, p. 49.

III

9

Undertrials: Their Rights and Reality

Rajindar Sachar

A visitor from some outer planet to this earth will be elated to learn about progressiveness of our legislation and further overwhelmed by the radical interpretation of laws by the Supreme Court. But alas, if he were to tarry a little longer, and devote time to find about the implementation of these laws, he will immediately realise the wide gap existing between laws and implementation. This will be true above all, about our laws regarding undertrials.

It is broadly accepted that the treatment given to its prisoners is one of the important test of a civilised and humane content of any nation.

Thus former Chief Justice Y.V. Chandrachud said, "Convicts are not, by mere reason of the conviction, denuded of all the fundamental rights which they otherwise possess...Likewise, even a convict is entitled to the precious right guaranteed by Article 21 of the Constitution that he shall not be deprived of his life of personal liberty except according to procedure established by law".[1]

Similarly, J. Krishna Iyer, speaking on behalf of the Court observed "the jurisdictional reach and range of this court's writ to hold prison caprice and cruelty in constitutional leash is incontestable. Thus it is now clear law that a prisoner wears the armour of basic freedom even behind bars and that on breach thereof by lawless officials the law will respond to his distress signals through 'writ' aid. The Indian human has a constant companion; the Court armed with the Constitution."[2]

Again J. Bhagwati observed "the prisoner or detenu obviously cannot move freely by going outside the prison walls nor can he socialise at his free will with persons outside the jail. But, as part of the right to live with human dignity and therefore as a necessary component of the right to life, he would be entitled to have interviews with the members of his family and friends and no prison regulation or procedure laid down by prison regulation regulating the right to have interviews with the members of the family and friends can be upheld as constitutionally valid under Articles 14 and 21, unless it is reasonable, fair and just".[3]

The deep consideration for undertrials was evidenced[4] where the Court reiterated that right to speedy trial is covered within Article 21 of the Constitution; the court directed the murder cases to be disposed of within 6 months by nominating Additional Session Judges. It also directed that undertrials who are in jail for more than one year and two years in cases under attempt to murder, cheating, kidnapping if they have been in prison for two years may be released even on their personal bond."

Again deep concern was visible when court recognised that many poor persons languish in jail because of poverty and directed that they be released on personal bond, because as the court said, "If they are poor and helpless, they languish in jails for long periods either because there is no one to bail them out or because there is no one to think of them. The very tendency of criminal proceedings for long periods by itself operates as an engine of oppression........ In a majority of these cases, whether instituted by police or private complainants, the accused belong to the poorer sections of the society, who are unable to afford competent legal advice........ It appears essential to issue appropriate directions to protect and effectuate the right to life and liberty of the citizens guaranteed by Article 21 of the Constitution. It is also necessary to ensure that these criminal prosecutions do not operate as engines of oppression."[5]

Notwithstanding all this oration, the reality is still very painful. This has been brought out in the incisive report of Ms. Justice Leila Seth, who enquired into the circumstances leading to the death of Rajan Pillai. Thus according to the report the congestion in Tihar Jail is horrible. Against a capacity of 3250 prisoners, average number of prisoners annually is 10,000; out of existing 9500 prisoners, 8200 are undertrials including 80 children.

One of the greatest injustice and violation of Article 21, in the case of poor undertrial, who has to remain in jail for his poverty, is the denial of his electoral right and denial of right to vote to elect his representative, which is a basic feature of the Constitution.

In a recent judgement[6], the Supreme Court unfortunately upheld the denial of law which debars the undertrial to exercise the right to vote, it is respectfully submitted that this judgement runs counter to the long established rights of the undertrial to exercise such rights in all other jurisdictions and under International Covenants. An examination of the recent decision of the Supreme Court upholding the validity of law which debars a slum dweller accused of even a minor offence from voting because he is languishing in jail, being too poor to offer bail bonds while permitting a rich accused facing charges of murder, rape or corruption to be elected as a Member of Parliament or the State Legislature highlights the incongruity and the contradictions in the situation.

A public interest litigation had challenged Section 62(5) of Representation of People Act, 1951 which denies to undertrials who are in prison or police custody the right to vote while permitting this right to vote to persons accused of heinous offences but outside on bail. The plea that this provision is grossly discriminatory as it favours the rich smugglers, blackmarketeers who could afford bail bonds against poor undertrials failed to persuade the court to hold this provision as unconstitutional.

The Court has upheld this restriction on undertrials by seeking support from the well accepted proposition that criminalisation of politics is the negation of democracy and thus subversive of free and fair election which is a basic feature of the Constitution and that this provision is enacted with that very objective.

A layman however would find absurdity and anomally in a law which at the same time permits a convicted person and sentenced to less than two years to contest election (even from jail) and vote at an election (if out on bail) even though sentenced for 10 years, and wonder as to how this discrimination advances the cause of fair and free elections.

The Court has also justified permitting a person in preventive detention to vote by postal ballot while denying the same right to undertrials in detention by holding that preventive detention is to prevent breach of law while imprisonment on conviction or during investigation is subsequent to the commission of crime and therefore, this classification is reasonable. Now persons under preventive detention are those against whom allegations are of indulging in smuggling and of narcotic offences. But even then such a person can only be kept in preventive detention if the same is held justified on a review by three Judges of the High Court. If in spite of this prima facie strong proof a detenue is permitted to vote at the election, pray what is the logic for denying the right to vote to a poor undertrial in jail, against whom the only allegation of guilt, and that too under a minor offence, say of affray or of a poor mill worker held in jail for allegedly violating a ban on meetings or processions. That too after an investigation by an inspector of police, and whom not even a magistrate has found guilty. This differential attitude against an undertrial would be in conflict with normal criminal jurisprudence and specifically with Article 84 of the Standard Minimum Rules for Treatment of Prisoner-adopted by the First United Nations Congress on the Prevention of Crime and the Treatment of Offenders, held at Geneva in 1955, and approved by the Economic and Social Council by its resolutions 663 C (XXIV) of 31st July, 1957 and 2076 (LXII) of 13th May, 1977 to the effect that "unconvicted prisoners are presumed to be innocent and shall be treated as such".

The finding of the Court is also counter to the right guaranteed by Article 25(b) of Human Rights guaranteed under International Bill of Human Rights, namely, International Covenant on Civil and Political Rights, which by Article 25(b) specifically provides that "Every citizen shall have the right and the opportunity, without any of the distinctions mentioned in Article 2 and without unreasonable restrictions: to vote and to be elected at genuine periodic elections which shall be by universal and equal suffrage and shall be held by secret ballot, guaranteeing the free expression of the will of the electors; which specifically recognises a right to vote and to be elected at genuine periodically election".

In U.K. right to vote is denied only if a person is convicted and during the time he is detained in penal institution. In Israel even a convicted person in jail is allowed to vote.

Notwithstanding the international law and conventions the Court felt the classification to be valid by holding that some elbow room must be available to the legislature in classification. But with due respect, the court has ignored the caution given by the apex Court more than 40 years back that through good faith and knowledge of existing conditions on the part of a legislature has to be presumed. That is so; yet to carry that presumption to the extent of always holding that there must be some undisclosed intention or reason for subjecting certain individuals to a hostile and discriminatory legislation is to make the protection clause of Article 14 a mere rope of sand, in no manner restraining state action. The protection afforded by the article is not a mere eye wash but it is a real one.

Another justification mentioned for upholding the law is that it would mean deploying larger police force for conduct of elections. But it was never pleaded that undertrials should be taken personally to polling booths to cast their votes, all that was claimed was the right to vote by postal ballot just like given to smugglers and others detained under preventive law. This did not require even one extra policeman to be deployed.

But what is of distorting consequence is the reason that as right to vote is subject to the limitations imposed by the statute and therefore, the challenge to any provision of election law cannot be made with reference to a fundamental right in the Constitution.

This finding contrary to Article 13(2) which mandates that any law made by legislature which contravenes any of fundamental rights in Part II (e.g. Article 14) shall be void. Thus the election law is no holy cow so as to claim immunity from the sweep and protection of Article 14.

The guarantee of equal protection under Article 14, according to earlier Supreme Court decisions embraces the entire realm of state action, even in the matter of granting privileges and contract. How then can it be said that statute on election law is immune from scrutiny under Article 14.

If the courts finding that Articles 14 and 21 cannot be invoked by a citizen in testing election law, grave consequences will follow. Thus assume that if parliament was to pass a law that only six feet tall and above persons or children of Ministers could alone vote at election could conceivably such a law be upheld and if so what becomes of the courts own dictum that free and fair elections are the basic feature of the Constitution.

Such a law would be completely subversive of our democratic constitution and would have to be held as null and void.

People are always keen observers as to who out of the executive or judiciary appreciates the felt needs of time and acts accordingly. In this judgement of undertrials, unfortunately with all its judicial activism, judiciary has felt helpless because of the wording of statute—even though it may have sympathised with the claim of undertrials. May be the executive/legislature in the fiftieth year of independence can come to the rescue of undertrials in prison who are being discriminated only because of their poverty.

REFERENCES

1. *D.B. Patnaik vs. State of Andhra Pradesh,* (1975), 2 SCR 24.
2. *Sunil Batra vs. Delhi Administration,* (1979), 1 SCR 392, p. 503.
3. *Francis Coralie Mullin vs. The Administrator, Union Territory of Delhi andors.* (1981) SC 746.
4. *R.D. Upadhyay vs. State of A.P. and ors.,* (1996), 3 SCC 422.
5. *"Common Cause" a registered Society through its Director vs. Union of India and ors.* (1996) 4 SCC 33.
6. *Anukul Chandra Pradhan, Advocate Supreme Court vs. Union of India and ors. JT,* 1997(6) SC 86.

10

Indian Prisons : A Survey

Sankar Sen

About appalling conditions in Indian prisons, many books and articles have been written. Reports of the All India Jail Manual Committee (1957-59), as well as the Annual Reports (1994-95, 1995-96) of the NHRC have highlighted the ills that bedevil the prison administration and advocated the need for both short-term improvements and long-term reforms. NHRC is trying to persuade the Central as well as State Governments to agree for a new All India Prisons Act whose draft it has prepared. The new Act is to replace the old and outdated Prisons Act of 1894.

Meanwhile, some quick and positive steps to improve the prison administration in the country are called for. In this connection it has to be borne in mind that the total number of prisoners in Indian jails is small when viewed against the prison population in many other countries of the world. Total number of prisoners in India, (as on 31-12-95) according to figures collected by the Bureau of Police Research and Development (BPR & D) was 226,158. Number of male prisoners was 219,873 and female prisoners was 6285. Of this, the number of undertrial prisoners was 163,092. This reduces the number of convicted prisoners to 63066. In a country of 970 millions the number of prisoners in jails, and particularly those undergoing imprisonment after conviction is no doubt very small. Indeed the prison population works out to be .023 per cent of the total population of the country.

The situation in India in this respect is to be juxtaposed against what is prevailing in some of the developed countries of the world. In USA today there are one and half million prisoners, and another three millions are under penal control outside prison.

Thus, nearly five per cent of adult males are under penal control. It is not, as a well-known penologist Nil Christe puts it "crime control, but a kind of war situation". In Russia also, there has been an exponential increase in the prison population. In 1993, Russia had about 573 prisoners per 100000 of population and in 1995, it was 687 per 100000 population. In India there were about 23 prisoners per one lakh of population in 1995. Prison population of China is also very high, but reliable statistics are not available. Today Russia and the United States are the two biggest incarcerators in the world. In Great Britain also prison population is going up. The present prison population in UK is about 60,000. It is by-product of a new policy of "get-tough-on-crime" and constitutes a departure from the old conservative British tradition represented by Winston Churchill who said that it was not decent to have so many poor people in prison.

In this connection it may be mentioned that academic research has shown little or no correlation between rates of crime and number of people in prisons. Increase in the incarceration is not necessarily followed by decline in crime. A study in the USA has shown that two States North Dakota and South Dakota each are virtually identical in terms of demographics and geography. South Dakota imprisons citizens at three times the rate of North Dakota but crime rate in both the states is roughly the same for several decades. (USA, Department of Justice, Bureau of Justice Statistics, August, 1995.)

However, the disturbing aspect of Indian prison condition is the overwhelming number of undertrial prisoners. In many jails of the country they constitute more than 90 per cent of the prison population. Presence of the undertrials along with the convicted prisoners has many distressing consequences. It causes 'contamination of crime'. Many inexperienced young men coming in constant touch with the hardened criminals get coarsened and spoiled. It is a fact that many gangsters recruit members of their criminal gangs from these borderline, yet redeemable, offenders admitted to jails. Further, constant movement of undertrial prisoners goes to create serious problems for the prison administration. They are carriers not only of narcotics and other contraband articles but also of contagious diseases.

Wolf Report

In the United Kingdom, Lord Wolf in his report on 'Prison Disturbances' (April, 1991) observed that because of overcrowding very often a substantial number of prisoners leave prisons more embittered and hostile to society than when they arrive. Lord Wolf proposed that for achieving humane and constructive prison regime, there should be a legal ceiling on the number of inmates in each prison which the Home Secretary should be able to extend only by obtaining parliamentary approval.

In America, the Supreme Court in two major decisions addressed itself to this overcrowding problem. In the case of *Wolf vs. Mcdonal*, 1974, involving pretrial detainees, the court, held that the principle of one, man, one cell cannot be read in the "Due Process Clause" of the Fifth Amendment. It held that the practice of putting two detainees in a cell meant for one person was not unconstitutional. In the case of *Rhodes vs. Chapman*, the court went on to conclude that the "Constitution does not mandate comfortable prisons". However, if overcrowding is not constitutionally impermissible, it no doubt tells on the health of the prisoners and affects the hygienic conditions. In Indian context, it is absolutely essential to take serious note of this problem.

At present, in Tihar Jail, there are about 9000 prisoners against the capacity of 2,500. In Meerut Jail, it was found during a visit of NHRC officers that against authorised capacity of 650 prisoners, there are about 3000 prisoners in which 80 per cent of them were undertrials. Overcrowded prisons do not have space, facility and resources to provide prisoners their normal work, training and other educational opportunities. It has a knock-on effect on other aspects of the prison administration.

The All India Jail Manual Committee (1957-59) strongly reccommended that there should be separate institutions for accommodating undertrial prisoners with adequate security and segregation facilities at each place where a central or district prison is located. This is necessary to relieve pressure on district prisons and work out suitable arrangements for dealing with the undertrial prisoners. The institution should be located near the court premises to reduce the problem and hazards of transporting the prisoners.

Transportation Problem

Indeed the problem of transporting the prisoners from prisons to courts and back is a recurring one. There are many complaints before the

NHRC from prisoners from different jails stating that they are not produced before the court on the dates of hearing because of non-availability of the police escorts. There was a harrowing case from Bihar where a prisoner could not be produced before the court for a year because of non-availability of police escort. The police, on the other hand, take the plea that it has no separate staff earmarked for escort duty of prisoners, and so they find it difficult to spare police for escort, especially when law and order problems erupt. Provision of separate staff for escorting the prisoners to courts and hospitals has to be considered seriously. The Supreme Court in the case of *Rama Murti vs. State of Karnataka* has suggested that escorting of prisoners should be done not by the police but by the prison staff and necessary steps should be taken for the purpose. It is necessary to quickly implement this recommendation.

Medical Facilities

Indian jails have very poor medical facilities. Mulla Committee in its report highlighted woeful lack of facilities for treatment of prisoners in jails. Disturbed by the rising incidence of deaths in police and jail custody, NHRC had issued instruction that reports of deaths in police and jail custody should be sent to it within 24 hours. During the year 1995-96, 308 cases of death and in 1996-97, 700 cases of death in jail custody were reported to the NHRC. One of the reasons for high incidence of death in jail custody is due to utter inadequacy of treatment facilities in jails. Indeed society has an obligation, as the Supreme Court has mentioned in Rama Murti's case, towards prisoners' health for two reasons. First, prisoners do not enjoy access to medical expertise that free citizens have and secondly, because of conditions of incarceration, inmates are exposed to more health hazards than ordinary citizen are. Prisoners, therefore, suffer from a double handicap.

For lessening the hardship of the undertrials, recently, the Supreme Court in a path-breaking decision *Common Cause vs. Union of India and others* has held that right to speedy trial is a part and parcel of right to life guaranteed by Article 21 of the Constitution. The court ordered release on bail of the accused persons whose trial is pending for one year or more attracting imprisonment up to 7 years and who have already spent 6 months to 1 year in jail. Cases, which are pending for more than a year but legal punishment is below one year imprisonment, could be closed and accused acquitted with court's orders. The court said that it will not allow criminal prosecution in the country to operate as 'engines of oppression'. It was hoped that this memorable judgement of the Supreme Court will usher in a new dawn for thousands of undertrial prisoners, but unfortunately the situation has not, for a variety of reasons, improved significantly eve after this judgement of the court. It is necessary for the court to appoint a committee to review the operation and impact of its judgement in reducing the number of undertrials in jails.

There is another handicap suffered by the undertrials. Section 62(5) of the Representation of Peoples Act provides that "no person shall vote in any election if he is confined in any prison, whether under sentence of imprisonment, transportation or otherwise. The law, thus, bars all undertrial prisoners who cannot arrange bail including those charged for minor offences from the right to exercise of their franchis. The Supreme Court, however has upheld validity of Section 62(5) of the Representation of peoples Act 1951. The court held that the classification of persons in and out of prison is a reasonable one. In view of restriction on the movement of prisoner, he cannot claim that he should be provided facilities to go and vote. In the judgement of the court, the restriction applies to all persons in lawful custody of the police, which includes a prisoner detained during the investigation before a charge sheet is submitted against him. On the other hand, a person convicted and sentenced to imprisonment but released on bail is permitted to vote. The court justified permitting a person in preventive detention to vote by postal ballot, while denying the same right to undertrials in detention by holding that preventive detention is to prevent breach of law, while imprisonment on conviction or during investigation is subsequent to commission of crime and, therefore, the classification is reasonable. The court has justified the restriction on the ground of criminalisation of politics is negation of democracy.

For improving prison management the idea of privatisation of prisons is being debated and discussed by the penologists. At present in the UK there are two prisons managed by the private sector. Six new prisons are being built and these will also be run by the private sector. This has become necessary because prison system has reached the maximum capacity of 60,000 inmates. In USA also a number of states are giving some correctional services and programmes to private firms. Indeed some areas of prison management can be considered for privatisation for better-care treatment of the prisoners. Certain areas of prison management can be privatised on an experimental basis by contracting particular services to private sector such as catering, medical care, maintenance of buildings, etc. Such a participation of private sector in prison management will tone up prison administration and allow prison officers adequate time to concentrate on correctional programmes, security and other administrative matters.

IV

11

National Human Rights Commission: An Assessment of its Functioning

G.S. Bhargava

To look back at the functioning of the NHRC during the last five years—it was established in October 1993—it is necessary to recall the attitude of the Government of India and the elite section of the population to human rights and their promotion in the run-up to the constitution of the commission. First and foremost, there was a widespread feeling, even among official circles, that with a democratic constitution guaranteeing fundamental rights enforceable by the courts and provision for periodical elections on universal adult franchise, there was no need for an institutional mechanism for monitoring and safeguarding human rights. The fundamental rights enshrined in the Indian Constitution are comprehensive and broadly cover the entire gamut of the provisions of the Universal Declaration of Human Rights. India's republican constitution came into force in January 1950, about two years after the adoption of the Universal Declaration of Human Rights by the United Nations. Although the UN Declaration might not have directly influenced the thinking of the Indian Constitution makers, they have drawn heavily on the American and Irish models in providing for a network of fundamental rights and their enforcement.

There have also been instances of the judiciary enlarging the scope of the rights. For instance, the Supreme Court interpreted Article 21 of the Constitution ensuring the right to life and personal liberty to cover prohibition of torture or inhuman or degrading treatment saying that right to life includes the right to possession of each organ of one's body. In an equally far-reaching judgement subsequently (in 1983) the court included the right to monetary compensation for deprivation of the right to life and liberty suffered at the hands of the Stater. (The case arose out of the wrongful detention in jail for 14 years of a person actually acquitted by a court.) That, incidentally, overruled the Government of India's reservation to the provision in the Human Rights Covenants that the Indian law did not recognise the right to compensation for rights deprivation.

These and similar other judgements of the courts created awareness of human rights among the people, although the expression in currency at that time was fundamental rights or civil liberties rather than human rights. The media also highlighted such pronouncements of the courts and welcomed them enthusiastically against this background, there was smug satisfaction that the human rights situation in the country did not need institutional or other props to be improved and that the violations of the rights brought to light from time to time were aberrations being set right by the judiciary under the law of the land.

More importantly, international human rights organisations like the Amnesty International and its American counterpart, Asia Watch, initially confined their focus to the human rights situation in India to Punjab and Jammu and Kashmir during operations by the police and the security forces against secessionist movements sponsored and sustained from across the border. Transborder terrorism is a continuing problem for India and the authorities are naturally sensitive to it. Public opinion also is generally supportive of Government measures, however draconian to overcome threats to the integrity of the country from secessionist violence. Against this background championship of human rights of victims of antiterrorist operations by the security forces sounded blasphemous and was openly resented on the platform and in the press. It was seen as promoting the psychological warfare by Pakistan, which kept up a relentless campaign against India in international forum. In other words, the political dimension was to the fore.

Thus the Government of India was not enthusiastic about a national institution to monitor the state of human rights in different parts of the country and set right their violations through ventilation of the incidents and corrective action on its own or through the courts. The first Human

Rights Commission Bill, introduced in the Lok Sabha on 14th May, 1993, fully reflected such an attitude. It was halting and replete with reservations on the objective of establishing a full-fledged human rights commission in the country and ensuring its autonomous functioning. The tendency was to see it as an unavoidable sop to international opinion which was becoming increasingly restive of India's record in safeguarding the human rights of its citizens inspite of the liberal constitution and the independent judiciary.

The draft legislation had been virtually mauled by human rights activists at home when the Parliamentary Standing Committee of the Ministry of Home Affairs was vetting the Bill. Either it had to be withdrawn or completely rewritten and reintroduced in Parliament which would have meant restarting the cycle of reference to a select committee, eliciting public opinion, making changes and then enacting it into law.

Apparently, the Government was loath to go through the timeconsuming process again and rightly so. It wanted the commission to be in place as quickly as possible obviously to overcome the increasing international pressure on the ground that the security forces countering terrorism in Jammu and Kashmir had been violating human rights on a large scale and with impunity and there was no credible mechanism for monitoring the situation and bringing the guilty to book.

Born in such trying circumstances, with scepticism abounding about its role and autonomy, the NHRC had to establish its credibility and live down the stigma of being a pooble of the establishment. If its record during the last five years has dispelled the misgivings about its functioning and commitment to the convention against torture is in no small measure responsible for it. Almost from its inception, the NHRC took up the issue. Although India had hailed the UN Convention against Torture and Other Forms of Cruel and Inhuman and Degrading Treatment or Punishment in force since 1984, it has taken more than a decade to fall in line with it, that, too, after persistent goading by the NHRC.

The former Narasimha Rao Government was not moved into action even when the NHRC pleaded evocatively in a formal letter in 1994 to the then prime minister that subscribing to the convention would be the fittest way of paying homage to Mahatma Gandhi in that 125th year of his birth. More eloquently, it referred to the large number of incidents of custodial deaths, rape and torture involving the police and other security agencies and established that recourse to third degree methods during investigation was responsible for them. Formal subscription to the UN Convention would reinforce the Government's credibility in dealing with the crimes. Thanks to the public awareness created by the NHRC campaign in support of signing the convention, it was included in the Common Minimum Programme of the ruling United Front when it was formed after the last general election to the Lok Sabha in 1995, and two years later, in October 1997, the Gujral Government acceded to the convention.

It is a healthy development in the context of the tendency towards jingoism among vocal sections of our people. International criticism of our conduct is wrongly viewed as an affront our national sovereignty. More importantly, having bound itself formally by the convention which Pakistan still has to sign, India will be in a better position to bring out Pakistan's sponsorship and sustenance of terrorism in Jammu and Kashmir and elsewhere in the country.

Significantly, the NHRC came into being five years ago, almost to the day of India signing the convention. It was established on 12 October 1993 by an ordinance, which is an unusual way of ushering in a statutory institution but the circumstances in which it happened have been recounted earlier.

Less tangible but equally important is the change in the mind set of at least the thinking sections of the population and the leadership of the security forces, including the police, brought about as a result of the activities and reports of the commission. Most visibly, even die-hard critics of 'busy bodies' meddling in sensitive matters of national security and maintenance of law and order—as a prominent newspaper editor dubbed human rights activists and High Court judges in 1995—are either muted now or not openly outraged by campaigns against violation of human rights. The top brass of the army and the paramilitary forces, not to mention the police, are more alive than ever before to the human rights dimension of their law enforcement activities.

An equally significant, and domestically more important, accomplishment of the NHRC is the burial of the Terrorist and Distruptive Activities (Prevention) Act (TADA). Enacted in 1985, it was meant to deal with the insurgency situation in Punjab and Jammu and Kashmir and was to be a temporary measure. Yet it remained in force for ten years until May, 1995 when it was not revived after the expiry of its extended term. Also, instead of being limited to the States revaged by terrorism, it had been thoroughly misused practically all over the country.

The most reprehensible aspect of TADA was its sanction of presumption of guilt of persons arrested under it and the shifting of the burden of proof of innocence to the accused. Further, it made confessions before police officers admissible as evidence, contravening a fundamental right, Article 20 (3), enshrined in our Constitution. (No person accused of any offence shall be compelled to be a witness against himself.) It also diluted the provisions of the Criminal Procedure Code in respect of time limit for investigation of offences and grant of bail to the accused. In short, it was what the doctor would order for riding roughshod over citizens' liberties.

Ironically, in 1994 about a year before the Government bowed to public opinion and allowed TADA to lapse, a conference of chief ministers had urged its retention on the statute book on the plea that the Supreme Court had not stuck it down. Both Rajiv Gandhi and P.V. Narasimha Rao, former prime ministers, would argue that terrorists infringed the human rights of their victims and as such could not use the alibi of human rights to stymie the police in quelling them. When the NHRC as a statutory organisation took up the issue, the Government had to rethink its strategy because its approach was unlike that of many other human rights champions.

For one thing, the commission had never shirked denouncing terrorism but juxtaposed its rejection of terrorist and violent activities with standing up for the life and liberty of victims of excesses by the police and other security forces. In the process, it established the need to respect the human rights of citizens while tackling insurgency, because ultimately the problems underlying terrorism have to be tackled politically. The two approaches have to go on simultaneously. Winning over the populace and involving them in countering violence are as vital as putting down terrorism.

Although the battle against TADA has been won by the lapse of the law, there are hundreds of TADA cases pending in the courts and the NHRC is rightly pursuing its campaign for their disposal. It has also included the Armed Forces (Special Powers) Act in use in Punjab and the north-eastern states and the Jammu and Kashmir Public Safety Act among the lawless laws to be repealed. This under the rubric of the task set to the commission under the law establishing it to review existing laws and implementation of treaties and other international instruments on human rights.

To start with, the commission sought amendments in the Protection of Human Rights Act, which is its charter to enlarge the area of its operation and augment its autonomy. Among the changes proposed by the NHRC—the Government has still to accept them—is widening the definition of human rights contained in the law. It wanted the definition to read as: "Human rights' means the rights relating to life, liberty, equality and dignity of the individual guaranteed by the Constitution or embodied in the International Conventions to which India is a party," whereas the Act sought to circumscribe the ambit by limiting the application of the rights embodied in international conventions to their enforceability by the courts in India. Reference has already been made to a 1983 Supreme Court ruling on payment of compensation for deprivation of human rights, rejecting the Government's contention that it had entered a caveat to that effect while adhering to the international covenants.

Whatever be the wording of the law, the Commission has been functioning on the basis of the enlarged concept of human rights. Thus, within a month of its inception of November 1, 1993, the NHRC took *suo motu* cognizance of newspaper reports of the killing of as many as 43 civilians in and around Bijbehare (near Srinagar) in Jammu and Kashmir in firing by the paramilitary force, the BSF. It happened a few weeks earlier during siege of the sacred shrine of Hazratbal in Srinagar by militants with a view of inflaming religious passions of the people. In the resultant tense situation the BSF had apparently ran berserk. After examining the findings of a magisterial inquiry by the State Government and the Staff Court of Inquiry set up by the BSF, the commission asked the Government to launch prosecutions against 14 BSF personnel against whom disciplinary proceedings had been launched. The Government accepted the NHRC's recommendation and took action against the offending BSF personnel, including a few officers.

More importantly, the Government of Jammu and Kashmir paid compensation in the shape of ex-gratia relief to each of the dependants of the 31 civilians killed in the firing. (The magisterial inquiry had established that the number of victims was 31 and not 43 as reported in the newspapers.) Compensation was also paid to 44 injured persons although the amount of compensation in the case of the injured was less than that recommended by the NHRC, it accepted it as interim payment to be adjusted against a final figure to be decided by the courts.

More important was the acceptance by the BSF authorities changes in the deployment pattern of the para-military force suggested by the NHRC to avoid similar incidents in the future. Alterations in the training schedule of the BSF personnel to emphasise respect for human rights and humanitarian laws, association of magistrates and civilian police, including women constables, with cordon and search operations, increase in the number of supervisory level officers with BSF units, strict instructions to ensure adherence to the principle of minimum use of force and preinduction training of four weeks for units before their deployment are among the changes effected as a result. In that connection special training courses were organised for the BSF with interaction by the NHRC and participation of the International Committee of the Red Cross.

In this connection, with a view to achieving transparency even in situations of terrorism and armed militancy, the NHRC has remained in touch with BSF and the army to make them accept the implication of accountability of their personnel impress for their actions in strife affected areas. As a result both the BSF and the army have been keeping the NHRC informed of incidents in which their personnel have been charged with violation of human rights in Jammu and Kashmir since 1990, two hundred and fifty-nine cases had been registered against the BSF and another 43 against army. In proven case, punishments ranging from ten years, imprisonment to dismissal or reduction in rank have been awarded. The army authorities are cagey about publicising such incidents on the ground that it will affect staff moral. So the NHRC keeps the details for verification by concerned non-governmental organisations and others.

Considering that under the Protection of Human Rights Act, investigation of complains of violation of human rights by members of the 'armed forces' (meaning the army and not paramilitary forces like the BSF) is technically beyond the purview of the NHRC, this is no mean accomplishment. It is interesting in this context that Ms. Patricia Gossman of Human Rights Watch (Asia Division) which has consistently upbraided India's human rights record in Jammu and Kashmir and other insurgency affected areas is on record saying, "We were not very hopeful at first about the formation of the commission and were concerned at the outset about the restricted powers it was given. However, we have been pleased so far with what it has been able to do and we'll see how much it is able to push against those constraints.... A friend of mine who works with an

Indian human rights group told me that the Human Rights Commission was doing more than many of the human rights groups."[1]

Meanwhile, the huge increase of the number of cases considered by the NHRC from 276 in 1994-95, the first full year of its functioning, (nearly 500 cases were considered by the commission in the five odd months from its inception till the end of the financial year, 31st March, 1994) to 11,153 in 1995-96 showed the awareness among the people of the human rights situation in the country and the willingness of the victims to approach the NHRC for relief. The most disturbing fact noted by the NHRC was the high incidence of custodial violence, including atrocities against women. As many as 444 custodial deaths were examined by the NHRC during 1995-96, excluding 39 cases of disappearance of persons arrested by the police. Quite a few fatalities, 308, were of persons in judicial custody. Other police 'excesses' probed by the NHRC during the year included torture of the suspects during investigation to extract confessions.

In the words of the annual report of the commission, 'a permissive approach to the use of third degree methods in investigation' and the 'wrong belief that such practices were necessary for the successful investigation of cases' were responsible for the bane. It also noted that most of those who are victims of custodial death and brutality belong to sections of society that are economically poor or disadvantaged, bringing into focus the societal aspect of human rights. Understandably, the NHRC has been able to pay adequate attention to this societal aspect of the human rights situation only recently because earlier it had concentrated on violation of human rights by the organs of the State. Considering the caste-ridden character of the Indian society and the general indifference of the upper castes to the rights of the socially underprivileged, this is a herculean task which the NHRC has now embarked upon with determination.

In the case of custodial violence and deaths, the NHRC is guided by the principle that it is for better 'to prevent such acts before they occur'. Accordingly, it has suggested changes in the Indian Evidence Act and the Code of Criminal Procedure. The first is to introduce a rebuttal presumption that injuries suffered by a person in police custody may have been caused by the police and the second is for doing away with the necessity of Government sanction for the prosecution of a police officer when a prima facie case of custodial violence has been established in an inquiry by a session court. Both the proposed changes have the sanction of the judiciary. The NHRC has further circulated to all directors-general of the police of the states the decision of the Supreme Court that person in custody is entitled to have a friend or a relative to be informed of this arrest and place of detention so that the police cannot get away with the plea of ignorance of violence or death inflicted on a suspect in their custody. In a couple of cases of proven custodial deaths, the NHRC has ensured that compensation due to the next of kins of the victims should be the liability of not merely the State Government but of the offending police officials as well. The purpose of these reforms is to provide an effective deterrent to aberrant behaviour by elements of the law enforcement establishment. Slowly but steadily, the NHRC campaign is having an effect as reports in the newspapers have shown lately. It has, above all, created aversion among the public towards such behaviour by the police and made the news media sensitive to such crimes.

However, the case of alleged mass cremation of victims of indiscriminate killings by the police in Punjab during 1991-93 is posing problems for the NHRC. It took a bizarre turn when the Union Government questioned the jurisdiction of the NHRC to handle the case. This was despite the fact that the Supreme Court had entrusted the matter to the commission after a preliminary inquiry by the CBI into charges that the Punjab police had cremated more than 2,000 bodies of persons killed in fake encounters. The disappearance of a human rights activist probing the outrage prompted the Supreme Court decision in December last year to "leave the whole matter to be dealt with by the Commission". It also added that "any compensation awarded by the Commission (to the dependants of the victims) shall be binding and payable".

When the NHRC began to investigate the charges and issued notices to the Union Government and the arranged police officers, among others, its jurisdiction to proceed in the matter was questioned by the Central Government itself, along with other respondents. IT contended that since the Protection of Human Rights Act under which the NHRC was constituted set a limit of one year from the date on which the act constituting violation of human rights is alleged to have been committed for inquiry by the commission, the Punjab case could not be taken up by it. When the commission rejected the objection, the Government has got the inquiry stayed to enable it to appeal to the Supreme Court.

Significantly, in its very first annual report (1993-94), the NHRC had urged the amendment of the provision to enable the commission 'to entertain a matter for inquiry beyond a year if it is satisfied' with the explanation for the delay. The Government has not heeded its plea. In the Punjab case, it is obvious why the matter could not be raised earlier.

The NHRC has also been striving to bring about systemic reforms of police, prisons and other centres of detention. It has been campaigning for implementation of the Police Reforms Commission urging, among other things, the insulation of the investigative role of the police force from extraneous considerations and the constitution of State Security Commission in each State to help the State Government 'to discharge its superintending responsibility in an open manner under the framework its superintending responsibility in an open manner under the framework of law'. A hopeful sign in this respect is a recent announcement by the Union Home Minister of the Government's intention to take up implementation of the reforms. Members of the commission have visited a number of prisons in the different States and came to the commission have visited a number of prisons in the different States and came to the conclusion the conditions in the prisons are generally marked by 'gross overcrowding, squalor and maladministration'. Since the system of jail administration in the country is antiquated with the Indian Prisons Act, 1894, introduced by the former British Government still governing it, the NHRC has set out to draft a new Bill taking into account the conditions prevailing and special arrangements for women and juveniles. As a result of the exertions of the NHRC, a new building with an additional capacity of 750 has been added to the Tihar Jail in Delhi, additional staff has also been provided and the medical facilities have been augmented. In Jammu and Kashmir, after on-the-spot examination of the conditions in jails and centres of detention, the NHRC has focussed on transparency, leading to association of the International Committee of the Red Cross with overseeing their functioning. As a result, several complaints about the conditions in the jails and the treatment of detainees are being attended to. As in other fields, what has been tried by the NHRC is a drop in the ocean of the work yet to be accomplished.

Other aspects of the NHRC's work regarding human rights education, rights of the child with reference to the fundamental right to free primary education, child labour, etc. are not being dilated here because they are being discussed separately. In short, besides investigation of human rights violation and redressing the wrongs including compensation for deprivation of rights, systemic reforms of police and prisons, institutionalisation of training in human rights for the security forces, spread of awareness of the importance of human rights and sensitisation of the public and the law enforcement agencies in the matter have been engaging the attention of the NHRC in the last four years. A lot needs to be done in these respects to ameliorate the human rights situation in the country but a good beginning has been made.

REFERENCE

1. Report of symposium on 'Kashmir : Resolving Regional Conflict', (Ed) Robert G. Wirsing, Kartikeya Publications, Meerut, 1996.

12

National Human Rights Commission: A View from Peoples' Front

Y.P. Chhibbar

Discussed here are a few points based on our People's Union for Civil Liberties (PUCL) experience and our interactions with the National Human Rights Commission (NHRC).

What has been our experience? From the very beginning, when the proposal of NHRC was being talked about, the PUCL had taken note of it because we had been discussing the need of some of such body in the country.

Before the present Act was enacted and Ordinance was promulgated, during that period a Bill was being discussed in the country and we in the PUCL, had discussed the provisions of that Bill and the fact was that the opinion was divided on whether such a Commission would be of any use and if the provisions that were being circulated were sufficient. Before we took a final decision at one of our National Conventions at Mumbai, there was a long discussion. It was decided on the first day that a small Committee of members who had expressed differing views should be constituted and the Committee should report the next day, so that a decision could be taken in the National Convention itself. The opinion that prevailed was that we should not write-off the proposed Commission.

* Excerpted from the transcript of the presentation on the subject at the national seminar (see n. page 25)

The argument was that it is going to be an institution, which will be created by an Act of the Parliament. Whatever may be the drawbacks, if an institution is established, in itself, it would be a good thing, it will be an achievement. An established institution can be reformed and improved; we can exert pressure through agitation, just as we had been doing, till the creation of some such forum. The main demand was that the government should be receptive to complaints about the violation of civil liberties and human rights. Our experience was that the common term that was used for activists like us by the press, and also by the leading politicians of the country, was "these human rights walahs". More than once, the Prime Minister of the country stood up in the Parliament and named PUCL as a foreign agent, as it was alleged that we were receiving foreign money from external sources. In such an atmosphere, if the government accepts the concept of human rights and establishes a Commission, it means the government is accepting the concept of human rights. This should be welcomed. We were, at the same time, clear in our minds that the establishment of such a Commission was no substitute of organisations like the PUCL.

There are a number of human rights organisations, which are very active in the country at the state or local level. It might be known to some people that one of the very leading members of the PUCL who was connected with another organisation also was so unhappy in the beginning that he said he will not be able to work in PUCL if this proposal was not opposed. Such was the initial degree of suspicion of the intentions of the government for setting-up such a Commission. After careful discussions it was decided that our reactions to the establishment of such a Commission should not be negative. But, we accepted the idea with reservations.

We publish a monthly journal, the *PUCL Bulletin.* In that journal we have published, from time to time, our reservations on the various provisions of the Protection of Human Rights Act, 1993 which created the NHRC and we are still agitating for changes in the statute. Our approach is that there may be weaknesses in the working of the Commission and there may be weaknesses in the law which has set-up the Commission. If some provisions of the Protection of Human Rights Act, 1993 are not up to our expectations then we believe that for those drawbacks/weaknesses we cannot fault the Commission because the Commission has to work under the Act. So, for such things we have to go on pressurising the government to make changes in the law. A very minor example can be given here. The act lays down in clause 6 (1) that a person appointed as Chairperson shall hold office for a term of five years. But no member shall hold office after attaining the age of seventy years. A situation can be visualised in which there may be no person qualified to be the Chief of the Commission. The Chairperson has to be a person who has been the Chief Justice of the Supreme Court and has to be less than seventy years of age. Mr. Justice Ranganath Mishra retired when he had served only for two and a half years because he achieved the age of seventy years. When he retired, there was only one person in the country who was eligible to be appointed the Chief of the Commission and it is known that the person had to be persuaded to accept the position—the present Chairperson. This is a weakness of the Act. This clause must be changed to say that the Chief of the Commission will work for five years, irrespective of age. Similarly, there is a weakness in the law with regard to the investigation of cases. I have been writing to the Commission as the General Secretary of the PUCL that the Commission also should do something about it.

The Commission has not been provided with an elaborate and full-fledged investigative machinery. That Act says that the Commission can utilise the services of any officer or investigation agency of the Central or State government. It has a skeleton machinery of its own for investigations but it cannot investigate all the cases. Its officers go personally to investigate the case. But each and every case cannot be investigated by them. So the Commission has to depend upon the organisation about which most of the complaints are addressed to the Commission, that is the police. There is a case pending with the Commission which we had sent towards the end of 1993, or beginning of 1994, from Bijnor, a small place in UP and it is still going on. The complaint is against the local police. Even if the local police officials are transferred, those who come in their place, have an in-built antipathy towards the complainants because they are complainants against the police. There is a feeling of brotherhood. The enquiry is also conducted by the police. There have been cases in which the NHRC has not depended upon the local police for investigation. Its officials have gone to investigate. But for such a situation or such weaknesses we cannot fault the Commission. We cannot pressurise the Commission on this score. For such weaknesses we have to pressurise the government; and we go on doing that.

Recently, we had our National Council meeting at Allahabad. The Council has set-up a small committee to review the Protection of Human Rights Act, 1993 and to make suggestions regarding necessary changes in the Act and also to evaluate the working of the Commission.

We have our branches in almost all the states. These branches also come into contact with the Commission. As and when necessary these branches write to me about their experiences with the Commission. State branches also come in contact with the State Human Rights Commissions. Based on such feedback, we have come to the conclusion that there are very few bureaucrats, members of the judiciary, members of Armed forces, etc., who have accepted the concept of Human Rights. There are some states, therefore, where the Human Rights Commissions leave much to be desired. This is a result of the atmosphere that was created in the country during and after the Emergency, which debunked Human Rights and branded activists in this field as anti-national.

We were told by our colleagues from one State that one judge from the lower judiciary threw out 35 human rights cases filed as PIL in a day without giving any explanation and imposed fines on the complainants of up to Rs. 5,000 for filing the case. The cases referred to rag-pickers in a town of that state. So, some members of the judiciary also have not accepted this idea. Therefore, the fight has to be on all the fronts, not only with the central government but also with the state governments, the local officials, and the judiciary. A directive from the Prime Minister, or directive from the Chief of the NHRC, or from any other Commission alone cannot solve this problem. These Institutions are no substitute for voluntary work; voluntary work must go on and on expanding its scope. The concept is new irrespective of the assertion that the Vedas have it, and that *Vasudhaiva Kuttumbakam* has been our slogan of human rights. I have always believed that how can a country that believes in untouchability and caste hierarchy say that we have always believed in human rights?

All times the concept of human rights is twisted to the advantage of some people. For example, K.P.S. Gill stands up and says, "What about the human rights of the police?" What is his interpretation Human Rights? "Their working conditions are bad, their pay scales are bad, nobody listens to them, the higher officer treats the junior functionary as servants." This is not a problem of Human Rights. But for the common people like us, who do not understand the meaning of human rights, Gill's or Shri

Tahir Mahmood's remarks is authoritative the latter said that seminar papers were not supplied to his and as such his human rights were violated.

We are not clear about the concept of Human Rights. When Gill says that Human Rights organisations do not care about the Human Rights of the Constable but they are very vocal about the Human Rights of the terrorist, he is taking advantage of this confusion about the meaning of Human Rights. That a person is a human being and therefore a person will be dealt with according to law: this right belongs to every human being, not a terrorist alone the police does not have to say that they are right to get hold of a person at random, shoot him down, and then say he was a terrorist. This atmosphere in our country is because of the conditions that are prevailing in some parts of the country. In the backdrop of terrorist violence, if the police says, "this person was a terrorist." We tend to belie them. But what is the use of having courts of law? The court has to decide whether the person was a terrorist. Only then that person can be sentenced, by the Court, not by Mr. K.P.S. Gill.

Newspapers are giving prominence to articles by K.P.S. Gill. K.P.S. Gill has become a symbol of this type of nonsense. There are other people also. His name is mentioned as a symbol. Newspapers are publishing articles; which show an utter lack of understanding of Human Rights. One newspaper once wrote that out, those who sit at home and pontificate can talk about Human Rights but those who face bullets have no time to do so. Does it mean that the entire law and order machinery should be given the freedom to decide on the spot whether a person was a terrorist and then sentence the person to death? Who is a terrorist? Mr. K.P.S. Gill, is one.

And then, what about the situations where there is no terrorism? Do Human Rights cease to exist in the JJ colonies? In police lock-ups?

So the establishment of NHRC has made this difference that there are now some important levels where this concept has been accepted, where there is an understanding of the concept. Also, the Judiciary, the Supreme Court especially, has played a very important role which has helped the NHRC and us also. The Supreme Court has now ruled that the International Conventions and Protocols that India has signed, can be enforced by High Courts, provided there is not specific Fundamental Right against them. These Conventions, without being adopted as a law by our Parliament, can be enforced and one should ask people who are shouting from roof tops against these "human rights *walahs,*" "Did you accept the Constitution of India when you entered into service? Fundamental rights are the rights of the people of the country and those fundamental rights relate to Human Rights. Do you accept the authority of the Government of India? And if you do, then remember that the Government of India is a signatory to these International Conventions. The most recent Convention that the Government has signed, which should have been done long ago, is the Convention against Torture. The Government is a signatory to such Conventions and how can you fault anyone for speaking for the ideas that are written in the Constitution?" Recently, we wrote a letter to the NHRC, about the DCP (Crime) of Delhi, who said in a meeting in Delhi that without torture nothing could be done. He went on to say that recently they had arrested the suspects of such and such case, but they did confess. The moment the police started beating them, within two minutes, they confessed; and then "on my personal intervention," he said it in the meeting, "no medical check-up was conducted on those people when they were presented in the Court, the next day". This was reported in the press. I sent this case to the NHRC. Our representatives from PUCL (Delhi) went to see the Police Commissioner who refused to see them. Later the Police Commissioner said that this was false, his officer never said that!

We have not yet accepted the idea of democracy in our psyche. Our democracy is only confined to voting and to elect a government. We have to learn to live democracy, and we, at least the activists, should be clear in our minds as to what Human Rights mean. This is what our attitude has to be and this is for what we have to go on working, in spite of the establishment of NHRC.

We have a very long-standing pending case with the Commission and have been writing to them about it off and on, concerning a member of our own National Council in Punjab who had complained against a Minister of State for having tried to molest a woman employee in the office. She represented that case against that person and the entire Department and Police Department turned against her. They started harassing her. She was transferred twice in a day. She sent her case to the NHRC. Mr. Justice Ranganath Misra said in a public speech at Ludhiana that he was helpless. Punjab Government was not doing anything in that case. Very recently she was asked by the Department as to by whose permission she joined PUCL and NHRC? They do not know what is

NHRC, and equate the NHRC with the PUCL. They have probably 'heard' that these two organisations are Human Rights organisations and she is member of these organisations. These are the people who are supposed to be the protectors of Human Rights because they have taken an oath to uphold the Constitution of India, which is the source of Human Rights in our country.

So this is how we view our relationship with the NHRC and our view of its working, its powers, etc.

There are several other commissions. We keep in contact with these other Commissions also at the national level and through our state branches; sometimes our local branches/district branches also contact these Commissions. The latest Commission that we have come to know about is the National Safai Karmacharis Commission. I do not know whether you are aware of it. It is a temporary Commission. According to law, it exists at present up to 2002, after that its term may be extended by the Parliament or it may be reconstituted. It appears that it is a make-shift Commission, but it is a National Commission. We came to know of this Commission, through an advertisement which they had published in the newspapers saying that this was a Commission established by law and such was their scope of work. On contacting, they were kind enough to send us a copy of the law under which they had been set-up. We requested them to send all the schemes that they had for the welfare of the Safai Karmacharis and what they had been doing uptill now.

Our Mumbai branch had moved the Mumbai High Court on the deplorable working conditions of the people who clean sewerage-lines in the city. These people have to dive into the sewerage-pipes to clean them. It may be a month of summers or that of winters. This is happening all over the country. The Mumbai PUCL went to the Mumbai High Court. The High Court appointed a Committee. That Committee made suggestions regarding measures to be taken for safeguarding their health, for their working conditions, prescribing the equipment that should be provided to them, etc. This is a very elaborate provision. We asked this Commission to get that judgement, the provisions of that judgement, implemented throughout the country. They asked for a copy of that judgement, which was sent to them. After that we have written them many letters on this subject, and also on other subjects, there has been no response. Then, there are other Commissions. Surely, the complaints that the Chairperson of the National Commission for Minorities has voiced today are quite valid, but our experience, has been that all other Commissions are very slow in responding. The National Commission for Women also does not respond.

One important thing is that we should (this goes for voluntary organisations as well as statutory Commission, other statutory bodies) realise that it is probably the duty of the Chief to run the institution as an Institution. Organisations can run round a person or through an infrastructure that has been created to sustain itself. In the case of the former the degree of activity, depends upon the level of activity, interest or initiative of the Chief. In such a case, what is going to happen after the retirement of this Chief?

The organisation has to be made a self-sustaining body. This goes for voluntary organisations, as well as statutory bodies. This way, the exit of the Chief will effect only the orientations of attitude, the hue may change, but it will not be discoloured. This is making an organisation into a Institution. On this score, we cannot fault the NHRC. The departure of Mr. Justice Ranganath Mishra, may have made some difference in the complexion of the working. May be the present Chairperson is not, an activist type, which Mr. Mishra was. But in the level of activity of the Commission, the effectiveness or ineffectiveness, whatever, of the Commission, there has been no deterioration because the Commission is becoming an Institution. There are weaknesses in the working of the Commission, even in the administration of the Commission because most of the people who have been posted to the Commission are from the bureaucracy, and the main problem we face is from the bureaucracy.

Members of the Commission may be convinced about the concept of Human Rights, etc., but the Registrars, Assistant Registrars, the lower staff, may be government bureaucrats in their minds. For them a reorientation course may be in order. The elements making the infrastructure have to be chosen carefully. This much cannot be said about all other Commission. If we have to remind a Commission to accept that a particular situation fell within its scope then that Commission has some weakness and that calls for rethinking. There may be some weaknesses in the attitude of the government towards other Commissions. This is a fact that the law under which the NHRC has been set-up is qualitatively different. The idea of the NHRC in the mind of the people also was much more clear. It is right when it is said that largely our idea of Minorities Commission is Muslim Commission. This is the psyche in our country. The anti-Muslim feeling is so strong that 'minority' is equated with 'Muslim'. There is an anti-minority feeling, and when we say 'anti-minority', in our mind there is always 'anti-Muslim'. Sadly, this is again a situation with which we have to cope as long as we are unable to mend it. This is a 'given' thing. Just as we have to fight for the acceptance of the idea of Human Rights, we also have to fight for the acceptance of the idea that Human Rights are for all-minority, majority, women, children, rich, poor, deprived. It is just that some need special attention.

An incident that took place at Dumka, Bihar. After a team had visited that place and its report was prepared, some people from Dumka came to PUCL. In the meanwhile we had received some communication from the Bihar branch of the PUCL also. The visitors related the entire incident in details. They also told what the NCM (National commission for Minorities) has done. Their complaint was that the Commission's report had evoked no response from the concerned authorities. Now, this is a situation that concerns, our anti-minority psyche. It might have been better if they had taken the case to the NHRC. The incident was largely concerned with deprivation of human dignity-parading a person naked for hours and making him march like that for long distances, and that too, in the presence of police and district officers. It was a gross violation of Human Rights of that individual. It was another matter that the person concerned belonged to a minority community. The NHRC could have taken action against those officers as to why they had remained mute spectators of the whole disgraceful drama. We wrote the NHRC that if this incident was true, which it was, the officers who permitted this whole thing to take place must be held guilty of failure to protect the Human Rights of the victim. This was a gross dereliction of duty. Photographs show a police officer walking along with the victim as if to protect his nudity. There may be a difference in our perception, but there are many situations in which a case can be more effectively treated as a case of Human Rights. In our mind at least, there is no conflict between the scope of work of one Commission and another. As long as people can get justice, complainants can get justice, whether from A, B, or C Commission, it does not matter. The main thing is that the complainant should not get an idea that no one is doing anything.

Sometimes people have come to us and told that they had gone to the NHRC and someone there advised them to go the PUCL. May be because it is known that our attitude is, that apart from dealing with cases of Human, Rights we should try to help everyone. The sufferers are generally poor people, deprived people who belong to minorities or women, or children. Even if their problems are not problems of Human Rights, we try to help them by giving suitable advice or by referring them to our members who are lawyers; sometimes they take up their case even if it may not be a Human Rights case, without any fees, etc.

Our attitude, therefore, is that this Commission or that Commission does not matter. The problem should be solved and our organisation's attitude is that even if it is not a Human Rights case, we do not turn the person back. We are not a government department and we, therefore, have greater flexibility. We work with people and, while working with people, we cannot have this type of attitude.

V

13

Human Rights : An Overview

V.M. Tarkunde

The United Nations Declaration of Human Rights was adopted by most countries including India on 10th Dec., 1948. It is appropriate that the celebration of the jubilee year of the attainment of national independence by India coincided with the celebration of the jubilee year of the Declaration of Human Rights. These simultaneous celebrations are appropriate because the movement for India's independence and the movement for human rights have been essentially for the same cause—the cause of the attainment by India of a fullfledged multidimensional democracy.

It is necessary to emphasize that for the majority of the people in India the national movement for independence was a negative movement, aimed at the removal of foreign rule. While the people in general wanted foreign rule to go, they were not actively conscious of the necessity of replacing it by a democratic regime in which they, the people, would have the power to shape their destiny. It is true that some of the fighters for national Independence were also inspired by the ideal of establishing a democratic regime in India. They realised that nothing much would be achieved by merely replacing a white bureaucracy by a brown bureaucracy and that we should aspire to replace foreign rule by people's rule in India. The fact, however, that the attainment of democratic freedom was not the conscious objective of the majority of the Indian people was the reason why the attainment of national freedom by India resulted in the formation of a very weak and superficial democracy in the country where the bulk of the people were not free either from political subjugation or economic exploitation. Imperialism, which was one of the impediments in the way of democratic freedom, was removed by the attainment of national independence, but the bulk of the people remained under the political and economic subjugation of the native vested interests. By the removal of foreign rule, India became a free country but the Indian people did not attain political or socio-economic freedom.

Like all other values, freedom is essentially an individual value. A society or a nation has no consciousness of its own; it is the individual who has consciousness and who either suffers from bondage or feels exultation in freedom. A society or a nation can be said to be free to the extent to which the individuals composing it are free. Since the Indian independence which was attained in 1947 did not result in the freedom of the Indian people, the struggle for Indian's freedom has to be continued even after the attainment of India's independence. This can be called the second movement of India's freedom, if by India we mean the Indian people, and aim to emphasize that this second movement of India's freedom should take the shape of movement for the full attainment of human rights.

Although the United Nations Declaration of Human Rights was adopted on 10th Dec., 1948, a more detailed enumerations and classification of human rights were made by two conventions adopted by the United Nations in 1960s—first, the International Convention on Civil and Political Rights and second, the International Convention on Economic, Social and Cultural Rights. Thus human rights were classified by the United Nations in five categories—Civil, Political, Economic, Social and Cultural. Civil rights are otherwise known as civil liberties and they are covered by the Chapter on Fundamental Rights in the Indian Constitution. Political rights (other than civil rights) are—the right to franchise, the right to free and fair elections and the right "to take part in public affairs directly or through freely chosen representatives" (Article 25 (a) of the first convention). The main economic rights are "the right of every one to the opportunity to gain his living by work" and "the right of every one to an adequate standard of living for himself and his family." The economic rights also include the rights of workers to form trade unions, to get fair wages and to work in safe and healthy conditions. Amongst social and cultural rights are the rights of equality among men and women, the right to marriage with the consent of both the spouses, and the right to education which shall be directed to the full development of the human personality. Primary education shall be compulsory and free, and secondary and higher education shall be progressively free. Physical and mental health is also recognised as one of the social rights.

The wide range of human rights, enumerated in the two United Nations Conventions, brings out the identity of the attainment of human rights with the attainment of a democratic state as well as a democratic society. If democracy is understood, not only as a form of government, but as a way of life, based on the humanist values of liberty, equality and fraternity, the attainment of human rights amounts to the creation of a democratic society of which a fully democratic state would be an essential component. It follows that the movement for human rights is a movement for the attainment of a democratic state in a democratic society.

Having considered the scope and significance of human rights, we may next consider the extent to which we have advanced in achieving them in the last 50 years. At present, the movement for human rights is overshadowed by a dismal political situation characterised by all-pervading corruption in the political and administrative apparatus of the country, by criminalisation of politics, and by the inability of political parties to form a stable government. It will be found, however, that if the movement for human rights is developed from below by voluntary organisations not interested in power politics, the situation is capable of being substantially improved in the not distant future.

In the region of civil liberties, some material improvements have been brought about in the post-independence period. The higher judiciary, the free press and the voluntary non-governmental organisations have succeeded to a considerable extent in protecting and promoting the fundamental rights (civil liberties) of the people. The broader interpretation given by the Supreme Court to Article 14 (equality before the law) and Article 21 (liberty of the person and of the life of individuals and the system of Public Interest Litigation have succeeded to a noticeable extent in establishing the rule of law and checking the arbitrary behaviour of politicians and public authorities. Of course, there are still many shortcomings in the attainment of civil liberties. The poorer section of society are still subjected to police torture during the investigation into offences, sometimes resulting in custodial deaths. Child labour and bonded labour remain in many areas, despite the laws passed to prevent them. The right to information is still a right only on paper and legislation in that regard is yet to be passed. Legislation is also necessary for protecting the right to privacy. But most to these matters are being handled by civil rights organisations and there is reason to believe that these shortcomings will be progressively removed.

Turning to political rights, other than civil liberties, franchise has been extended to all persons above the age of 18 years. Elections are still far from free and fair, but there is a strong demand for electoral reforms and an enactment for that purpose is on the anvil. People's participation in the governance of the country is likely to be gradually extended on account of the panchayat system made compulsory by the 73rd Constitution amendment and municipalities with ward committees by the 74th Constitution amendment. Panchayats and municipalities will be initially dominated by political and economic vested interests, but there is reason to believe that the growing awakening among the people coupled with the work of voluntary organisations will result in more power going into the hands of the unprivileged majority, first in rural areas and then in towns and cities. In fact, the empowerment in the people, particularly in gram panchayats, should now be the main work of voluntary non-governmental organisations.

In respect of economic rights, some limited progress was made by the abolition of the zamindari system, by laws to make the tiller the owner of the soil, and by labour legislation for fair wages and healthy conditions of work to the working class. There are, of course, large loopholes in the implementation of laws for agricultural reforms, particularly the Agricultural Land Ceiling Acts, as well as in the application of labour laws to labour employed in small unorganised industries, which employ the bulk of industrial workers. Above all, poverty remains almost as much as before, with about 40 per cent of the people remaining below the poverty line. The alleviation of poverty requires improvement in agricultural production, promotion of small-scale industries, and the development of other labour intensive undertakings such as road construction, house building, reforestation of depleted forest lands, etc. A great deal of improvement is possible by promoting watershed management in rural areas. Although the problems of poverty and unemployment or underemployment remain acute, they are being handled with determined efforts by voluntary organisations, often with the participation of the people and the support of state governments.

The same cautious optimism can be entertained in respect of social and cultural problems, such as communalism, casteism, gender equality and the prevalence of blind faith among the people. In all these directions, not much can be expected from the central and state governments, but a great deal can be done by grass-root organisations with the help of the people who are gradually getting conscious of the fact that they must work voluntarily for the improvement of their conditions of life, without depending solely on the machinery of the state.

The problem of corruption remains the greatest stumbling block to the country's progress in all directions. There is, however, a growing consciousness amongst the people about the evil of corruption and this consciousness is likely to increase in the near future. A countrywide movement against corruption can be launched by voluntary organisations with the help of the people at large and with the machinery of the Lok Pal, the Lokayuktas and vigilance officers who may be appointed by the central and state governments.

In considering these problems, one should realise that the Indian people have gone through eleven general elections, that each election has been a source of political education of the people, and that there is a noticeable rise in the people's appreciation of their political, social and economic rights. This awakening of the people, although very slow, is quite noticeable. With its help, human rights organisations working on a voluntary basis can meet the grave problems with which we are faced and see that there is a gradual improvement in the political, economic, social and cultural atmosphere in the country. Human rights have been attained by us only to a small extent up to now, but the future of the human rights movement is bright, and there is every reason to hope that the country will advance in the direction of a more genuine democratic state and a more genuine democratic society in which the people will enjoy human rights to an increasing extent.

14

Fundamental Rights and the Reality

Shanti Sadiq Ali

As a prelude to the discussion on the subject, some pertinent points may be noted.

Gandhi was one of the greatest human rights activists in India. In his constructive programme for the socio-economic upliftment of the nation, he identified every facet of Indian life that needed remedial action unemployment, poverty, untouchability, Hindu-Muslim unity, women and child welfare, environment, sanitation and health and grass-root development. This programme was carried on side by side with the national liberation movement. It has firmly committed itself to social reform and justice, elimination of foreign control and attaining of self-sufficiency.

With independence India faced new challenges. The institutions inherited from the colonial period were not found to be adequate they needed to be modified or even radically transformed to meet the burgeoning expectations of a people now more politically conscious.

At the political level, India was easily able to opt for the classical democratic pattern of a competitive party system, because of the existence of various political parties and their varying interests in pre-independent India. Even though the Congress party, regarded as representing largely the national "bourgeoisie", initially held the monopoly of power opposing interests were able to challenge its authority with varying success. Today it is out of power in the vast Hindi speaking belt and the southern states and West Bengal.

During the period 1947-79, "Nehruvian model" was dominant in the economic policy formulation called the mixed economy, with democratic planning as the technique and socialist pattern as the objective. But the model did not work as anticipated. The major constraint was foreign exchange for industry. The border problems with China and Pakistan further weakened the Indian economy, compounded by a major food crisis, necessitating massive food imports. The World Bank, in Mrs. Gandhi's regime, forced India to devalue the rupee. The two oil shocks were further adversely affected the Indian economy and led India to accept certain conditionalities from the International Monetary Fund (IMF).

Rajiv Gandhi, who responded positively to the policy of marketisation, privatisation, liberalisation and globalisation, reshaped the Post-Nehruvian economic period. But India faced two serious problems: fiscal instability and the huge foreign debt. The foreign exchange crisis in 1990-91 resulted in India selling all her gold reserves to meet the import bills. When India approached the World Bank and IMF, they gave it the Anderson Memorandum containing the Structural Adjustment Programme (SAP) which the Narasimha Rao Government was obliged to accept. The SAP has put limitation on the government priority on social programmes, such as basic education, primary healthcare, access to clean drinking water and family planning services, though the Government insists its reforms will have a "human face".

Critics of the impact of this New Economic Policy (NEP) assert that it will make the poor people more vulnerable. The NEP and the new GATT (General Agreement on Tariffs and Trade) rules facilitate, in multiple ways, the recolonisation of India. The farmers are going to lose their freedom even to choose the seeds, which they like. The Transnational Corporations, if allowed to function without any control, will after sometime seize the entire production. There will be a rise in unemployment due to labour saving techniques, and a large number of traditional workers will lose their jobs. Already 30 per cent of India's population is living below the poverty line. It would also destroy our inherited knowledge and techniques, waste-dumping, such as the highly polluting pig dung from the Netherlands, and industrial waste from Australia, Canada and USA, which India has already experienced, will increase.

NEP coincides with the challenge of a society in ferment. Today communalism and caste divisions are rife, secessionism and separatism is on the increase, the tribal community is raising its head, women, downtrodden and marginalised, though they may be, are also increasingly conscious of their rights. On the other hand, the Supreme Court of India has been upholding the Constitution and taking the side of the poor, who turn to it for justice as a last resort. There is also a vigilant press which courageously portrays the ills of society.

India has ratified both the Covenants in 1979. The Covenant on Economic, Social and Cultural Rights states that each party is progressively required to undertake steps to create conditions conducive for the basic minimum for decent existence, essentially by legislative means, and to the maximum of its available resource, individually and through international assistance and cooperation. Indivisibility of rights is well recognised. As such, civil and political rights are equally important. The UN Declaration on Human Rights to Development (1986) also states that the promotion of one set of rights cannot justify the denial of other human rights.

Let us examine the fundamental changes, which have taken place in India in the current historical situation as far as these two sets of rights are concerned.

The Ingredients of the Indian Constitution

The Indian Constitution has been described as "first and foremost a social document. The majority of its provisions are either directly aimed at furthering the goals of social revolution, or attempt to foster this revolution by establishing the conditions necessary for its achievement." This is understandable in the light of India's backwardness, when attained independence, it highlighted India's commitment to the principles enshrined in the two Covenants—economic, social and cultural as well as civil and political rights. Article 51 A of the Constitution spells out the fundamental duties of every citizen. Duties are therefore an equally important part of human rights as envisaged by Gandhi.

Politically, India has opted for a federal democracy with a powerful centre. The core of the Constitution is the concept of unity in diversity. Unity is sought to be forged in diversity by a common citizenship, irrespective of race, religion or language to preserve the composite culture of India.

Religious tolerance and equal treatment of all religious groups and protection of their lives and property and of places of worship, in the country, is an essential part of secularism enshrined in the Constitution.

Panchayati Raj—Grass-Root Democracy

There has been a vacuum between the Parliament and local bodies. The situation has been rectified by the 74th Constitution Amendment, which has made it mandatory now to constitute civic bodies and also to hold regular elections which was not being done earlier.

Apart from civic election, Gandhi's concept of gram swaraj (village autonomy) which, he felt, could alone empower the people, has been realised to a great extent now. All the states have brought their laws governing the Constitution had powers of rural panchayats (village republics) into conformity with the Constitution (73rd Amendment) Act of 1993.

The present law, with statutory sanctions, also makes the periodical conduct of elections mandatory and reserves a fixed proportion of seats in the panchayat bodies for the underprivileged, including women. This will ensure the survival of the Panchayati Raj system in the functional sense. But self-government at the local level in respect of activities directly affecting the lives of the people is still a far cry because of India's feudal background. Compounding the situation is the allocation to every member of parliament with power to sanction schemes to the value of ten million rupees, through the Collector, in his or her constituency. This will necessarily have an impact in the political field.

However, Panchayats are the instruments of central policies and programmes and are expected to carry out centrally sponsored development programmes. This is also seen as an inhibiting step.

However, a heartening aspect is that women are now playing a greater role in Panchayats and their participation is much higher than male-headed Panchayats. But ineffective women get elected as Serpent and then make way for their husbands to become the "Sarpanch Sahib". These are the findings of a report of "strengthening" Panchayati Raj institutions.

The Election Commission imposed a number of restrictions to cleanse the quagmire into which caste, criminalities and corruption have thrown our electoral system. The introduction of the Identity Card to prevent duplication or impersonation of voters, is one of its most welcome improvements. In addition, the Commission has circulated a list of 23 "don't" for political parties and prospective candidates. The Commission earlier assumed powers to withdraw recognition of national and state parties for the non-observance of this Model Code of Conduct. Now the demand has been made to exclude persons convicted of corruption from contesting elections.

Clearly the Indian Union is not a federal system. The framers of the Indian Constitution had strong "centralist" tendencies, believed fervently that only a strong centre could work for the common and general interest to the country.

The overriding powers enjoyed by the centre, however, if used to serve partisan interests of the party in power, can cause irrepairable damage to the Indian polity, as was the case in the misuse of the centre's discretionary powers by dismissing duly elected state governments.

In India, the centre has also retained its dominant position in the matter of legislation as the laws passed by the state legislature are subject to Presidential assent. The Central Government's powers have been enlarged while the scope for autonomous action by the states has been abridged.

Decentralisation of power, however, is the essence of democracy. The common man would feel part of the power sharing only when local bodies and institutions were given their due importance. The states have been demanding greater devolution, particularly in the financial sphere.

Though the founding fathers of the Constitution provided a parliamentary form of government on the British model, in which Parliament is supreme, they also gave a place of primacy to the judiciary in the scheme of governance.

In these troubled times, in which India has fallen, the Supreme Court is being looked upon not only as a guardian of our democracy, but as a continuing fountain of justice. Seen once merely as an interpreter of law, the Supreme Court is now increasingly giving the impression of a self-styled institution which relates to people and democracy on its own terms. The Supreme Court has played a commendable role in resolving many controversial issues that touch the daily lives of all Indians.

To furnish an example a major lacuna still seemed to exist on the question of compensation until a general principle of law was laid down in January, 1990. Basing its judgement on Article 32, the Apex Body has, for the first time, laid a sound legal basis for the claim of compensation for infringement or violation of fundamental rights.

But a major tragedy of the Indian polity is the increasing loss of credibility of the judiciary at the lower level. The entire criminal justice system is under sever strain and it has virtually broken down in some states. Many cases pertaining to heinous offences have been pending in the courts for as long as over 10 years. The criminal justice system has become so complex that criminals with clout and resources can remain out of the clutches of the law indefinitely.

The ordinary constable who constitutes the core of police system in India has a very low status and "poor image". He is ill-equipped to carry out more reliable investigative procedures.

The National Police Commission went into the entire working of the police system and made salutary recommendations. But these have yet to be adopted. In the meanwhile the Police Act of 1861 remains practically unaltered. Political considerations and caste loyalties are taking primacy over improving the efficiency and performance of the police.

Freedom of Press

Indian journalism has played a commendable role during the freedom struggle and whenever democracy was in jeopardy. Article 19 of the Constitution guarantees, by inevitable implication, the freedom of the Press as a Fundamental Right.

But now the Fourth Estate is in peril and it is being called upon to resist the very real possibility of the foreign media coming into the country. This issue is currently in the centre stage of national debate.

Freedom of the Press is not an end in itself but a means to the end of a free society. If that end is threatened then the means, namely press-freedom, must necessarily come under control. Many countries of the world which have accepted freedom of the Press do not permit foreign entry in that field for obvious reasons. These non-citizen newspapers are beyond Indian control because their assets and their masters are located outside our frontiers.

Concluding Observations

From the above, it is clear that the struggle for human rights is being waged under very trying and difficult circumstances will grow as efforts are made to make human rights education to generate wider awareness. The process is still at a preliminary stage.

In spite of the judiciary taking the lead in ensuring that the principles of the Constitution acquire stronger legal and moral authority as a prime constituent of governance, India is still far from adhering to international norms of human rights and justice as, among other things, there has been a lot of interference from various quarters, particularly at the lower levels.

There is virtual collapse of the present party system in the political life of the country. How will the vacuum be filled? Perhaps a national (coalition) government at the centre could be the answer.

The people at large find themselves without genuine leadership. At the same time communalism, casteism and social militancy, borne out of sheer turmoil and deprivation, rather than any ideological spur, are spreading. This requires a new kind of transition to a different political order, more decentralised and federal. This would mean decentralisation in the sense of a greater role for civil society and its further democratisation than mere devolution of the machinery of the state which has suffered a sharp decline in legitimacy. A feeble effort towards transition can be seen in the newly installed panchayati system, where women, the Scheduled Castes and Tribes are given more representation, but it is too early to warrant its success.

The demand is there by the states, which are clamouring for more powers and a truly decentralised polity. In a society as diverse as India, the principle of universality must take full account of particularly — the flowering of a truly multiculturalism. The founding fathers reconciled the demands of universality and particularly in their own way but India has outgrown the union principle. Today a search for new sources of strength and sustenance need to be explored, while bearing in mind the need to preserve and indeed nurture liberal democracy and its constituents-secularism, pluralism, toleration of dissent and communitarianism.

Rural poverty continues to be a massive problem in India. This is evident in the striking deficiencies in the form of high infant mortality rate, low literacy rate and as many as 300 million people suffering from abject poverty.

Since 1990-91, when India launched the new economic reforms, poverty in the villages has deteriorated, not improved. During the last three years, an interesting indicator of how the poor are getting poorer and the rich richer, is evident from the fact that the per capita consumption of food grains has dropped from 510 grams a day to 465 grams a day since the New Economic Policy was introduced. Simultaneously the sale of cars has gone up by 34 per cent and that of luxury cars have virtually doubled.

Moreover, the social clause in GATT will hit the already precarious plight of labour in developing countries, like India. Ironically, the poorer nations are being asked because they are poor. Once this social clause is brought into the picture, Indian products will became unsaleable in the West. One is not averse to the entry of multinationals in certain areas which require high and sophisticated technology, at the same time, one is opposed to open invitation to multinationals in the consumer and core sectors.

15

State of Socio-Economic Rights

N.R. Madhava Menon

One of the greatest accomplishments of civilisation in the 20th century is the acceptance of human rights as an integral part of governance for which the state, whatever its form, has accepted obligations and accountability. Today the United Nations may be characterized as a human rights maintenance organization, clarifying, promoting and monitoring the human rights related activities of governments the world over. There is hardly a constitution which does not speak of the rights of the individual vis-a-vis the state and the mechanisms whereby they are to be made accessible to the citizens. There is a strong NGO movement supported by an increasingly activist judiciary and an independent media to monitor human rights violations and to seek accountability of the powers that be at different levels of government. Admittedly, there is a human rights ideology emerging everywhere informing and illuminating public policy and governance with varying degrees of success against strong currents of authoritarianism and abuse of power.

In India, the story of this progress towards democratic governance based on human rights is indeed impressive during the last fifty years though the picture is not as rosy as one would expect. Communal politics and violence are still real threats to peace and fraternity. Corruption in government and public life is eating up whatever progress made so far and is constantly making the life of the ordinary citizen miserable. Increasing criminalisation and decreasing efficiency of the law enforcement apparatus pose a real and imminent danger to the fragile human rights situation in the country. Militancy and terrorism in some parts of the country complicate the situation tending to brutalise the security forces and in the process, expose the hollowness of the human rights record of an otherwise peace-loving nation with rich cultural traditions. While a lot still remains to be done both in policies and programmes, no one can deny that the "right consciousness" acquired during the last few decades in the country is capable of sustaining itself hopefully with increasing efficiency in the future. Given the democratic nature of the polity, given the commitment to rule of law and independence of the judiciary, one can argue that at least in the area of civil and political rights, the future holds out promises which can put India in the forefront of nations honouring human rights.

Poverty : A Threat to Human Rights

However, the picture is not so reassuring when one looks at the state of social and economic rights. Poverty is indeed the greatest threat to human dignity and a nation which cannot provide for the basic needs of all human beings has no prospects for good governance. Statistics in this regard is shocking and the reality is shameful for every self-respecting citizen. Some take satisfaction by arguing that socio-economic rights are not rights in the strict sense of the term. Others point out that the situation is same or even worse in most parts of the developing world and therefore the Indian State cannot be particularly accused of rights violation. Yet another group even go to the extent of saying that individuals themselves are the cause of their poverty and the State cannot be blamed for their condition! Unfortunately, the rights in liberal societies. During the days of the Cold War, the Communist Bloc countries and others following a middle path were giving equal, if not greater, attention to poverty eradication justifying it in terms of the right to equality. In capitalist societies, the emphasis was more on freedom and liberty and equality was considered a natural result of a free society. The role of the State in building an egalitaring social order has been rather minimal in Western capitalist societies where individual choice (assuming that they did have choices) was taken to be the key for rights and good governance. Of course, the condition of western societies, many of them being former colonial powers, was much different because of historical reasons. Poverty in absolute terms was a negligible phenomenon in the developed world. Till the breaking up of the former Soviet Union and the disintegration of communism in Eastern Europe, poverty jurisprudence gave a different ideological thrust to the "Rights Debate" in nearly half the world. The rights discourse was more friendly in social and economic rights and state organs took the responsibilities in this regard very seriously.

With the advent of competitive free market economy and globalisation in trade relations, a situation is fast emerging which does not augur well for marginalised and underprivileged sections of society. The name of the game is survival of the fittest and there is no level playing field for the late starters. The State is expected to withdraw from economic operations and the market, dominated by the economics of developed countries, will dictate policies for production and distribution of wealth. Individualism and consumerism will be the dominant ideology and equality which cannot support it may not find acceptance in the rights discourse. While the middle and upper classes may reap the benefits, the lower classes may suffer increasing deprivation because of labour displacement as a result of changes in the agrarian economy. This is already evident in places where agriculture is changed to cash crops or when fishing is mechanised to suit an export market. With rising level of consumption on the part of the urban middle class and the inability of the state to adequately support the social welfare sector, there is every likelihood of social tensions resulting in terrorism and violence which again impacts adversely on the poorer classes. The pressure on the state for reduction of subsidies and for limiting the public distribution system is indicative of the trends which a weakened state will find increasingly difficult to resist. The inevitable consequence of such a development is starvation for those living below the poverty line. It is in this context, human rights discourse will have to examine the prospects of better implementation of right to live, right to education, right to health care and clean environment, right to work, right to food, right to housing, etc.

It seems difficult to reverse the march of globalisation and marketisation absorbing Third World economies. The only option seems to be to take advantage of emerging opportunities while ensuring the basic needs of those who are outside the competitive market. Human rights language is what state entities and world bodies understand. However, human rights technology does not at present provide adequate techniques and tools to realise basic human needs ever though the

Universal Declaration and Bill or Rights contain guarantees in this regard. There is indeed a poverty in the laws and legal institutions when it comes to the protection of socio-economic rights to the same level of civil and political rights. This is where the legal community will have to work with the economists and other social scientists for evolving acceptable norms and procedures in the introduction of human rights discipline in the municipal and global markets. The next few years are crucial for India and its human rights commitment, we cannot afford to fail lest posterity should blame us for lip service to human aspirations and the right to be human.

SOCIO-ECONOMIC RIGHTS AND THE UNIVERSAL DECLARATION OF HUMAN RIGHTS

In 1976, the International Covenant on Economic, Social and Cultural Rights came into force with 35 State Parties ratifying it. India ratified it later. Today more than 125 State Parties have ratified it. The different right recognized in the Covenant are described in Articles 6 to 15.

Economic Rights

Article 6 – Right to Work, Vocational Guidance and Training.
Article 7 – Right to Just and Favourable Condition of Work.
Article 8 – Right to form and join Trade Unions, Right to Strike.
Article 11 – Right the adequate standard of living including Food and Shelter.

Social Rights

Article 9 – Right to Social Security.
Article 10 – Rights of the Family, Mothers and Children.
Article 12 – Right to Physical and Mental Health.

Cultural Rights

Article 13 – Right to Education.
Article 14 – Right to Compulsory Primary Education.
Article 15 – Right to participate in cultural activities and to enjoy Scientific Progress.

There is no International Court for Human Rights, nor is there at the current stage of international law, a possibility to address individual complaints or State complaints about alleged violations of the rights enshrined in the Covenant on Economic, Social and Cultural Rights. The Covenant does include a system of obliging State Parties to report on the "measures which they have adopted and the progress made in achieving the observance of the rights recognized herein" (Article 16).

The reporting procedure to the Covenant on Economic, Social and Cultural Rights had a slow start as the UN was more concerned with Civil and Political Rights. In 1985 the UN established a Committee on Economic, Social and Cultural Rights of 18 independent experts which meets annually for three weeks to review the States reports. The Committee started its work in 1987. It revised its procedures, gave comments on the contents of specific rights and in 1990 issued revised guidelines for the submission of reports by States. The reports are to be submitted every five years. The reporting guidelines have no legal force and are merely recommendations concerning the reporting procedures. However, they do contribute to standard setting and, in this sense, is a landmark in the process of strengthening these rights.

The Committee on Economic, Social and Cultural Rights entertains additional information from non-governmental organisations and encourages participation of NGOs in the preparation of the reports and in their publication in the respective countries after submission.

While thousands of reports on violations of civil and political rights are submitted to the UN Centre on Human Rights every year, reports on violations of economic, social or cultural rights have practically been negligible. If socio-economic rights have to assume a better status in the Human Rights agenda of the United Nations, States as well as NGOs should start taking them seriously, monitor and report its violations to the UN Human Rights Centre and evolve techniques and tools to direct international efforts for better protection of basic needs. The parallel reporting procedure for NGOs now evolved by the Economic Rights Committee in Geneva provides an opportunity to get the system work for the advancement of socio-economic rights.

It is now acknowledged that Human Rights are indivisible, and as such, there cannot be sufficient protection for civil and political rights without equal protection for social and economic rights. In fact, claims of equality and non-discrimination have often revolved around social security benefits. The reason offered for the grouping of human rights into two distinct categories was that socio-economic rights, unlike civil and political rights, were not immediately realisable and could only be achieved over a period of time as resources become available. The nature of State obligations differed in the two sets of rights.

Whatever the reasons for the prioritisation of human rights and the relative neglect of socio-economic rights in the past, today experience has revealed the indivisibility of rights and the importance of enriching individual capabilities rather than overdependance on restructuring political and economic systems. Education and health care are needed to find employment and to lead free and fulfilling lives. It is perhaps the realisation of this obvious connection which compelled the United Nations to call the Social Summit of 1995 at Copenhagen. The proceedings of this World Summit constitute a reiteration of the States Parties commitment to work towards the early eradication of poverty and to provide a favourable climate for enjoyment of socio-economic rights.

Socio-Economic Rights and the Indian Constitution

The bifurcation of human rights in the International Bill of Rights seem to have influenced the treatment of human rights in the constitutions throughout the world. Civil and political rights are given greater importance and put in a higher pedestal in terms of enforceability and respect. Social and economic rights are treated as judicially not enforceable directives or policy guidelines for the governments. Thus socio-economic rights came to be regarded as the exclusive domain of the executive and legislative branches of the government with the judiciary having to do very little in terms of their enforcement. The Indian Constitution reflects this dual approach to human rights. While Part III dealing with Fundamental Rights deal largely with what are called civil and political rights, Part IV titled the Directive Principles of State Policy incorporate what the International Human Rights Instruments designate as socio-economic rights. Concerned with the importance of the latter for realising the goals of the Preamble, the Constitution makers while excluding the courts from enforcement of socio-economic rights, declared that "they are nevertheless fundamental in the governance of the country and it shall be the duty of the State to apply these principles in making laws (Article 37)."

The broad scheme of Part IV on Directive Principles of State Policy reflect the range of socio-economic rights (or entitlements recognized by the Indian Constitution.)

Article 38	:	State to secure a social order for the promotion of welfare of people.
Article 39	:	State to direct its polity towards securing equality in the matter of access to resources.
Article 39A	:	State to secure equal justice and free legal aid to the poor.
Article 41	:	Right to work, to education and public assistance in cases of unemployment, old age, sickness, disablement and of undeserved want.
Article 42	:	State to make provision for just and maternity relief.
Article 43	:	State to secure a living wage and decent standard of life as well as full enjoyment of leisure.
Article 43A	:	State to secure participation of workers in management of industries.
Article 44	:	State to secure a uniform civil code.
Article 45	:	State to provide for free and compulsory education for all children until the age of 14 years within a period of ten years from the commencement of the constitution.
Article 46	:	State to promote the educational and economic interests of Scheduled Castes, Scheduled Tribes and other weaker sections.
Article 47	:	Duty of the State to raise the level of nutrition, standard of living and public health.
Article 48A	:	State to protect and improve the environment, to safeguard the forests and wildlife.

It is often pointed out that the civil and political rights in Part III are couched in negative language injuncting the State from doing certain things. Of course, there are exceptions where affirmative action is expected of State for fulfilling some of the obligations in the Part (Articles 15 (4), 16 (4). For a long time, the judiciary adopted an approach of helplessness and treated socio-economic rights as subservient to fundamental rights (civil and political rights). This philosophy permeated the civil society as well. It was taken for granted that no viable legal claims against the government can arise for non-fulfilment of obligations under Part IV which contained the socio-economic rights. The dominant view has been that the courts are ill-equipped to adjudicate socio-economic rights, because (a) these rights are not precise and well articulated (b) they involve complex question of competing social policies (c) they require substantial resources the disposition of which only elected bodies can decide and (d) the adversary system is ill-suited for organizing public goods in the best public interest.

There is an impression in society that governments are expected to provide socio-economic services free of charge to all citizens which tend to support the separation of these rights from the civil and political rights. Primarily betterment of standard of living is the responsibility of individuals. State obligations are intended to supplement these individual efforts whenever and wherever needed and to enhance the capacity of individuals to achieve such conditions on all equal opportunity basis. Those who cannot meet basic needs and have no opportunities should be the responsibility of the State.

The Indian Supreme Court had to abandon its earlier approach of aloofness and detachment with Part IV. Invoking the mandate of Article 37 that the obligations of Part IV are "fundamental in the governance of the country and therefore binding on all three wings of government, the Court evolved a strategy of seeking support from Directive Principles of state policy for interpreting the scope of State obligations in respecting Fundamental Rights. In this exercise the judiciary also sought assistance of international treaties and agreements obligating States Parties to enforce socio-economic rights. What emerged from an activist court is a new human rights jurisprudence obliterating the division and prioritisation of rights and giving a fresh lease of life in honouring socio-economic rights. Through this process of judicial activism during the last two decades in India, the following socio-economic rights are judicially declared as enforceable fundamental rights as they form integral part of (a) right to life and personal liberty (Article 21) and (b) right to equality (Article 14) :

(1) Right to education, especially primary education
(2) Right to health
(3) Right to livelihood/Right to work
(4) Right to a clean environment
(5) Right to development

The story of this transition of socio-economic benefits (entitlements) into fundamental rights is still unfinished. What is means in real terms to the citizens is not clear. It did focus public attention on the obligations of government in the realisation of these rights and have put some pressure on legislatures and governments to adopt policies and programmes directed towards early realisation of these rights. Beyond this, the judicial initiatives remained unfulfilled in delivery of social justice to the poverty-sticken masses of the country. The judiciary has also been cautious about directing the government to undertake expensive socio-economic programmes even if they are fundamental for the fulfilment of basic needs of people. Only when the governments have shown marked recalcitrance in meeting its own legislative mandates or fulfilling constitutional obligations thereby putting the lives of citizens in jeopardy, that courts directed for governmental action involving budgetary resources. Public interest litigation, judicial activism and human rights consciousness among the general public have contributed to the emergence of a new era in the enjoyment of socio-economic rights. If it is sustained for some time, there is bound to be some difference in the prevailing climate of frustration and despondency. Political and social action is bound to pick up momentum with judiciary showing the directions and monitoring the implementation. Other institutions outside the judiciary now available for human rights protection will also support the initiatives which may tend to generate the necessary momentum for better realisation of socio-economic rights.

16

Role of Institutions of Higher Education

K.P. Saksena

Human rights are essentially the rights of the people, both as individuals and in groups; persistence vigilance and live actions by the people themselves for protection of human rights are essential. Human rights activists, individually or organized in groups (commonly refer to as NGOs), could play and have been playing a significant role in championing the cause of human rights, registering protest against their violations and creating general awareness about the observance of, and respect for human rights. Likewise, lawyers, teachers, journalists and professional organizations could contribute their part. There are other wide varieties of ways and methods which could be used to seek the objectives. But undoubtedly the most vital contribution that could be made is by having a programme of teaching about human rights at all levels of education.

The Universal Declaration of Human Rights (Art. 26.2) gives expression to this proposition when it declares that:

> "Education shall be directed to the full development of the human personality and to the strengthening of respect for human rights and fundamental freedom. It shall promote understanding, tolerance and friendship among all nations, racial or religious groups..."

The first International Congress on the Teaching of Human Rights (Vienna, 1978) elaborated this point by *inter alia* stating that "human rights education and teaching must aim at fostering the attitudes of tolerance, respect and goodwill towards fellow human beings", and that teaching about human rights is a continuing process and should embrace all levels of the educational system—from primary school to university level, to professional education as well as out of school or university settings.

Indeed, an essential pre-requisite for progressive realization of human rights is popular awareness of and support for universally accepted human rights norms and standards.

II

Teaching of human rights at all levels of education is, of course, essential. However, human rights education in the institutions of higher learning—universities and institutions providing professional education, has importance of its own.

While teaching at primary and secondary levels or adult literacy or post-adult literacy should not unnecessarily burden the students with specific texts; here the focus should be on inculcating an attitude of self-esteem, respect for ideas and beliefs of other people and plurality of culture and of fostering an attitude of tolerance and removal of prejudices. What is needed at these levels is not so much the question of any specific curriculum—human rights dimension could be added to the existing curriculum—as of providing orientation programme on human rights for teachers, appropriate school settings and cocurricular activities. At higher education level we could go further. Here, students have reached, agewise, enough maturity to imbibe the meaning and evolution of the concept of human rights, norms and standards spelled out in various international instruments and also to discuss in depth specific human rights issues in the context of concrete social, economic, political realities with emphasis on struggles, needs and aspirations of the people. Secondly, and more importantly, institutions of higher education produce civil servants, law enforcements officials, lawyers, doctors, scientists, teachers, journalists and so on whose work makes a vital difference in progress of the community, country and society at large. The underlying assumption, at the level of higher education, is that human rights education would lead to a more enlightened society, and those holding positions of responsibilities would not engage in human rights abuse or to tolerate them on their part in the society. Indeed, those having higher education would be equipped with better capability to resist authority when abused and to promote respect for, and protection of, human rights.

Regrettably, while almost all countries of Europe and North America and some in Latin America[1] have introduced human rights teaching at various levels including higher education, precious little has been done in India.

Some abortive attempts have been made here, since 1980s. As a follow-up to the International Congress on Human Rights (Vienna, September 1978) UNESCO addressed communications to governments of various member states requesting that steps be taken, if not already taken, to introduce human rights education at all levels. These educations were passed on the University Grants Commission (UGC), which, in turn, appointed a Commission under the Chairmanship of Mr. Justice S.M. Sikri (other members included jurists and senior lawyers) to consider ways and means of promoting human rights teaching in the country at all levels of education. It prepared a blueprint by December 1985 and UGC sent the same to National Council of Educational Research and Tranning (NCERT), and to various universities; since then the report has been gathering dust.

An attempt to introduce human rights teaching in all Indian universities was also made, in 1985 when a national symposium was convened by Human Rights Centre (HURITER), Jawaharlal Nehru University with the support of National UNESCO Commission and U.G.C.; the then U.G.C. Chairman, Mrs. Madhuri Shah took keen interest and also inaugurated the symposium

Recognising the fact that introduction of new curricula or the revision of the old ones had to be initiated and approved by the academic council and other appropriate bodies of the university concerned, the attempt was to prepare broad guidelines in collaboration with the 'official' representatives of various universities. Subsequently, these representatives could take initiative within the framework of their respective universities. Hence, the Vice-Chancellors were requested to send a senior faculty member, as 'official participant' of the University to the national symposium. Consequently, senior faculty members representing 29 universities—from Madurai to Warangal to/Delhi and Chandigarh, from Bombay, Pune to Varanasi, to Calcutta and Guwahati, participated in the three–day national symposium. In addition, other participants included eminent human rights activists, educationists, exponents and jurists. Although the symposium was supposed to confine its deliberations to human rights education at university (undergraduate) level, but the participants thought it appropriate to cover all levels of education. Its recommendations covered the entire range of education from primary to secondary to higher to university/professional levels, etc. Subsequently, its recommendations were published[2] and widely circulated to all universities and educational institutions. Subsequently, it was learnt that participants did attempt to introduce human rights dimension in the curricula of their respective universities. However, there could be no follow-up by the organisers for lack of resources; the UGC did not extend any further support after the retirement of Madhuri Shah, as Chairman, in 1986. Thus, the initiative, despite wide collaboration obtained, did not move further on the desired course.

Of late, there have been much "intellectual" activity—seminars, workshops, studies, reports, etc., as a preliminary, to introduce teaching human rights at various levels of education. Indeed, it is gratifying that there is wider awareness of this need, and that National Human Rights Commission (NHRC) has taken initiative, on priority basis, to promote teaching human rights at various levels. Consequent to its (NHRC) pressure, so it seems, the Ministry and national institutions such as UGC, National Council for Teachers Education (NCTE), have become more 'active' in 'planning' for teaching human rights. Several universities have introduced courses on "International Human Rights Law". A few universities have also introduced "post-graduate Diploma Course on Human Rights"[3].

But the question is: have we made the necessary preparatory work to move ahead on what would be not only long but continuous journey.

III

While discussing the role of institutions of higher education, it is necessary that we turn to some of the misgivings which are widely prevalent including among those who bear the responsibility for conducting higher education—that human rights is a Western concept being imposed by the powers-that-be and that, in India, our priorities should be different.

This kind of thinking is perhaps partly because Western countries have been increasingly using human rights issue as a political weapon, and also assuming the role of self-appointed guardians of human rights. Thus, partly as a resentment against Western aggressive instance on human rights issues, even highly educated people in India and other non-Western countries very often treat human rights issues as one being imposed on them by the West. Another reason seems to be that world-wide movement for human rights is largely controlled by the Western based transnational NGOs. Invariably all of them lay emphasis on civil and political rights, based their reports as if sitting in judgement on the happenings or mishappenings in the non-Western world; economic, social and cultural rights and the factors responsible for their denial and the deeper, structural causes of injustice are ignored.

Further, human rights literature is also dominated by the Western authors who trace the origin of the concept to Greco-Roman period and highlighting, the Western traditions and contributions of Western philosophers[4]. They hardly make even a passing reference to cultures and traditions of other regions. Unfortunately, most of the non-European authors, too, have written their books on material and ideas borrowed from Western authors. This holds true in most of the Indian publications, if not all, on human rights.

What is more unfortunate is that one of the premier institutions in India, which prepares textbooks for secondary, higher secondary and senior secondary education has recently brought out a publication,[5] which reproduces text of international legislations, some relevant national legislations and excerpts from the Indian Constitution. It is intended to serve as background informative material for teachers with the purpose of promoting human rights education. A commendable initiative, indeed. However, the introduction, by a senior faculty member, traces the origin of the concept of human rights beginning the renaissance in Europe and that important landmark in its development are the American Declaration of Independence, the French Declaration and the Bolshevik Revolution in Russia.

Indeed, the origin of the concept of human rights could be traced not from any specific period or specific region or culture but from the dawn of civilisation—when human beings first started living in groups.

It should be recalled here that nature has bestowed men with two related characteristics: first, he is an individual, second, he is a social being. No person can be his/her natural self in solitude; he/she needs fellow human beings around—living in groups or in organised community is natural to him/her. It was but inevitable that at one stage or the other of the evolutionary process, human-persons started living in groups. In all areas and eras, they must have implicitly or explicitly, in legal or social terms, agreed on certain norms of social behaviour, defining the rights and obligations, on the basis particularly nature of socially accepted claims of the individual and restrictions imposed by the need of maintaining social order.

Thus, each civilisation developed its own norms. In India, they found expression in Panchayat system; well defined duties of the ruler and obligations of the ruled. However, here the emphasis was on duties rather than on rights. As Mahatma Gandhi has aptly noted : if everyone performs one's duties, everyone's rights would betaken care of.

There is more to the evolutionary process. Human rights basically implies the availability of those conditions which are essential for the development of the innate characteristics which nature has bestowed him/her with as a human being. It also implies basic principle of "live and let live" and respect for other species. Throughout history, India's tradition has been respect for all human beings irrespective of one's religion, race, colour, etc. Vedic philosophy, Buddhism, Christainity Jainism, Islam, Sufism, Sikhism, etc. all lay emphasis on universal brotherhood. India was perhaps the first country in the world where freedom of religion, freedom of expression accompanied by right to dissent were part of our way of life. In European region, kings fought bloody wars amongst themselves for centuries until freedom of religion and of expression became an accepted norms as late as early 18th century.

In brief, the concept of human rights is not the "monopoly" of Western civilisation. Indian traditions and cultures, as of other regions, have made their own contribution to the evolution of the concept.

In the evolution of the concept Asian way of life, its cultures and traditions, especially of China and India had made solid contribution. This aspect is well reflected in the writings of various scholars, both European and non-Europeans.[6]

To cite a ready reference of an article which appeared in SPAN Magazine (New Delhi, September 1995), it carries an article by an eminent American human rights exponent, Prof. Charles Norchi (Harvard University), who is also Director of one of the oldest human rights NGO based in New York—International League for Human Rights. In that article, the author notes in his concluding observation:

> In the final analysis, human rights is really about human dignity—a notions familiar to India's civilisation, centuries before the West was even born.

This is not to say that human rights education should focus on India's contribution alone; this would amount to chauvinism, something which goes against the very concept of human rights, but teachers/students should know that concern for human rights is not something "foreign" but rooted in India's centuries old history, culture and tradition.

IV

Another argument that we come across is that we do not need human rights education. Our priorities, in the present situation should be different; a large segment of the people in India do not have basic necessities of life, like food, shelter, and clothing; hence, the priority-concern should be to concentrate on practical efforts for the removal of hunger, poverty and other social evils. How human rights 'teaching' some people ask, was going to help these helpless people? Another point, emphasised is that India, as several countries in other parts of the world, are experiencing turmoil, insurgency, terrorism, etc. Therefore, we in India, cannot indulge in such 'theoretical' exercises as teaching about human rights.

These arguments may appear plausible to many but a closer look at the realities must lead to a different conclusion. The turmoil and turbulence which these countries arc experiencing partly because some aggrieved people feel alienated from society; such a situation warrants a compulsory need for human rights education—an education which not only provides understanding of ones own rights (and duties also) and, therefore, inculcation of self-esteem and recognition of ones own rightful place in society, also fostering of an attitude of tolerance, goodwill and removal of prejudices towards fellow human beings. It is partly because the educational system did not give attention to human rights dimension that there is turmoil and turbulence in various countries; of course, there are other varied factors involved.

Let us look at another aspect; in larger part of our country, especially in rural areas hierarchical social order unfortunately is still prevalent;

while a small percentage of people enjoy privileged positions, comforts and luxuries, majority do not have enough to eat; a comparatively small percentage of students have opportunity to go for higher and professional/ technical education, a vast majority do not. That is why those who are the privileged ones need to be taught human rights to create awareness and recognition of the rights of those who are unfortunate and the exploited ones.

There is more to the situation; take the tragedy that was unleashed in Bhopal a decade ago. There were, of course, complexities of factors involved, including negligence on the part of Union Carbide—a transitional corporation. However, it was a grim reminder to us that while the benefits which scientific knowledge and its application through technology have brought to mankind are immense. On the other hand, certain rapid advances in nuclear energy, biochemistry, biology, and medicine have posited threats to human personality and its physical and intellectual integrity and to human environment. It is, therefore, essential that teaching of various disciplines in natural sciences should emphasise that scientific research and its application should be so directed as not to posit a threat to human dignity and human rights.

Again, day in and day out, we hear about police atrocities; most glaring of them, police torturously blinding the alleged 'professional criminals' in Bhagalpur jail. True, a number of socio-economic factors were behind this gruesome tragedy. But such tragic incidents bring forth a pertinent questions; Isn't it essential that professional training to law enforcement officials should include human rights education? To that extent, should not the administrators, engineers, technocrats, doctors and nurses, acquire during their training and professional education, the necessary understanding of human rights dimensions involved in the discharge of their duties.

This is, of course, not to say that human rights education alone has the answer to all the problems. Nonetheless, if education is to provide the intellectual basis for understanding and resolving important contemporary social problems, education at all levels will have to deal with teaching about human rights.

V

The term human rights education implies the entire process of social life by means of which individuals and social groups learn to develop consciously within, and for the benefit of, the national and international communities, the whole of their personal capacities, attitudes, aptitudes and knowledge. This process is not limited to any specific activities.

As it goes without saying, institutions of higher education do have a crucial role in developing the individual awareness of the ways and means by which human rights can be translated into social and political realities, both at national and international level.

Here, obviously, the teacher concerned bears a heavy responsibility in exercising his discretion what to teach and how to impart human rights education, taking into account the discipline and professional training students are getting equipped with, and also keeping in mind the social realities and needs and aspirations of the people concerned.

This bring us to the most important pre-requisite: "The teachers, instructors' training and education in human rights education, it is obvious that, however, carefully planned education programme may be, it will have little impact in the hands of the teachers', lacking the necessary motivation, training and informative material for carrying it out. (In teachers' training orientation programme, periodical workshops and seminars on human rights issues could play a purposeful role.)

Curricula and the examination system have to constitute the core of human rights teaching, which, of course, remains the exclusive responsibility of the appropriate bodies of higher institutions which should keep in mind that teacher concerned is given wide discretion in picking up specific themes and methods of teaching, as well as evaluation. In a general way, some observations are made here.

In social sciences and humanities, for instance, introducing a separate compulsory course on human rights should not create much of a problem. Indeed, in some disciplines, such as political science, economics, sociology, law, etc. Human rights dimensions could conveniently be added in the existing courses in addition to a separate course.

In case of natural science, we know that recent developments in sciences have, of course, brought to mankind immense benefits, but at the same time, this is also true that rapid advances in biochemistry, biology, physics, electronics, medicine and, of course, Nuclear Energy have posed serious threats to human personality and its physical and intellectual integrity. As such teaching about human rights in sciences including medical sciences is very much desirable. In the first instance, the role of science needs to be spelled out. This would involve examples from agriculture, health/medicine, communications, transport meteorology, etc. Further, attention to those aspects where the application of science and technology lead to violation of human rights, such as radiation hazards, abuse of drugs, abuse of electronics and computers in violation of the rights of privacy, environmental pollution and ecological imbalance, use of human subjects for experimentation, especially in the fields of medicine and psychology including artificial insemination, manipulation of human embryos, transplantation of organs, pre-natal sex diagnosis, etc.

As regards students of medical sciences, specific attention should be drawn to the "Principles of Medical Ethics" relevant to health personnel, particularly surgeons and physicians as spelled out (on the recommendations of WHO Council for International Organisation of Medical Scientists), by the UN General Assembly Resolution 37/194 (December 1982).

As regards training programme of law enforcement officials, besides understanding human rights dimensions of their responsibilities, they should be made aware of Code of Conduct for Law Enforcement officials, Rules Regarding Detention and Treatment of Offenders—Standard Minimum Rules for the Treatment of Prisoners, Standard Minimum Rules for the Administration of Juvenile Justice—adopted by the UN General Assembly, over a period, on the recommendation of various United Nations Congresses on the Prevention of Crime and Treatment of offenders, which meets periodically and in which Indian delegation composed senior law enforcement officials and jurists.

Within the limited space it is not possible to go into details. However, some basic points need to be noted. Firstly, while emphasising the universality of human rights and universal brotherhood, teaching needs to be adopted to socio-cultural settings, as well as to national and local realities. It is true that the principles underlying human rights are universal but teaching would be reduced to theoretical exercise if the approach is not based on real problems; teaching procedures and methods need to be adopted specifically to live problems and to social conditions in a particular country in a given time.

Secondly, there is need for action-oriented research. As we all know, for instance, bonded labour, child labour have been one of the most perennial evils of our society; the Government has passed a legislation abolishing bonded labour and strict regulations regarding child labour, yet both continue unabated. Then again, bonded labour, is of a different kind; traditional bonded labour in rural areas; then there are bonded labour in urban areas—brick kilns, construction work, glass industries, carpet industries, etc. What is needed is an in-depth research based on fieldwork to bring forth the entire set of problems, both economic and social, which are keeping the continuance of, for instance, bonded labour. What are the socio-economic factors responsible for child labour?

Of late, it is gratifying to note that various universities have undertaken research work on human rights problems. At Jawaharlal Nehru University, during the last two decades, more than 20 theses/dissertations on themes relating to human rights have been completed leading to the award of Ph.D./M.Phil. Degrees. The subject covered range from India and International Covenants on Human Rights, to Child Labour, Rights of the Disabled Persons, Bonded Labour in specific areas and so on. Other universities, such as Delhi University, Bombay University, Guwahati University, Banaras Hindu University, Pune University, Aligarh Muslim University, have encouraged scholars to undertake research work on human rights themes.

Research scholars and faculty members have contributed several research articles to various journals and also write-ups on various issues relating to human rights in national and regional newspapers. However, work has progressed in a haphazard manner. For one thing, a teacher/supervisor has to keep the interest of students in mind and let him/her to decide about the specific areas of research work. There has been also lack of coordination and exchange of information. As such topics chosen for research projects have been repetitious of the work already done. Thus, several aspects of human rights problems in India, which demand action-oriented research, have not been touched upon. It is true that universities should exercise their autonomy but we have to avoid duplication and repetition which sometimes amounts to plagiarism.

We have to build-up some research arrangements, as we find in the USA, where all topics, as approved for Ph.D. thesis, submitted should necessarily be accompanied by a 600 words abstract, is also registered with the same Centre. Further, both the list and dissertation abstracts are published periodically. Thus, duplication or repetition of research topics is not permissible. What is important is that micro-filmed text of Ph.D dissertations are conveniently available. Here, in India, perhaps Association of Indian Universities should take initiative in this regard.

Further, for building up a viable and meaningful programme, it is essential that there should be network of documentation/information centres with research facilities at national, regional/state and local levels. Such units/centres should serve as depository of the texts of international instruments—Declarations, Covenants, adopted by the UN/UNESCO/ ILO and other international organisations, as also relevant documents and reports prepared by these organisations; such units/centres should collect and disseminate information on national and international human rights legislations, as well as information relating to syllabic materials and instructional guides for all levels of education and availability of material towards setting of priorities for effective human rights research.

It is also necessary that these units/centres should function as an autonomous unit/centre and not as part of the general library. Documentation system and cataloguing of human rights material is very different from that of a library. Documentation Centre in-charge should be one who has excellent knowledge of human rights material, including the material published by UNESCO and the United Nations. What is more important is that he should be familiar with human rights information and documentation system as spelled out by HURIDOCS International.

Needless to say, we have yet to make a beginning in the desired direction. Curricula in various disciplines have to be restructured, reading material has to be prepared, programmes for cocurricular, extracurricular activities for promotion of human rights education have to be introduced. What is perhaps most important is orientation and training programme of teachers—motivated and dedicated to the promotion of respect for and awareness of human rights and also well equipped with necessary informative material.

REFERENCES

1. For on overview of human rights teaching programme in these continents, see, - "Systems and Programmes for Human Rights Teaching in Latin America and the Caribbean" (UNESCO Document SHS-87/CONF.401/INF. 6), prepared by the Inter-American Institute of Human Rights, San Jose, Costa Rica; and-

"Methods and Programme for Teaching Human Rights in North America and Western Europe" (UNESCO Document SHS-87/CONF.401/INF.9), prepared by the Human Rights Research and Education Centre, University of Ottawa, Canada. These two studies were presented at the UNESCO International Congress on "Human Rights Teaching, Information and Documentation", Malta, August-September 1987.

2. The Teaching of Human Rights: Proceedings of the First National Symposium on Human Rights Teaching in India at University (undergraduate) Level, May 9-11, 1985 (New Delhi: HURITER, 1985).
3. As per information available with the Research Wing of NHRC, following ten universities have been identified by the UGC to establish new department for human rights: (1) Andhra Pradesh University, Waltair, (2) Panjab University, Chandigarh; (3) Jammu University, Jammu; (4) Aligarh Muslim University, Aligarh; (5) Cochin University, Cochin; (6) Banaras Hindu University, Varanasi; (7) Delhi University, Delhi; (8) Rajasthan University, Jaipur; (9) Karnataka University, Dharwar and (10) Kurukshetra University, Kurukshetra.
4. In 1965, UNESCO convened a Round Table in London "to discuss this most controversial issue–whether or not, the concept of 'human rights' was peculiar to and inherent in Western philosophical traditions." Its participants were drawn from different geographical areas, traditions and cultures (India was represented by Romila Thapar). Here, again, those who dominated the deliberations argued for the Western thought and philosophy. For them "acceptance of the Universal Declaration of Human Rights by nations outside Europe is a victory of Western thought..." (UNESCO International Social Science Journal, vol.XIII, No. 1, 1996, p.8).

   Some of the conclusions reached were that Universal Declaration, the first 21 of its articles in its form and terminology represents preponderance of Western philosophy.

   However, totality of Universal Declaration also represents the values of various traditions and religions; respect for human rights and dignity, tolerance, importance of the criteria applicable to individual and group relations in social life, observance and safeguarding of those criteria, including contractual obligations and so on. ("Final Report of the Round Table Meeting on Human Rights" reproduced in UNESCO, Teaching of Human Rights, Voluntary IV, 1985, p.76).

   In 1947, UNESCO had also organised a symposium of eminent persons and scholars representing various cultures, traditions drawn from different parts of the world. Proceedings reproduced in Human Rights Comments and Interpretations, a symposium by UNESCO (London: Allan Wingate, 1949).
5. Reference here is to Arjun Dev, et.al. eds, Human Rights: A Source Book (New Delhi: NCERT, 1996.)
6. This aspect has been well elaborated in an address (Dr. Nagendra Singh Memorial Lecture), by Judge (C.G. Weeranmantry) of International Court of Justice, reproduced in Indian Journal of International Law, December 1996.

17

Human Rights in India: A Survey

V.S. Mani

Human rights of the individual are "those conditions of social life without which no man can seek, in general, to be himself at his best[1]. Human Rights have to do with the all round development of the human being in harmony with that of his fellow-beings in the totality of the relations in a society. The concept of human rights is necessarily evolving in nature apace with the evolution of human civilization in the context of a changing social, political, economic and cultural milieu. It is, therefore, a daunting task for anyone to assess the state of implementation of human rights in a society. The arrogance of sitting in judgment over the human rights performance of the society apart, it is a function often tainted by a preferred perception and prioritization of human rights *inter se* and an eclectic identification and impressionistic evaluation of human rights situations. The exercise usually ends up in a fault-finding judgement, without taking into account the intrinsic correlationship of the development of the individual with the development of the society, and without addressing the question of social and economic costs of conditioning the correlationship between the individual and societal development. For these reasons, the present study does not claim to be a comprehensive and holistic assessment of the human rights situation in India or an elaborate prescription of preventive and remedial measures. Its aim is rather modest: to present a general overview of the human rights situation in India, as the nation celebrates the Golden Jubilee of its independence.

The ethos and problems of a developing ancient oriental society like the India must first be understood before an acceptable standard of rights performance assessment is evolved. Indeed, the non-derogable rights to life and dignity do provide a universal bottom line. Yet, to look at a society purely through that looking glass is to ignore the ground realities in the midst of which the human rights culture has to nurture.

The Vision of the Makers of Modern India

Since the days of the Indus Valley Civilization down to this day, the Indian culture has been the product of syntheses of diverse cultures and religions that came into contact with the enormous Indian sub-continent over time.

The Indian culture perceives the individual, the society and the universe an organic whole: Everyone is a child of God, and all fellow-beings are related to one another, belonging to a universal family. Religious prayers would ask of God to make all peoples of the world happy. The same cultural ethos rang in when Mahatma Gandhi said:

> I do not want to think in terms of the whole world. My patriotism includes the good of mankind in general. Therefore, my service to India includes the services of humanity[2].

While the ancient texts tend to emphasize the principle of equality between individuals, there is no doubt that there was always a gap between the ideal and the ground reality. Humans in any society have never been equal *inter se* and there have always been dominant groups/classes seeking to monopolize social and material benefits unto themselves and deprive others from access to them. Stratification is the bane of all societies. In India, for instance, the caste system arose from the principle of division of labour as a method of social organization. However, over a period of time, those castes which could gain power and wealth, such as the Brahmins and the Kshatriyas, exploited the society and its institutions. The chasm between the religious, scriptural norms and practice grew wide.

The historical responses came from Buddhism and Jainism, both of which emphasized the principles of equality, non-violence and denial of materialistic pleasures. The religious reformers like Sankara then took upon themselves the task of purification of the Indian society, through a process of synthesis of new thoughts. Subsequently, the advent of the

Muslim rulers from the north brought with them the teachings of Islam. This historical process of synthesis, aided by enlightened reformers, and great kings like Ashoka and Akbar, now forms the foundation of the amazing phenomenon called the Indian culture.[3] On it stands the co-existence of and mutual respect for diverse religious and philosophical beliefs and subcultures.

While the dubious credit for the unification of India must largely go to the British rule, the British achieved it with systematic destruction of the traditional social, political and economic institutions, and exploitation of the social and religious weaknesses of the Indian masses in furtherance of the cause of British imperialism[4]. The British stood to gain by sharpening the caste and religious differences in the society in pursuit of their divide and rule policy[5]. In the Indian cultural history, the British colonial period shall remain the Indian equivalent of the "Dark Ages".

The renaissance came about thanks chiefly to the rise of nationalism and religious and social reformers. The leaders of Indian nationalism have, however, been a new breed of men and women of vision synthesizing the traditional cultural values with newly imbibed ideas of the American and the French revolutions. Mahatma Gandhi was the foremost among them. His test of freedom has always been what benefit it would accrue to the poorest of the land. "Whatever can be useful to starving millions is beautiful to my mind. Let us give today first the vital things of life and all the graces and ornaments of life will follow". His ambition, he said, was "to wipe every tear from every eye"[6].

The ultimate welfare of the poorest of the Indians was Gandhiji's fundamental yardstick. He dreamt of an India "in which the poorest shall feel that it is their country, in whose making they have an effective voice, an India in which there shall be no high class and low class of people, an India in which all communities shall live in perfect harmony ..... There can be no room in such an India for the curse of untouchability or the curse of intoxicating drinks and drugs.... Women will enjoy the same right as men"[7].

Addressing the nation on the threshold of independence, Jawaharlal Nehru declared in the same vein:

> We shall look to the common and forgotten man of India and seek to bring him relief and raise his standard of living. We shall continue our fight against the curse of untouchability and other

> forms of enforced inequality, and shall especially try to help those who are economically or otherwise backward. Today millions lack food and clothing and houses, and many are on the verge of starvation.[8]

Thus the leaders of India's independence struggle had already set a clear "Indian" human rights agenda for action even as the nation was emerging independent. Small wonder, the new legal and political norms and institutions reflected this agenda, although it was left to these institutions and ultimately to the people of India to evolve and redefine these norms through the ever changing national political and social processes.

The Constitutional and Institutional Framework of Human Rights

The Constitution of the Republic of India, which came into force on 26th January, 1950, with 395 articles and nine schedules, is one of the most elaborate fundamental laws ever adopted. The Preamble to the Constitution pledges to secure to all the citizens of India Justice—social, economic and political, liberty—of thought, expression, belief, faith and worship, Equality—of status and of opportunity; and Fraternity assuring the dignity of the individual and the unity and integrity of the nation. Two parts of the Constitution embody most human rights, distinguishing between judicially enforceable fundamental rights and rights not so enforceable, namely Part III and Part IV.

The judicially enforceable fundamental rights, which encompass all seminal civil and political rights and some of the rights of minorities, are enshrined in Part III of the Constitution (Articles 12 to 35). These include the right to equality, the right to freedom, the right against exploitation, the right to freedom, of religion, cultural and educational rights, and the right to constitutional remedies.

Judicially non-enforceable rights in Part IV of the Constitution are chiefly those of economic and social character. However, as Article 37 makes it clear, their non-justiciability does not weaken the duty of the state to apply them in making laws, since they are "nevertheless fundamental in the governance of the country". Additionally, the innovative jurisprudence of the Supreme Court has now read into Article 21 (the right to life and personal liberty), many of these principles and made them enforceable.[9]

In the scheme of the Constitution, there exists a separation of powers among the legislature, the executive and the judiciary, with the judiciary being fiercely independent of the other two, charged with the task of enforcing the constitutional norms, including human rights, and adjudicating upon all interindividual, interinstitutional disputes.

In order to monitor implementation of the constitutional objectives for the welfare of the weaker sections of the nation, the central government has appointed a National Commission for Minorities, a National Commission for Scheduled Castes and Scheduled Tribes and a National Commission for Women. The appointment of a National Commission for Backward Classes is now on the anvil. The National Human Rights Commission (NHRC) came into being in 1993 by virtue of the Human Rights Protection Act, 1993. The freedom of the Press is monitored chiefly by the Press Council of India since 1979.

A network of laws, too wide to be portrayed *in extenso*–in this essay, exists to give effect to the broad range of human rights recognized in the Constitution. It must be noted, however, that the human rights enumerated in the various multilateral treaties to which India is a party,[10] and also found in the Indian Constitution and laws have not been defined in identical terms in the latter, nor are all the rights mentioned in the treaties specifically recognised in the Constitution and the laws *in extenso*.[11] However, the innovative jurisprudence of the Supreme Court seeks to update and harmonise the Indian law with the emerging international norms, and application of these norms taking into account the special conditions obtaining in India. It would seem, therefore, that the guarantee of life and personal liberty in Article 21 of the Constitution is adequately all-pervasive of all human rights, both present and evolving.

Implementation of Human Rights

The Right to Development

Article 28 of the Universal Declaration of Human Rights, 1948 recognizes that "Everyone is entitled to a social and international order in which the rights and freedoms set forth in this Declaration can be fully realised". Closely following this, Article 38 of the Indian Constitution requires the state to "strive to promote the welfare of the people by securing and protecting as effectively as it may a social order in which justice—social, economic and political—shall inform all the institutions of the national life". This indeed is the ultimate objective of the whole Part IV of the Constitution. The right to development has now come to be recognized as "an inalienable human right... in which all human rights and fundamental freedoms can be fully realized".[12] It is also recognized that "The human person is the central subject of development..."[13]

The right to development in India is grossly impeded by the stupendous nature of the developmental problems which India faces. At the root of these problems are poverty, illiteracy and overpopulation which form a vicious circle each contributing to the other. While the British could be blamed for the conditions in which the country found itself in 1947, the succeeding governments have not done enough for the eradication of poverty and illiteracy and reverse the process of population explosion. At independence India's population was around 360 million, it is now touching 950 million. In 1970 some 16 per cent of the population was below the poverty line, now it has risen to 37 per cent of the current population.[14] These problems have a multiplier effect on all other social and economic problems.

In 1992, the top 20 per cent of the population accounted for more than two-fifths of the total consumption expenditure, while the bottom 20 per cent had a share of a mere 8.5 per cent of the total consumption. The top 10 per cent spent eight times as much as the bottom 10 per cent.[15] There are parts of India, such as the tribal belts of the Districts of Kalahandi and Bolangir in the state of Orissa, exposed to "the scourge of poverty, malnutrition and even starvation" attributed to repeated crop failures, inhuman exploitation of the tribals and politicization of human calamities, with the administration "woefully unequal to the task".[16] Evidently, the poverty eradication programmes started with a new zeal since the seventies have failed to mitigate, let alone prevent, such human tragedies.

The Government of India has announced plans of setting up a nationwide public distribution system whereby availability of 10 kilograms of foodgrains per head per month at cheapest rates is ensured for each family below the poverty line.[17] The ninth five year plan (1997-2002) is likely to have a special thrust for rural development "with poverty alleviation programmes as its major component". These would encompass programmes for reduction of rural unemployment, land reforms, improved access to water resources, drought prone area programme and desert development programme. The Chief Ministers Conference of January

1997 had identified "seven basic minimum services", namely safe drinking water, primary health services, universal primary education, public housing assistance to the shelterless poor, better nutrition for children, road linkages with all villages and habitations, and public distribution system for the poor.[18] The Prime Minister of India has recently admitted that over 400 million Indians are illiterate,[19] despite the fact that the first fifty years of expansion of educational facilities have credited India with one of the largest educational infrastructure in the world.[20] The shelter shortage of by 1997 was estimated to be 7.57 million dwelling units.[21]

The process of globalization and liberalization, now afoot in India, has not found favour in certain quarters and the fear that it is harmful for the uplift of the poor is often expressed. It is contended that trade liberalization has led to decline in foodgrain production and consumption.[22] It would hit hard the landless rural communities due to the loss of traditional markets, and deprive them of food entitlements and purchasing power.[23]

The International Labour Organisation, in its *World Employment Report for 1996-97*, cautioned against economic liberalisation on all fronts at one go as it would lead to sharp increases in unemployment, underemployment and poverty. While economic reforms are essential, they should be pursued in a phased manner, accompanied by programmes to strengthen the productive capacity of the poor, development of rural infrastructure, credit schemes and improved access to education and health services.[24]

India has registered a discernible level of development for the last fifty years on many fronts. It has also mastered some of the most modern technologies such as those in the fields of communications, space and nuclear energy. However, the magnitude of the problems engendered by poverty, illiteracy and population explosion has apparently dwarfed these achievements and demand greater and more sustained efforts. In the meantime, the Indian society will continue to be bedevilled by the maladies of inequality and exploitation, unless the governmental efforts are equally complemented by committed non-government ones.

The Right to Life and Personal Liberty

A number of situations involving violation of the right to life and personal liberty at the instance of state agencies such as the security and police forces, are being reported in the media by non-governmental organizations, and the National and State Human Rights Commissions. They relate not only to areas where there exist serious threats to internal security such as terrorism and insurgency, but also other areas as part of the law and order problems. A standing fact finding committee of the Legislative Council of Bihar (the first ever legislative committee appointed to investigate human rights violations in any State in India) is reported to have observed that human rights violations were common in the State and the "main targets have been the depressed and exploited classes, the dalits, women and children. The police and bureaucracy is [sic: are] responsible for most crimes and most violations are a result of untempered police attitudes towards the common man".

Instances of custodial violence—violence by the police to human being during custody, such as torture, inhuman or degrading treatment, rape and killing—have been reported in the national media. They include violence against prisoners. A number of such instances have eventually reached the National Human Rights Commission, the High Courts and the Supreme Court.

Instability in the North East (Nagaland, Manipur, Tripura and Assam) has been the result of terrorism, insurgency and intertribal conflicts. Added to these is the politics—both national as well as local—to shroud the real problem, namely economic backwardness. The borderline between a secessionist claim and a claim for autonomy is often determined by the political games which the parties to them play. Terrorism elsewhere in India has also principally been spawned by politics, but often taken advantage of by the unfriendly neighbour across the border. Mindless acts of political expediency by political parties, besides economic and other causes, have contributed to terrorism in Punjab, and Jammu and Kashmir.

The Indian army and paramilitary forces have often been pressed into service to meet the challenges of terrorism and insurgency, as the police force is not adequately equipped to meet such threats to civil life. While there are claims of rights violations by army and paramilitary forces some of which have been found proved by the National Human Rights Commission and the Indian judiciary, the army claims that its human rights record has generally been "exemplary".

There have been instances of use of excessive force and violations of human rights by these forces. Often behind these is the soldier "losing his balance". The question of taking *impromptu* revenge to terrorist acts apart, "little or no leave, absence of 'soft' postings, difficult living conditions, indifferent food and, above all, constantly facing the prospect of dying is enough to try the mettle of even the bravest soldier and psychologically push him over the edge"[25].

The police, a state subject, have been largely an ill-equipped, under-trained, overworked and underpaid force. Their work has considerably expanded over time, but they are seriously handicapped for lack of resources. They have been politicised by succeeding governments, but the latter have been slow to bring in necessary improvements in their pay, conditions of work and techniques of crime investigation. Given the wretched conditions of life in which an ordinary policeman lives, it would require considerable persuasion and resources to make him feel human.

Apart from police reforms, a number of areas of criminal justice have been identified by the judiciary, the National Human Rights Commission and the Law Commission of India for reforms and to make the system of administration of criminal justice humane. The recent public outcry against some of the human rights violations by the security forces resulted in the termination of the Terrorist and Disruptive Activities (Prevention) Act, 1985-91 (TADA), whereby the police and other security forces committed abuse of powers, and both the Supreme Court[26] and the National Human Rights Commission came down heavily on such abuses. There is also mounting criticism against the Armed Forces (Assam and Manipur) Special Powers Act, 1958, the National Security Act, 1980 and the Public Safety Act, 1978, which have lent themselves to be abused by the security forces.[27]

In terms of the actual working of the Indian criminal justice system with its delays, cumbersomeness and costliness, there exists a strong view that the system is "indifferent and perhaps [a] little hostile to the poor and the weak, such as women, children, physically, economically and mentally handicapped groups, prisoners and the like.[28] What is more important, however, is that the human rights culture should percolate through all the segments of the criminal justice system.

Rights of Women

Two principal facets of rights of women in India are highlighted here, namely the problem of equality with men, and trafficking and other undesirable practices and atrocities against women. Underlying these are the age old attitudes and customs of an ancient male dominated society. While violations of women's rights are not unknown in other societies, including the developed ones, what aggravate them in the context of the Indian society are poverty, illiteracy and some of the rationally and morally untenable social customs, such as dowry, sati, etc.

The right to equality in the context of women has many aspects—equal pay for equal work, equality of opportunity, equality before law, political equality, equality of status and so on. A number of laws exist in the statute book. However, implementation of these laws has left much to be desired.

Parliament enacted the Indecent Representation of Women (Prohibition) Act in 1986 to expand the law of obscenity contained in the Indian Penal Code, 1860 and to counter a growing tendency of indecent representation of or references to women in publications such as advertisements, which is derogatory of women. However, the implementation of this Act has not been effective.

Despite the Suppression of Immortal Traffic in Women and Girls Act, 1956, poverty has pushed a number of women into one of the oldest professions in the world.[29] Coordinated action is called for not only to retrieve and rehabilitate them, but to prevent their exploitation.

There has been a significant increase in reported crimes against women atleast in certain metropolitan cities like Delhi.

Parliament is currently considering a law to reserve 33 per cent of the seats in the Lok Sabha (the Lower House of Parliament) and the state legislative assemblies. This follows the 73rd Constitution (Amendment) Act, 1986 which reserved 30 per cent of seats in councils at village, block and district levels. However, the male dominated political parties have so far stalled all attempts at getting the measure adopted into law.

In order to address the problems of implementation of women's rights, Parliament enacted the National Commission of Women Act, 1990. While the Act empowers the Commission to investigate, examine and review all matters relating to the safeguards provided for women under the Constitution and other relevant laws, the Commission feels that its powers are not equal to its tasks, and that it should have power to prosecute/summarily decide on cases of violation of gender justice. Also, there should be commissions for women at state and district levels as well.[30] Given the traditional male domination in the Indian society, the Commission has a most unenviable task.[31]

Freedom from Bonded or Forced Labour

Despite the constitutional interdiction, poverty and illiteracy continue to be the breeding grounds for exploitation of humans keeping them often in perpetual bondage. The Bonded Labour (Abolition) Act adopted in 1976 has been an attempt to implement Article 23 of the Constitution. However, the indigent circumstances keep people in bondage and their exploiters reaping profits from their cheap or free labour. The Supreme Court's decision in the *Bandhua Mukti Morcha* case injected a fresh momentum in efforts to eradicate forced labour.[32] It led to a 1985 amendment to the Act of 1976 to broaden the application of the law. It also led to further Court judgements declaring that labour on payment of unreasonably low wages amounts to forced labour prohibited under the law[33].

Pledging one's labour or the labour of one's children for little or no wages in repayment of a debt has been the bane of India's problem of rural indebtedness. Clearly, no effective answer to it is in sight except long term economic development. In the meantime, there will continue to be reports of forced or bonded labour.[34]

Rights of the Child

India became a party in 1992 to the International Convention on the Rights of the Child, 1989, following popular demand. There is no doubt that all human rights (save perhaps the political rights) must apply to the child, as they are essential for the development of the human beings.

While the rights of the child call for a comprehensive treatment[35], we shall confine to its two aspects in the context of the Indian society which have lately highlighted the need for urgent affirmative action. They are the incidence of violence against children, including violence by the criminal justice system, and the practice of child labour.

1. Violence against Children

Trafficking in children is prohibited under the Suppression of Immoral Traffic in Women and Girls Act, 1956 (strengthened by an amendment of 1986). Yet the Act is not wellimplemented.

The National Crime Records Bureau's report on "Crime in India" has reported a rise in crime against children in recent years. There are also reports of growing violence against street children in many urban areas.

Parliament enacted the Juvenile Justice Act, 1986 principally for "the care, protection, treatment, development and rehabilitation of neglected or delinquent juveniles. The Act improves on and replaces the Children Act, 1960 and other various state enactments on the subject. It creates the following new offences: cruelty to juvenile, employment of juveniles for begging, giving a juvenile intoxicating liquor or narcotic drug or psychotropic substance, and exploitation of juvenile employees. It provides for juvenile homes for neglected children and special homes and observation homes for delinquent juveniles. However, for lack of resources the number of such juvenile homes so far established has been limited. Also, some of those few which exist are not properly run, even a brutal murder of an inmate by another took place in a Delhi Observation Home.

The National Crime Records Bureau's data indicate that juvenile delinquency continues to show a declining trend. In 1994 it recorded a 17.2 per cent drop over 1993. A total of 5,962 cases were registered against juveniles in 1994, and 38.4 per cent of juvenile in custody were awaiting trial. A disturbing trend, however, has been the introduction of juveniles to serious crimes.

2. Child Labour

Large scale exploitation of children for a free or cheap labour has been a bane of independent India.

There is no reliable data on the exact number of children being exploited at work. In India the estimates range from 20 million to 100 million. Children are engaged in a variety of industries or vocations—making of matches and fireworks, carpet making, glass bangle-making, brasswares, plastic and rope weaving, salt extraction, incense stick production, diamond cutting and polishing, biscuit-making, steel rolling and chips recycling, domestic work, prostitution, construction industry, etc. This painful reality exists despite the Employment of Children Act, 1938 (amended 1985), the Child Labour (Prohibition and Regulation) Act, 1986 (which prohibits employment of children in hazardous occupations and regulates it in others), and other laws like the Factories

Act, 1948. Indeed, child labour exists more in unorganized sector than in organized, which makes its detection difficult, although some of the NGOs seem to be doing extremely effective work in this regard.[36]

The Prime Minister of India in his Independence Day address to the nation on 15th August, 1994 pledged elimination of child labour from all hazardous industries by the year 2000. The government's hands are now being forced by a revolutionary Supreme Court judgement of 10th December, 1996[37]. The Government has been given a period of one year to implement this decision. One hopes that the Supreme Court's initiative will operate as the much–awaited shot in the arm. It would appear that there is also scope for private initiative.

The rights of the girl child have received a special emphasis the world over recently. India is notorious for its neglect of the girl child. The problem is multifaceted, it encompasses foeticide, female illiteracy, social discrimination, child marriage and so on. There is a need for changing social attitudes through a process of social mobilization. There is also a need for concerted administrative, legal and social action to eliminate inequality of the girl child, female foeticides and female infanticides.

Rights of the Scheduled Castes and Scheduled Tribes

As seen already, for historical and socially wrong reasons, the Indian society perpetrated a system of exploitation and dehumanization of some of the socially and economically most backward classes. These classes, as identified in a Schedule to the Constitution, are known as the Scheduled Castes and Scheduled Tribes. Majority of them are below the poverty line. The legal and political system provides for a range of measures of affirmative discrimination in their favour, such as reservation of seats in legislatures, reservation of jobs, reservation of seats in educational institutions, special scholarships, etc. Yet much of their lot is yet to cross the Rubicon of inequality, and still subjected to indignities, humiliation and harassment by some of the members of more advanced classes in society. The rationale behind the Scheduled Castes and the Scheduled Tribes (Prevention of Atrocities) Act, 1989 has been to stem the atrocities against them and to strengthen the constitutional interdiction.

Also, in 1990 the Constitution was amended to establish a seven-member highlevel National Commission for the Scheduled Castes and the Scheduled Tribes to investigate and monitor all matters relating to the safeguards provided for Scheduled Castes and Scheduled Tribes, to examine specific complaints of violation of rights and safeguards, and to make recommendations to the government for effective implementation of these rights and safeguards.[38]

Despite these legislative measures, atrocities against the Scheduled Castes and Scheduled Tribes are being reported whether as part of custodial violence, bonded labour, violence against women or other human rights violations. The Commission on Scheduled Castes and Scheduled Tribes has expressed concern over the rise in the number of such atrocities. Protection of land rights has become a crucial issue.

The answer to the economic backwardness of these classes appears to lie in spread of education, not necessarily in reservations or measures of affirmative discrimination. The reservations or affirmative discrimination has a knack of benefiting more advanced segments of these classes, and in the process, other less fortunate ones remain left in the lurch. Problems of tribals too cannot be solved within the framework of reservations alone.

The recent Indian politics have thrown up another issue—Protection of other Backward Classes (OBCs). It is true that the Indian society is highly segmented and that there are other backward classes other than the Scheduled Castes and the Scheduled Tribes, which need special attention. However, the approach to meet the problem of bringing social justice to these sections of people adopted by the government appears to be two-pronged—one, creation of a system of reservations, and two, determination of OBCs based on caste rather than economic criteria. Both tend to be populist measures aimed at "vote-grabbing through causing social divisions". There is much truth in the statement: "Today backwardness is neither a social stigma nor a handicap. It is the politician's chartered vehicle to power and pelf"[39].

Minority Rights

The term "minority" has not received adequate definition in the Indian context, although it is clear that the Indian context is different from the European. Article 30 of the Constitution speaks of "all minorities, whether based on religion or language". While it does not deny the existence of minorities identified on criteria other than religion or language, the current political vocabulary accepts only religious and linguistic minorities.[40]

The founding fathers of the Constitution were indeed more keen to ensure the protection of religious minorities as part of the transition of India into independence.[41] The partition of India into two countries resulted from the false apprehensions that the majority community in India would not ensure the rights of a minority community. Yet India has had a tradition of tolerance and social synthesis of diverse religions, a tradition lately marred by the rise of groups and political parties advocating religious fanaticism. The politics of religion have to do with this more than anything else. Such groups were responsible for the pre-planned destruction of the Babri Masjid in December, 1992 which fomented considerable ill-feelings leading to several riots aimed more at one community than the other. Happily, the religious fanaticism is confined to small groups and the Indian electorate has time and again endorsed secularism and forced many of these groups even to moderate on their policies.[42]

The National Commission for Minorities Act was enacted in 1992 aimed at protection of religious minorities such as Muslims, Sikhs, Buddhists, and Parsis. While the legislation and the Commission need strengthening, much more can be done by the Commission than what it has been able to achieve so far. Spread of secular education will go a long way in providing a firm foundation for development of minorities in India. There is enough law to protect various religions, or to prevent misuse of religious institutions for purposes other than religious.

The Rights of the Disabled

The rights of the disabled came to be formally recognized in India only recently, although they are readily read into Article 21 of the Constitution. According to one estimate, there are about 60 million disabled persons in the country belonging to various categories of disability.[43] These categories include, the blind, the deaf, the dumb, physically handicapped, the mentally retarded and the mentally ill. In the context of the Indian society, the disabled suffer from social stigma of various degrees, and this, more than other factors, stands in the way of their claims to equality and social justice.

Thanks to the pressure exerted by the NGOs, Parliament adopted the

Persons with Disabilities (Equal Opportunities, Protection of Rights and Full Participation) Act in 1995. However, the NGOs feel that there is considerable tardiness on the part of the government in the implementation of the law. The 1995 law awaits formulation of rules and regulations, and appointment of the Central and state coordination committees as well as the executive committee and the Chief Commissioner of the Disabled Persons. While there are reservations of seats in the universities, no such provision exists for the school level education yet. Therefore, the legislation largely remains merely on paper, despite its coming into force on 7th February, 1996.

Regardless of any legislation, the Indian society has done precious little for a "barrier-free environment" for the handicapped. The public buildings, public transport system, public places, all unfortunately remind one of this.

Similarly, the Mental Health Act, 1993, which replaced the archaic Lunancy Act, 1912, has not come into force in all states, despite the requirement that it be implemented by 1st April, 1993. A number of judgements of the Supreme Court have revealed the shabby management of some of the 37 mental hospitals in the country.

It is, however, gratifying to note that the social awareness about the need for protection of the rights of the disabled[44] and also the awareness on the part of the disabled themselves of their rights, has been gradually growing.[45]

Catalysts of Rights Implementation

The ultimate responsibility for implementation of human rights falls on the state and its legislative and executive machinery. The state has the unenviable, yet complex, duty to protect and promote individual and group rights as well as to umpire the conflicting claims to rights, against the overall requirements of the development of the society.

The Indian polity has, over time, and particularly in the post-Emergency era, evolved four principal catalysts of human rights implementation, which have developed new, often effective, strategies to catalyse rights implementation. They are the judiciary, the NHRC the NGOs and the communication/information media.

A. The Judiciary

One of the three organs of government, the judiciary has become a vanguard of human rights in India. It performs this function mainly by innovative interpretation and assumption of its jurisdiction, and, more importantly, by innovative interpretation and application of the human rights provisions of the Constitution. The Supreme Court of India has in fact declared that it has a special responsibility "to enlarge the range and meaning of the fundamental rights and to advance the human rights jurisprudence"[46].

We have already seen that the Supreme Court of India and the State High Courts have broad powers under the Constitution in respect of enforcement of fundamental rights and that they have liberally interpreted these powers. The major contributions of judiciary to the human rights jurisprudence have been twofold: one, the substantive expansion of the concept of human rights under Article 21 of the Constitution, and the other, the procedural innovation of public interest litigation. Since the role of judiciary in promotion of human rights has received more than adequate coverage in a number of legal journals and the media, no attempt is made here to elaborate the above points.

B. The National Human Rights Commission

India enacted the Protection of the Human Rights Act in 1993 more in response to considerable international pressure than the domestic pressure, chiefly to ward off the criticisms it encountered on human rights violations in the terrorism or insurgency affected areas. Be that as it may, this was a piece of beneficent legislation in that it established a new national human rights institution, namely, the National Human Rights Commission (NHRC).

NHRC's functions are extremely broad, pursuant to section 12 of the Act—to inquire, either *suo motu* or on a petition, into human rights violations, intervene in court proceedings, visit jails or other places of custody, review human rights safeguards and make recommendations, review factors, including terrorism, inhibiting the enjoyment of human rights, study international instruments on human rights, undertake and promote research, spread human rights literacy and awareness of safeguards among the masses, encourage NGOs, and institutions working in the field of human rights, and perform any other functions that NHRC may deem necessary for promotion of human rights.

NHRC has so far given priority to civil liberties—custodial deaths, state violence against civilians, torture and other cruel, inhuman or degrading treatment, custodial rape, disappearance from custody, atrocities against vulnerable sections of the society such as women, children and the disabled (including dowry deaths, bonded and child labour), and promotion of human rights education and training. Indeed in its very first year of existence, NHRC proposed to the government that its role be restricted, by defining "human rights" under section 2(1) (d) to mean "the rights relating to life, liberty, equality and dignity of the individual...." In 1996, the Commission has also included in its priorities the issues of prison reforms and undertrials.[47]

NHRC has pledged that it would strictly observe the principles of autonomy and transparency. Its reports and the *Human Rights Newsletter* seek to fulfil both, by reporting the activities of the Commission.

NHRC earned considerable prestige and reputation by its *suo motu* action in the case of the *Bijbehara* incident (in Jammu and Kashmir) in which there were press reports of death of about 60 civilians as a result of firing by security forces. Upon investigation, it recommended disciplinary proceedings against 14 members of the security force, prosecution after a magisterial inquiry, payment of compensation, and a review of circumstances and conditions of deployment of security forces. NHRC's Annual Reports and the *Newsletter* regularly cover the various investigations by the Commission. The Commission also took a lead in building up public opinion which forced the government to terminate the TADA.

A recent development is the use of NHRC by the Supreme Court as an investigative arm of the Court.[48] On a public interest relating to cremation by the Punjab Police of several dead bodies as 'unclaimed' during the past few years, the Supreme Court described the issue as a "flagrant violation of human rights on a mass scale", and asked the Commission to launch a thorough probe and "determine all the issues raised by the petitioner", including the question of payment of compensation.

So far the states of West Bengal, Himachal Pradesh, Madhya Pradesh and Assam have established State Human Rights Commissions. The State of Jammu and Kashmir has announced its decision to set up a Commission in that state. The Chairperson of at least one State Commission, viz., Himachal Pradesh, seems to wear more than one hat, other than the charge of the Commission, not necessarily conducive to the effectiveness of the Commission.

An overview of the year 1996 shows that the main strength of NHRC is its access to the media to build up a climate of human rights. It was in the news rather intermittently.

There are complaints from some NGOs that NHRC has not lived up to the principle of transparency, as it does not give NGOs full access to its activities. A criticism one could offer is that NHRC is increasingly becoming bureaucratized in its internal structure—with its personnel chiefly drawn from government. One may also fault NHRC's bureaucratic approach to evolving human rights syllabii for teaching purposes. The Commission should, but does not seem to, offer assistance in the effective functioning of other national institutions like the National Commission on Minorities, on Women, and on the Scheduled Castes and Scheduled Tribes. Indeed, part of the blame on this count should rest with the Chairpersons of these Commissions themselves who are *ex officio* members of NHRC. Further, the Government, on its part, has at times failed to respect the independence of the Commission, as is illustrated by the appointment of two of the Commissioners as state governors.

In sum, however, NHRC is doing landable work in the field of human rights implementation, its main contribution being its role in the spread of human rights awareness and education, particularly among the security forces of the state.

C. Non-Governmental Organizations

There are a number of NGOs, both national as well as international, performing useful work in the monitoring and implementation of human rights. Indeed, there are NGOs with political or other motives and those wedded to selfless service. At times, it is difficult to discern one category from the other. In the face of allegation of misappropriation by certain NGOs of funds received from the Union Welfare Ministry, the Ministry decided to constitute a 15–member committee to study the working of NGOs attached to the Ministry.

Among the foreign or 'international' NGOs, the Amnesty International (AI), the Human Rights Watch/Asia (HRWA) and the International Commission of Jurists (ICJ) are prominent in the field of civil and political rights. AI and ICJ were highly rated in India for their reports on human rights violations in India during the emergency (1975-77). However, the recent situations of terrorism in Jammu and Kashmir and in Punjab have led to highly exaggerated reports of rights violations by these bodies, and non-notice of government responses to the specific cases raised with it. Until recently, these foreign NGOs ignored the heinous human rights violations perpetrated by terrorists and militants. They also fail to focus on the role of Pakistan in terrorism in India.

The recent revelation of a bloomer in AI reports seem to have led to explanations from AI which in turn revealed that certain terrorist organisations, active in India earlier, had access to AI. Despite a record number of killings and other violations of human rights to its credit, a terrorist organisation was reported to be an "international member" of AI.[49] If the newspaper reports are to be believed, at least so far as India is concerned, AI's credibility can only be retrieved if it launches a full scale and open (transparency?) inquiry into the genuineness of its India-related members.

There are a number of Indian NGOs which perform useful work in various fields of human rights—social welfare, old age care, health and community medicine, assistance to depressed classes, women's welfare, child welfare, rehabilitation of bonded labour, rehabilitation of people uprooted by economic development projects, welfare of the disabled, consumer rights and so on. The chief problem with these NGOs is that there is a lack of coordination of their activities in terms of their fields of activity, territorial area, and target groups of their activities. Indeed, at times, they reveal a sense of rivalry.

At least among the Indian NGOs in the field of civil liberties, there is a complaint that the government is too readily responsive to foreign NGOs, but does not treat the Indian NGOs at par with them.

By and large, NGOs have arrived on the Indian human rights scene and have begun to play an important role not only in monitoring human rights violations, but equally in rehabilitation of victims and promotion of implementation of rights.

D. The Media

The information media is an important arm of any modern democratic polity through which the people enjoy their freedom of information. The freedom of information, the democratic right to know, is crucial in making all other human rights effective and providing an important safeguard for the enjoyment of all those rights. Traditionally, the vehicle of public information has been the press and now thanks to modern technology, the media. The 'Fourth Estate' plays a crucial role in a large democracy like India. India has about 1,500 newspapers.

The period of national emergency saw, for the first time, gagging of the free Press. Many depended on BBC for 'impartial' news about India. Small wonder, the freedom of the press or media became a watchword for human rights after emergency.

Under the Indian Constitution, the freedom of information is implicitly covered by Article 19 (freedom of speech and expression, freedom of trade) and Article 21 of the Constitution.

Disposing off a case of contempt of Court against the editors of two newspapers recently, the Supreme Court remarked:

> It is the duty of a true and responsible journalist to inform the people with accurate and impartial presentation of news and his views after dispassionate evaluation of the facts and information received by him to be published as a news item.

The editor of a newspaper or a journal, the Court said, has a greater responsibility to guard against untruthful news and its publication. "If the newspaper publishes what is improper, mischievously false or illegal and abuses its liberty, it must be punished by a court of law". While a free and healthy Press is indispensible to the functioning of a true democracy, the Court said, the freedom of the Press is subject to reasonable restraints.[50]

Since the 1970's the Indian media has played an extremely important role in sensitizing people with information about governance, development, science and technology, foreign relations and so on. However, lately it has also come in for criticism, as highlighted by the above Supreme Court decision. There is a decline in journalistic credibility, as noted by the Chairman of the Press Council of India as well as President K.R. Narayanan. Recently, due to the media preoccupation with the trivia, personality cult, one-sidedness, and instant news as against in-depth investigation,[51] senior journalists feel that the media shies away from important people's issues such as tribal issues, that it is losing social content and becoming a consumer product with a manager overshadowing the editor. The Press has also come in for rough treatment by terrorists/ insurgents, and some individual politicians. The media has a tendency to launch "trials by the media", even sentencing by the media, while a Court proceeding is underway.

Taking the totality of impact of the media for the past two decades, despite the above pitfalls, one must recognize that the contribution of the media, in revealing and highlighting human rights causes, has been most impressive. A colonial law relating to official secrecy, the Official Secrets Act, 1923, remains an impediment in the effective exercise of the freedom of information.

In fact all the above four catalysts of human rights have before them a broad field to be covered with some adequate coordination, something that is not attempted effectively so far.

REFERENCES

1. This is an abridged version of IWOCHR Occasional Paper No. 4, H.J. Laski, *A Grammar of Politics,* London, 4th edn., 1960 reprint, p. 91.
2. Jawaharlal Nehru, *The Discovery of India*, New Delhi, 1946, 12th Impression, 1992, p. 420.
3. In Nehru's words, "There is nothing in Indian history to compare with the bitter religious feuds and persecutions that prevailed in Europe. So, we did not have to go abroad for ideas of religious and cultural toleration; these were inherent in Indian life." See Nehru, n. 2, p. 382.
4. Brooding over the prospects of the British leaving India, Tagore said: "But what kind of India will they leave behind, what stark misery? When the stream of their centuries of administration runs dry at last, what a waste of mud and filth they will leave behind?" Quoted by Nehru, n. 2, p. 499.
5. See Nehru, *ibid.,* Chapter 7, pp. 289 ff.
6. Quoted by Nehru, n. 2, pp. 363-64.
7. Quoted by Nehru, n. 2, p. 363.
8. First broadcast over the national radio as Vice-President of the Interim Government of India, 7 September 1946. Reproduced in *The Hindu* (Madras), 9th September, 1946.
9. See Justice Sujata V. Manohar, "Judiciary and Human Rights", IJIL, vol. 36, 1996, no. 2, pp. 39-54, at pp. 40-46.
10. India acceded to the 1966 Human Rights Covenants on 27th March, 1979. For the text of India's instrument of accession, see IJIL, vol. 20, 1980, pp. 118-19.
11. See P. Chandrasekhara Rao, *The Indian Constitution and International Law,* Delhi, 1993, p. 145.
12. Article 1(1) of the Declaration on the Right to Development. UN General Assembly Resolution 41/128 of 4th December, 1986. For a comment on the Declaration, see Danilo Turk, "Right to Development as a Human Right", in K.P. Saksena (ed.), *Human Rights Perspectives and Challenges,* New Delhi, 1994, pp. 171-85.

13. Article 2(1), *ibid.*
14. The Planning Commission had put it at 37.27 per cent in 1993-94. The then Deputy Chairman of the Commission, Madhu Dandavate said: "If the number of people are more, we have to accept that fact. As for the resources, we have to manage with what we have...." *The Hindu* (Delhi), 27th December, 1996, p. 1.
15. See World Bank, *World Development Report, 1996*, cited in *The Hindu*, 16th September, 1996, at p. 16.
16. Editorial, "Criminal Neglect", *The Hindustan Times*, 27th November, 1996, p. 13. See also Srimoy Kar, "Natural Calamity, Human Greed", *The Indian Express* (New Delhi), 10th November, 1996, p. 9.
17. *The Hindu*, 3rd January, 1997, p. 1. *The Hindustan Times*, 3rd January, 1997, p. 10.
18. *The Hindustan Times*, 10th January, 1997, p. 17.
19. *The Hindu*, 9th January, 1997, p. 20.
20. The statement of the Minister for Human Resources Development, *ibid.*
21. "A Grey Revolution for Shelter", *The Hindu*, 8th October, 1996, p. 9.
22. "3-Year Campaign on 'right to food' planned", *The Hindu*, 23rd November, 1996, p. 3.
23. See "Peoples Charter for Food Security", *The Hindustan Times*, 14th October, 1996, p. 10.
24. *The Hindustan Times*, 28th November, 1996, p. 17.
25. See Rahul Bedi, "Uncivil Conflicts", *The Indian Express*, 28th December, 1996, p. 9.
26. The Supreme Court also largely 'humanised' TADA in its application. See *Kartar Singh vs. State of Punjab, Judgements Today* (Delhi), 1994 (2), no. 9, p. 423, *Hitendra Vishnu Thakur and others vs. State of Maharashtra, Judgements Today*, (1994) (4), no. 4, p. 255; *Sanjay Dutt vs. The State, Judgements Today* (1994) (5), no. 17, p. 540.
27. See for instance, *Amnesty International Report 1995*, pp. 156 ff. The criticism has been noted by the National Human Rights Commission - see NHRC *Annual Report 1994-95.*
28. K.D. Gaur, "Poor Victims of Uses and Abuses of Criminal Law and Process in India", *Journal of the Indian Law Institute (JILI)* (New Delhi), vol. 35, (Part II) (1993), pp. 183-232, 'Conclusion' at p. 230. See some of the case law which he cites to support his conclusions.
29. Indeed, the problem of trafficking in women is endemic in the whole of South Asia. According to an estimate, during the last ten years over 200,000 women and children were brought to India just for onward "dispatch" to other countries. *The Hindustan Times,* 2nd January, 1997, p. 8.
30. "Commission sought for Women's Rights", *The Hindu*, 19th February, 1996, p. 20.
31. For the first time when the Commission organised Lok Adalats (People's Courts) for quick disposal of a number of complaints at Jabalpur, Madhya Pradesh, it had

to bear the brunt of the male ire. See Usha Rai, "New Chairperson Attacked", *The Hindustan Times*, 3rd October, 1996, p. 6.

32. *Bandhua Mukti Morcha vs. Union of India, All India Reports (AIR), 1984, Supreme Court*, p. 802.
33. See, e.g. *People's Union of Democratic Rights vs. Union of India, AIR, 1985, SC*, p. 1473. This case related to contract labour for certain government works.
34. For some of the recent reports, see G. Prabhakaran, "Bonded Labour still in many Kerala areas", *The Hindu*, 30th October, 1996, p. 9; "Government crackdown on illegal kilns saves 120 labourers", *The Indian Express*, 21st December, 1996, p. 2.
35. See, e.g. B.S. Padmanabhan, "Wither Child Rights", *The Hindustan Times*, 8th December, 1994, p. 13.
36. According to a recent report, 58 bonded labourers (29 men, 9 women and 20 children, who were under forced labour in the stone quarries of Pichopa, Dadri Division, Bhiwani District of Haryana and paid only some ration (and no wages), were released by the local Magistrate at the timely initiative of the Bandhua Mukti Morcha (Movement for the Liberation of the Bonded Labour) (BMM)—see "58 bonded labourers rescued", *The Hindustan Times*, 2nd October, 1996, p. 5.
37. The judgement in *M.C. Mehta vs. Union of India* reported and commented upon *inter-alia*. In *The Times of India* (New Delhi), 11th December, 1996, p. 1, *ibid.*, 12th December, 1996, p. 10 ("Price of Innocence"), Editorial, "Another Declaration", *The Indian Express*, 12th December, 1996, p. 8.
38. The Constitution (Sixty-fifth Amendment) Act, 1990, amended Article 338 of the Constitution.
39. See Editorial, "Backward Indeed", *The Hindustan Times*, 14th November, 1996, p. 13.
40. Imtiaz Ahmad, an eminent Indian political sociologist, rightly argues that the term "minority" has been narrowly defined in India. "Further, inequities exist at every level of segmentation of social community .... Every social community in India is a minority at some level of social segmentation or another. It is problematic in the Indian context to speak of some social communities as minorities and contrast them with the majority....Everyone in Indian society is in one sense or the other is disadvantaged ...." He therefore recommends contextual indices of deprivation to determine a deprived minority. "Defining Minorities in India", *The Hindustan Times,* 17th October, 1996, p. 13. See also his "Limits to Group Claims", *The Hindu*, 27th November, 1996, p. 10. But see Tufail Ahmed, "Need to redefine minority", *The Hindustan Times*, 9th September, 1996, p. 12.
41. See, e.g., Nehru, n. 2, pp. 382-83.
42. According to Asghar Ali Engineer, "In all riots which took place in 1996, one does not see any political party provoking them. These riots were the result of local incidents, not of planned provocation. Organising riots does not seem to be a paying proposition, at least for the present". See his "Communalism and Communal Violence", *The Hindu*, 10th January, 1997, p. 10.

43. "Act on disabled 'only on paper'", *The Hindustan Times*, 30th October, 1996, p. 5.
44. A number of seminars/workshops are being reported - see *The Hindu*, 19th October, 1996, p. 2 (visually handicapped); *The Hindu*, 28th December, 1996, p. 20 (mentally retarded children: their number is around 500,000 in India); Satyen Mohapatra, "Mentally Retarded: What they need is a Mother's Touch", *The Hindustan Times*, 26th November, 1994.
45. As Ms Anuradha Mohit of the National Association for the Blind is reported to have said recently: "We are a marginalised section of society, yet we are more aware about our rights now than ever before". See "Disabled protest against Govt. apathy", *The Hindustan Times*, 3rd December, 1996, p. 3.
46. Rao, n. 11, p. 148. He cites in support *Ajay Hasia vs. Khalid Mujib, AIR, 1981, SC*, p. 487 at p. 493; *M.C. Mehta vs. Unikon of India, AIR, 1987, SC*, p. 1086, at pp. 1089, 1097. Rao, however, raises but keeps open the questions whether it is the legitimate function of the Court to transcend the text of the Constitution, and whether this in fact advances the cause of human rights.
47. See an interview of the new Chairman of NHRC, Justice M.N. Venkatachaliah, "For justiciable human rights", *The Hindu*, 30th December, 1996, p. IV, See also "Rights of child, civil liberty top NHRC agenda", *The Hindu*, 30th December, 1996, p. 2.
48. The Committee for Information and Initiative on Punjab vs. State of Punjab, *The Hindu*, 13th December, 1996, p. 20.
49. Vijay Dutt, "Have terrorists taken over Amnesty?", *The Hindustan Times*, 7th December, 1994, pp. 1 and 15.
50. See, "Don't misuse Press Freedom", *The Hindustan Times*, 20th September, 1990, p. 12. The case about a false report condemnatory of the judiciary, involved the editors of *The Tribune and the Punjab Kesari*, two newspapers.
51. "Media full of trivia, says Press Council meet", *The Indian Express*, 17th November, 1996, p. 7.

18

Human Rights and Globalisation

K.P. Saksena

While human rights have been universalised and internationalised and some international mechanism to monitor their observance have been instituted, the State remains the protector and guarantor of these rights. That is so, not only because there could be no global authority, free from power politics, to guarantee just implementation of rights to all irrespective of one's race, colour, religion, nationality, etc., but, more importantly, human rights are intrinsically bound up with socio-economic and cultural conditions which differ from country to country. As such human rights can be realised and enjoyed in the country where individual lives, and enforced under the laws and institutions of respective countries. Realisation and protection of human rights, therefore, depends on the extent to which the government of the country concerned is democratic and responsive to the needs and aspirations of the people. They depend on popular participation in all sphere of State's activity. Again, human rights belong to the people and it is the vigilance and capacity to resist the authority when abused by the people themselves which would ensure observance and protection of human rights.

There is another dimension to the situation and a critical one, too. While people and the concerned national governments bear the overall responsibility, it is also a reality that no country today, particularly, the developing ones like India, are "masters" of their domestic affairs. What happens in the outside world and international economic system impinges on human conditions and therefore human rights within the domestic jurisdiction of a State.

The other reality is that external factors operating at global level are managed by a coterie of industrialised powers of the North—the Group of Seven now Eight.[1] Their control is so deeply entrenched, both historically and institutionally, as to be beyond the influence of governments and people of developing countries constituting the South or the Third World.

In brief, in the contemporary world, global factors operate to the advantage of the industrially advanced nations at the cost of developing countries. There is more to the situation.

As the world stands on the threshold of the 21st century, it is engulfed by a phenomenon that has come to be called "globalisation"—the world rapidly being turned into an integrated whole via international trade, internationalisation of production and financial markets and the internationalisation of consumer-culture, promoted by an increasingly networked global telecommunication systems.

How could this world, characterised by an enormously disproportionate distribution of wealth and technological advancement, be integrated into one global whole? What impact globalisation is going to have on more than 180 "sovereign" nation- states when their own socio-economic conditions are so vastly different and when they are not on a "level-playing field"? A more important question is: how the forces of globalisation, moving as they are, at an escalated pace, going to affect the day-to-day lives, i.e. human rights, of the people, particularly that of India, having different needs and aspirations.

As a prefatory to the discussion on these and related questions, let us look at the factors that led to the current pace of change and intensity of challenges which the globalisation presents.

Genesis

The genesis of various facets of globalisation that we are witnessing today could be traced to the Colonialist-Imperialist era which had its beginning in the 17th century when Europeans successfully attempted to reach various parts of the globe, through trade and flag—armed intervention followed by occupation. By the 19th century, Europeans had occupied 76 per cent of the earth surface; almost all countries in South America, Africa and Asia came under colonial rule of one or more European powers. And the world became Euro-Centric.

The Colonialist-Imperialist era also coincided with industrial revolution in Europe and North America; colonies provided the raw material and also markets for goods manufactured in respective metropolitan countries. Expanding industries and possibilities of earning further profits at a still higher rate were at hand in the form of land and resources and cheap labour. To ensure full utilisation of these new possibilities, the European powers extended their grip on the whole world. Territories not yet under their occupation were forcibly seized, sometime by outright war and military action, sometime in the disguised form of "treaties" imposed on local rulers by a combination of sheer deceit.

The overall objectives were to keep the Colonial people divided and in political subjugation, to destroy their local industry and potential for economic development and to make possible the maximum exploitation of the people and the country's resources.

It is pertinent to note that until mid-18th century, West Asia, India, China and other East Asian countries were major international trade-centres. A British trade expert, Daniel Defoe, for instance, expressing the common perception, warned in 1728 that England attempted of building up its textile mills faced uphill struggle in competing "with China, India and other Eastern countries." The problem was, he noted, that "they have the most extended manufacture and the greatest variety in the world; and their manufacture push themselves upon the world by the mere stress of their refineness and cheapness." What followed was the British rule over India was gradually extended after the battle of Plassey (1756) and Britain imposed policies which crippled India's textile industry. An eminent scholar notes "Britain itself would have been deindustrialised by the cheapness of Indian caliocoes protectionist policies had not been adopted".[2] A century after Daniel Defoe, historian Horace Wilson observed that without protection, the mills of Paisley and Manchester would have been stopped in their outset, and could scarcely have been again set in motion, even by the power of steam. They were created by sacrifice of the Indian manufacturers. It was because of British rule that Indian industries including steel, shipbuilding, and other manufactures could not make any progress.[3]

Thus, the North comprising advanced industrialised countries now advocating market economy and free trade built up their industrial advancement and wealth at the cost of what is known today as the Third World by resorting to protectionism.

It is not necessary here to go into the historical details but to emphasise the following:

(a) The two world wars that the Europeans fought ended in the emergence of USA, as dominant global power, both in economic and military terms; in 1949 UN economic survey indicated that US share of the entire world income amounted to 49.9 per cent; to ensure growing economic ascendancy and to promote reconstruction and prosperity of its European allies it established such institutions as IMF, IBRD and GATT;

(b) Colonial-imperialist era gave birth to trading companies and business corporates having their base in today's industrially advanced North; and

(c) The second world war also led to the demise, at least politically, to the colonial-imperialist era. From the ruins of the old colonial empires emerged, starting from India, nearly 100 countries to "sovereign Statehood". However, what was of added significance was the fact that these new nations, politically independent and legally sovereign constituting in terms of numbers and size of population, a vast majority emerged in a world which continues to be dominated by the European[4] powers possessing a history of political culture and involvement at international level, since Colonial-Imperialist era. In other words, the new states find themselves (as the title of a book succinctly states) *The Weak in the World of the Strong.*[5]

Transnational Corporations (TNCs)

The colonial system matured, by the end of the 19th century, as capitalism or monopoly capitalism; the advance of industrial techniques in the 19th century, the growth of large scale industries and concentrations of economic power in the hands of a relatively small number of major companies and banks provided the background for the emergence of large business corporates what are widely referred to as multinational corporations (MNCs), and what in the UN terminology are aptly called transnational corporations (TNCs). During the cold war period, the domain of their activity was largely confined to the West and those of the developing countries which were having political and military ties with the West. But the ending of the Cold War have led to their unbridled sway over world economy, intruding on the economy of almost all countries, including Russia (erstwhile Soviet Union), Eastern Europe, non-aligned countries and also Communist China and Vietnam.

TNCs have huge funds and technical knowhow which the Third World countries are very much in need for their economic development. The reach and magnitude of their impact on world economic development can be gauged by recalling that the total assets of some of the largest TNCs exceed the GDP of many medium-sized countries. For example, US-based General Motor's revenue for the year 1997 amounted to $168.3 billion, which exceeded the combined GDP of Indonesia and Pakistan. (Indonesia: $15 billion; Pakistan: $45 billion). Again, the combined revenue of 2 US-based business corporates—General Motors and Ford Motors ($ 147 billion) is nearly equal to India's GDP ($324 billion).[6] All the major TNCs are based in industrialised countries of the US, Europe and Japan. Their role in world economy has been the most contributory factor to globalisation.

TNCs can play and are playing significant role in economic development of the developing countries. But their motivating force is profit; they exploit cheap labour and resources of the country where they operate. Thus, in many cases role of TNCs runs counter to, and in conflict with, the mandate of the State to protect and safeguard the human rights of its people. This conflict arises out of divergence between the profit objectives of the TNCs and the socio-economic goals pursued by national governments. Since these corporations are operating like octopus in several jurisdictions, the nation-states are helpless in taking measures to eliminate the conflict.

There is no doubt that TNCs can act both as engines of development and the destroyers of it. The TNCs could help bring in foreign direct investments (FDI), instituting training facilities to the local employees, setting up expansion of export trade, introducing modern management techniques for increasing productivity and providing for adequate safeguards for the community against hazards from the nature of manufacturing operations.

Unfortunately, in all the surveys made by the UN Centre for Transnational Corporations, none of the positive traits could be perceived. On the contrary, whatever gloss the apologists of TNCs may give, the glaring fact is that these TNCs in their operations have been found to adversely affect the economic and social rights of the people as also the economic and social policies of the state. Such a damage results by: (i) increasing the cost of processing of manufactures or semi-manufactures; (ii) withholding needed capital investment or technological improvement; (iii) depriving the country concerned of its export earnings by transfer pricing and through exports in a condition fetching a lower market value; (iv) by exploiting local labour by offering only survival wages and not taking the steps for elimination of unhealthy working conditions; (v) polluting their environment and disturbing the ecological balance; (vi) exposing the local population to hazards arising from leakage of lethal gases and chemical manufacture.

The 1984 accident at Union Carbide owned Pesticide Plant in Bhopal (MP) was a clear example and one of the most tragic events of the 1980s. The facts of the case are so well-known all over the world that it is unnecessary to set tremor again.

Another aspect requiring consideration from the human rights angle is the exploitation of the labourforce. The ILO report indicates that even while labour is organised through trade unions but they are no match to TNCs gigantic bargaining power. TNCs have integrated worldwide economic system which allows them to easily exploit the local labour by not giving equal pay for equal work, allowing labour to live in unhealthy and filthy conditions, taking advantage of their total helplessness particularly when they are unorganised.

Indeed, labour is increasingly losing its bargaining position because it remains immobile and stays at place or country it belongs to. On the other hand, TNCs are free to move with their capital, machinery and equipments from one country to the other in search of cheaper labour and resources/raw material.

The situation has further aggravated by the refusal of TNCs to provide any guarantee of environment and the possibility and the threat of temporary or permanent transfer of their operations to other countries. Structural adjustment policies have reduced the capacity of the state to address inequality and denial of labour rights.[7]

It is ingriguing that instead of laying down a code of conduct for TNCs, the industrialised countries, as represented in OECD, are preparing drafts for Multilateral Agreement on Investment (MAI). In February '97, a 147-page negotiating text was leaked and is now available on Public

Citizen's Tradewatch Web page of the Internet. The draft bans any restriction on "repatriation of profits" and the movement of capital. It also bans "performance requirement" and prohibits governments (of developing countries) from treating foreign investors differently from domestic investors and authorises TNCs to sue national governments for failure to meet the MAI's terms.[8]

The industrialised countries of the North where TNCs have their base, while promoting free play market forces in their own country, have also laid down rules and regulations and parameters within which TNCs and private entrepreneurs could operate, but there are no such rules and regulations on international level. The United Nations attempted to do its part of monitoring their activities and preventing their misuse of power. For several years United Nations also tried to work out a "code of conduct" for TNCs but after more than two decades of negotiations and drafting of the code, the attempt was abandoned in the late 1980s. In January 1992 the United Nations department concerned with TNCs was abolished under US pressure.

Debt Crisis

Another contributory factor has been the debt crisis. Debt crisis broke into public awareness in the late 1970s, although it was brewing up since the early 1950s, as a result of policies of US and its allies to promote export of their capital goods and cold war strategies.[9]

The developing countries after gaining independence soon discovered that the prices of primary commodities and semimanufactures they exported were going down and capital goods and equipments they imported for their economic development from industrialised countries were going up. They also learnt that their currency had no value beyond their national frontiers; whatever they needed to import, have to be paid in "hard currency", variably in US dollars which they could earn only through their export. It was inevitable that any country that, over the long term runs a trade-deficit would run out of both dollars and the ability to borrow them. Thus, the options for the Third World countries were either to slow down their plans for economic development and stop running into trade deficit or borrowing. The first option was bound to adversely affect the interests of industrially advanced and developed countries of Europe, North America and Japan. These countries knew that they could maintain their continuing prosperity and economic growth only if they have expanding markets in developing countries to sell manufactured goods and equipments and continuing sources of cheap food and raw materials.[10] Hence, they came out with plans for development grants, loans, "development aid" which meant: "buy now pay later". The IMF and World Bank became ready instrument of strategies of US and its allies. Even the United Nations apparatus was used, for the same purpose, by instituting such programmes as of UN Technical Assistance (TA) and the Expanded Programme of Technical Assistance (EPTA).[11]

It should be noted that between 1956 and 1972 (before the oil price hike) all major Third World countries like Argentina, Brazil, Chile, Ghana, India, Indonesia, Pakistan, Peru and Turkey were knocking the doors of the "Paris Club"[12] seeking rescheduling of payments for debt services and debt owed to government creditors.

By 1970s, the debt burden of the developing countries had reached a crisis proportion. The oil price hike by Organisation of Petroleum Exporting Countries (OPEC) further aggravated the crisis. By that time, the Third World as a whole was approaching the 'break-even' point at which debt service exceeded new capital inflows. It was open secret that many debted countries would default and seek moratorium. It is deeply ironic that at this moment commercial banks with headquarters in North America and Europe chose to abandone their long-held skepticism on the safety of international lending and began to throw hundreds of million of dollars at the Third World countries, which were already in heavy debt.

One explanation could be that OPEC price-hike in early 1970s generated huge petro-dollars which were invested back in industrialised countries of the Europe and North America in real estate or placed in deposits with commercial banks. Thus, commercial banks were loaded with money and were faced with the problem of finding profitable outlets for their money. They found ready customers in the Third World countries particularly the non-oil producing countries who had suffered much because of oil price hike. They needed money which was readily offered to them by the commercial banks. Once they failed to pay the interest and instalments, they were obliged to borrow higher amount to avoid default, to pay the arrears and debt servicing; thus got caught in "debt-trap". It is intriguing that not only non-oil producing countries but oil exporting countries such as Indonesia, Venezuela, Mexico and Algeria also got snared.[13]

A special study prepared by the World Bank in 1993 showed that from 1980 to 1992 developing countries have paid more than $400 billion as interest and part payment of debt. Thus, there has been a reverse flow of capital from the South to the North. Despite this repayment of debt, the total debt burden is still at a mind-boggling figure of $1.4 trillion.

As a consequential to continuing debt crisis (i) developing countries constituting the South not only lost the momentum of their steadily growing "collective self-reliance" but increased their dependence on the industrialised North; (ii) already in a state of vulnerability they could not resist the pressure of opening their economy to global market forces; (iii) reverse capital flow from the South to the North added to expansion, in quantum and mobility, of what is referred to as "global money".

Global Money

A phenomenon characteristic of globalisation is global money or capital which is owned, controlled and managed (invested or diinvested) not by any government or intergovernmental agency but by non-governmental institutions or non-territorial centres of power and speculators who indulge in the sale and purchase of domestic currencies, resulting in sharp decline or rise of exchange rates of a national currency specifically of the developing countries. Let us take the case of recent East Asian currency turmoil (1997); until early 1997, East Asian countries—South Korea, Taiwan, Hongkong, the Philippines, Thailand, Indonesia, Malaysia and Singapore were referred to as East Asian economic giants or 'new tigers' who had made good because of their market economy and free flow of capital. But then suddenly between July-October 1997, currencies of the region fell against the dollar by 21 per cent to 34 per cent to 150 per cent. Thus gears of hard economic games were wiped out by a few weeks run on a country's currency. How did this happen?

Global currency market is dominated by speculators and financial investment institutions. Not so many years ago there were only 7 stock markets around the world in which one could invest. Now there are more than 90 stock markets, including the Bombay Stock Exchange. However, New York, London, Frankfurt and Tokyo remain the main financial markets. They are so instantaneously linked to one another that there is a virtual single "global" financial market. Investors can now buy and sell securities wherever and whenever they wish, 24 hours a day. The motivating force is profit and these investors easily panic or get too excited or act as such; they withdraw their investments by selling the stocks. Worse still, there is neither any international law nor any global authority to enforce rules for currency-trading.

Thus, years of hard won economic gains can be wiped out by a few weeks' run on a country's currency, as it happened in case of Mexico (1994) and of East Asian countries (July-October 1997). Who is responsible for this slippery state of affairs, and who are the beneficiaries?

The US sponsored Bretton Woods system had laid down, in 1946, a fixed exchange rate; each currency was related to the dollar and dollar value was fixed as 35 dollars equivalent to one ounce of gold. The situation was compromised by introducing SDRs in 1969 and was completely given up in 1973 when President Nixon floated the US dollar to give full autonomy to the nation-state for monitoring fiscal affairs. At the same time, the United States also expanded emission (additional printing) of dollar currency and most of the industrialised countries, encouraged by the new "floating exchange rate system", simultaneously pumped up their money supply.

Over the period, floating exchange rates have been causing extreme currency instability as an enormous mass of "world money" is being created by currency trading.

As Peter Drucker, the eminent economist, in his recent article[14] observes: this money is being created by currency-trading as "virtual money" rather than real money. "It fits none of the traditional definitions of money, whether standard of measure, storage of value or medium of exchange. It is totally anonymous but its power is real." The volume of this money is so gigantic, the author goes on to say, that its movement in an out of a country have greater impact than the flows of financing, trade or investment. This money has total mobility because it serves no economic function. And because it serves no economic function and finances nothing, this money also does not follow the economic logic or rationality. It is volatile and get easily panicked by rumour or unexpected event.

Currency speculators, as noted earlier, are creating havoc in the economies of developing countries as was demonstrated recently in the so-called New Industrial Giants (NIG) of East Asia.

Reagan-Thatcher: Market Economy

The Reagan-Bush administration in the US (1980-92) and that of Margaret Hilda Thatcher in UK (1979-91) aggressively promoted market economy. The two powers, in conjunction with their European allies, first attempted to weaken the economic and social sector of the UN system arguing that UN economic and social programmes promote "statism".[15] Further, in various international fora they introduced resolutions recommending private enterprises and market economy as the panacea of all socio-economic problems of developing countries. Their efforts paid dividend as a result of ending of the cold war and the fast changing international scenario. In 1990, they did succeed in getting adopted (by the UN General Assembly) a set of resolutions[16] which endorsed private entrepreneurship and market economy. This was for the first time when the world organisation made recommendation in support of a particular economic system. It is intriguing to note that these resolutions were supported by all countries, including Soviet Union (now Russian Federation) and East Europeans, with one exception that of Cuba which voted against. Thus, market economy became the major thrust of not only industrialised nations but also of UN Development Programmes and international agencies.

What is meant by private entrepreneurship or free market economy? That means that government should not own or control means of production and distribution; it means that economic activities should be left for private entrepreneurs or businessmen. It is argued that under private entrepreneurship all economic activities would lead to better and more production of goods and services, both in terms of quality and quantity. Again, incentive of profit and competition among private entrepreneurs or business corporates, it is argued, would be beneficial for the economy of the country and add to the overall prosperity of the people. Such arguments also again reemphasise that TNCs with massive capital and technical knowhow and based in the industrialised countries of the North, should be allowed, without any restriction, to operate in the Third World countries or the South.

What began as a post-war corporate (TNCs) expansion has now, in the post-cold war era, become a global movement of capital, technology, and culture at a much faster pace than ever before. Free movement of goods and capital is being proposed to the Third World countries as a panacea of their economic and social problem. TNCs, international agencies like IMF and World Bank and their media spokespeople have been saying that free markets promote economic "growth" and "progress" and "globalisation".

In this prescription really that good or does it merely provides a facade to the real objectives? To find an answer, it is not necessary to recall here in some detail what all colonial-imperialist countries used to argue that they are the engines of "progress" and "modernisation". Similarly it is not necessary to recall US involvement in other countries affairs since the 19th century to promote its economic interests.

President George Bush during the years 1989-91, frequently talked about the beginning of the New World Order (NWO) under the unchallenged leadership of the United States of America and predicted that the "21st century will be another American century".[17]

National Security Adviser, Anthony Lake, while announcing the "Clinton Doctrine", in September '93, noted: "throughout the cold war, we contained a global threat to market democracies; now we should seek to enlarge their reach. The new world opening before us he said, presents immense opportunities to move forward to consolidate the victory of democracy and open markets".[18]

A year earlier, Thomas Friedman, the chief diplomatic correspondent of the *New York Times* had written that "America's victory in the cold war was a victory for a set of political and economic principles: democracy and free market", and added that "free market is the wave of the future—a future for which America is both the gatekeeper and the model."[19]

Indeed, globalisation, in its present form, is an off-shoot of American imperium.

Rhetoric and Reality

What we have discussed above, bears out that process of globalisation, we are witnessing today, is the produce of concatenation of parallel, but interlinked set of developments the expanding role of TNCs, the debt crisis, the emergence of global money, ending of the cold war, disintegration of the Soviet Union, accompanied by an aggressive push to market economy. To cap it all came, beginning the last decade of this century, revolutionary innovations in informations and communication technology.

There is enough historical and empirical evidence, as analysed in the preceding pages, to suggest that globalisation has its genesis in the institutions of exploitation and domination that have had their beginning in the colonial-imperialist era.

One is reminded here of Harold J. Laski's observation, made wayback in 1947, when the UN Commission on Human Rights was preparing draft of the Universal Declaration of Human Rights. Laski has forcefully argued that unless institutions so well entrenched both at national and global level, were removed, the Declaration would only raise "false hopes" and its contents on human rights "have not prospect of being fulfilled".[20]

What is happening today in the name of globalisation is that the lopsided world economic system which operates to the advantage of the industrialised countries at the cost of developing countries is being imposed on the latter at a time when they are burdened with heavy debts and adverse balance of payment; they are in a most vulnerable state and have no capacity to resist the "imposition".

Globalisation demand of developing countries, to remove all trade barriers allow free flows of goods and capital, which would usher in economic growth and development, so the rhetoric goes. However, the industrialised countries of Europe and North America themselves are resorting to protectionist measures and formation of regional trade blocs.[21] Thus, while consumers goods produced in industrialised countries could have unrestricted entry in developing countries but goods produced, for instance, in India cannot have the same unrestricted access in North America or Europe.

Writing in *International Herald Tribune* (September 25, 1997, editorial page) a well-known economist, William Pfaff has warned that:

> Trade between the West and countries in the non-Western world may destroy subsistence agriculture, co-opting Third World farmers into production for the international marketplace, while their societies are made dependent on imported foods....Local artisanal production can be wrecked by international competition, causing more unemployment than the new employment produced by international investment. The social and cultural consequences of this may be very serious.

He goes on to add that free trade is of mutual benefit when the countries trading goods are roughly at the same level of industrial development and have sophisticated economic structures and legal system as in case of trade between the United States and Europe and Japan. But

> when barriers between advanced and backward economies are destroyed, a new form of human exploitation can follow, resembling that of colonialism in the 19th and early 20th centuries, complete with new forms of indentured labour.

Viewed in the context of human rights it should be noted that free market economy sets the goal of more production at less cost and more profits; glossed over in this approach is the "human face" and day-to-day problems faced by the common people. Such an approach not only ignores human rights aspect but further widens the gap between the rich and the poor and aggravates what Peter Drucker calls "social crisis".

The UNDP's *Human Development Report 1997* provides arresting evidence of how globalisation and the systematic violation of human rights go hand in hand. Its statistics provide gloomy confirmation of the fact that many countries are worse off today than they were one, ten or thirty years ago and that the global distribution of income is the worst it has been for at least three decades. The report indicates that in 1997 thirty developing countries have registered a decline in their 'human development index', a construct based on life expectancy, literacy and income—more than in any other year since the UNDP began publishing its annual reports in 1990. And the share of the world's poorest 20 per cent in global income is only 1.1 per cent, down from 2.3 per cent in 1960. On average, the world's richest 20 per cent earned 78 times more than the poorest 20 per cent. In 1960, they earned only 30 times as much.

Of course, not everybody in the global economy is suffering. Last year, the UNDP said the assets of the world's 358 billionaires exceed the combined annual incomes of countries with 45 per cent of the world's population. This year, we learn that the sales of the world's top six firms, at $716 billion, exceed the combined GDP of South Asia and Sub-Saharan Africa.

While business corporates have further enriched themselves the common people in industrialised countries have suffered. To take an instance, a woman Addie Brown in South Corolina, USA was well satisfied with her job at $65 a day with Kingstree's biggest employer, Baxter Healthcare. Then Baxter closed South Corolina plant, laid off hundreds of workers and moved production to far off Malaysia where young women turn out the same Baxter latex gloves for barely $8 a day.[22]

As noted by American historian, Paul Kennedy, "globalisation attempt to merge socio-economic conditions of industrially advanced countries with developing countries when the US and the European Union are currently earning about $85 a they are not on a level-playing-field, could face gales ahead. He draws attention to the fact that the Third World workers in day. How on earth, he argues, one can reconcile their legitimate interest with nearly 1.2 billion Third World workers who earn less than $3 a day. Kennedy foresees "a colossal depressive force upon real wages in the richer countries" and "mounting public discontent", in both richer and poor countries.[23]

According to OECD Report 1997, the number of unemployed workers in the industrialised nations has trippled to 35 million since 1970s. Popular protests against economic policies and further stringent measures (to reduce national deficit budget) in many European countries have been made. In France and other European countries people resorted to streets and crippling strikes.

In most of the industrialised countries, business corporates have increasingly acquired domineering influence over the top echelon of the government and its policies. Thus, a fear expressed by President Eisenhower in his farewell address (1961) regarding the role of military-industrial complex has not only come true, but a new nexus has been added what economist Jagdish Bhagwati refers as treasury wall street complex.[24]

In a recent pole conducted by *Mother Janes (1997)*, a US investigative magazine, "81 per cent strongly or partially agreed with the statement that "our (American) system of government is democratic in name only. Special interests run things." The magazine further reported that some 400 multi-millionaires head various business corporates, contribute massive funds (by utilising many loopholes in the funding restrictions) to politicians and get what they want—reduction of state tax, corporate tax and capital-gain tax, government sponsorship for investment and market in developing countries, erosion of the minimum wage, subsidies in the agriculture and armament industries and reducing government's ability to regulate corporate behaviour.

Jean Fancois Dulat, a sociologist claims that many of the decisions that are handed down by Brussels are perceived by the people as being "pro-big business". They encourage large financial conglomerates at the expense of the small investor or entrepreneur. But above all they penalise the salaried individual.[25]

Globalisation is a reality; one cannot escape its forces. The real choice of governments is not how to fight globalisation but how to manage it. In a way, globalisation posits a challenge to the concept of nation-state. At the same time, it is the nation-states—the practice they adopt, the arrangements they enter into and the safety net that they provide—that will determine whether we exploit or be exploited by globalisation which represents the most potential force of this era.

The developments could be fully utilised by creating better conditions for the realisation of human rights. Market economy and global money could be utilised for more production at minimum cost and economic growth could alleviate poverty. Globalisation could be utilised, especially the global media, and information technology, to remove illiteracy, superstitions, etc. and to generate wider awareness of human rights issues. It could be utilised by drawing attention of the governments and the people to violation of human rights happening anywhere in the world. This could help promote public opinion and moral political pressure on the governments concerned.

All this could happen if certain prerequisite steps are taken. For instance, international institutions such as IMF, World Bank, government creditors and commercial banks should either accept moratorium on debt or should write them off. Indeed, debtor countries have already paid more money by way of debt servicing, interests and annual part payment of the principal to the creditors, such a move alone would help bring developing countries to a level-playing field in competitive global economy.

Globalisation could lead to mutual benefit provided the powers-that-be are ready to have an equitable management of global economy, an international code of conduct for TNCs and an equitably managed global institution to regulate global money—the rapid flows of investment that moves in and out of developing countries as investor's sentiments change.

As long as seven industrialised countries (nominally eight, with the inclusion of Russia, which itself is now a "basket case") decide exclusively all matters relating to global trade and commerce, fiscal and monetary transactions—which are also of vital concern to the rest of the world representing 3/4th of the world population, globalisation would amount to a hegemony and domination of a few over the rest of the world. Such a global system, where prosperity of few depends on exploitation of the many, amounts to the very negation of the concept of universal concept of human rights.

India's Experiment

Until 1991, India largely adhered to the policy of a state-regulated closed-economy and followed a policy of economic development aiming at equity, i.e., economic growth with social justice, removal of poverty, unemployment and social deprivation as well as regional disparities. For nearly 40 years, it did not very much opened up to Foreign Direct Investment (FDI) and exercised its discretion of such offers on case by case basis.

To pursue its objectives, India attempted to regulate the industry and market through licensing-controls and other bureaucratic practices, in the belief that market forces alone cannot achieve growth with equity, it was seeking. That belief was, of course, correct; it is a well recognised fact that market forces, if they are fully competitive can at best achieve efficiency in production but not of distributive justice.

India for long relied on Indian private entrepreneurs and Public Sector Units (PSUs) to do their part, but they failed, with few exceptions, even in the achievement of efficiency. At the same time, economic growth rate have been very slow because of the framework adopted was inward looking and counter-productive and India continued to have a declining share of world trade. From 2.5 per cent in 1947, it has come to less than half of one (0.59) per cent. Moreover, public sector enterprises became very dominant and unprofitable and had a multiple effect because they were at the commanding heights (e.g. providing infrastructure). Another problem was the rampant, inexplicable expansion of licensing. The failure to achieve equity—elimination of poverty was partly a result of the failure to achieve economic growth and more so because of rampant corruption.

Indeed, what was worse was that a system of regulated economy gave birth to bureaucratisation, red-tapism and corruption. The analyses presented in the preceding chapters of this book bear out how after 50 years of India's independence, extreme poverty, illiteracy, denial of basic human rights and widespread corruption are still rampant.

There was widespread discontentment with the way the Indian economy was being 'managed' which was leading us no where. But then by 1991-92, because of forces of globalisation and other external factors (Gulf War and stoppage of "overseas remittance" from West Asia, etc.), India's foreign exchange reserves had reached an alarmingly low level—$1.2 billion in June 1991. It was also no longer in a position to meet its debt ratios, which had reached a figure of $92 billion. Even then the short-lived coalition government in 1990-91 was hesitant to open up its economy and to carry out necessary reforms. But after the elections and advent of new government, India decided to take the necessary steps and to approach IMF and IBRD for massive loans to meet its financial challenges.

IMF/World Bank conditionalities for development aid or loans to promote market-economy are wellknown. They assured India of their assistance provided India was ready to open its economy to market forces. Subsequently, IMF assistance and structural adjustment loans from the World Bank (December 1991) helped India to face the financial challenges.

Earlier, in June 1991, India initiated new economic policy by devaluation of the rupee, macro policy changes to liberalise its economy, sought Foreign Direct Investment (FDI) cut down subsidies, and opted for free-trade and market based policies.

What may appear as if India acted under compulsion was in a sense, is continuation of the policy pursued, though haltingly since mid-1980s.

Thus, India began its experiment with the forces of globalisation, beginning 1991. We are experiencing changed situation in certain respects. Once significant development has been better annual economic growth ranging between 5 per cent to 7 per cent (from an average of 3 per cent in the preceding decade). However, in many ways the life of a common man continues the same way as it has been before "liberalisation".

Scores of TNCs have established their business, in collaboration with the Indian partners or independently. Indian markets are flooded with consumergoods. Foreign made colour TVs, cellular phones and various models of cars—German, French, Japanese, South Korean, Italian, cosmetics, textile, readymade clothes, shoes, etc., have flooded the market. Food joints such as Kentucky Fried Chicken (KFC),

MacDonalds, Pizza Hut have their restaurants and food shops all over India. The two cold drinks—Pepsi and Coke, have captured soft-drink market. The Indian companies have vanished. Arrival of TNCs have increased rentals and market value of real-estate, manyfolds depending on the site and the precise locality in the metropolitan towns. On the other hand, Delhi itself continues to experience acute shortage of power and water supply. States like Bihar, U.P., Madhya Pradesh, Rajasthan continue to be worse state in terms of power and water supply.

Of course, prices of electronic goods such as colour TVs, computers, refrigerators of various makes, which are now easily available, have came down, while the prices of essential commodities of day-to-day needs such as vegetable, food grain, edible oil, etc., have gone up. There is rush from villages to metropolitan towns and number of slum dwellers have increased many fold in Delhi and Mumbai.

It is too early to draw conclusions whether the so-called "liberalisation" would turn out to be a blessing or a curse in the context of realisation and protection of human rights.

The point is that where objective of policy is economic development with equity, liberalisation of markets must be attended with positive action for poverty alleviation, primary education, improved nutrition and regional balance. It is true that without deregulation of licenses and permits and opening up of the markets, costs of inefficiency can easily surpass the benefit of any other positive action. But without such other positive actions and deliberate policies of the government, deregulation alone cannot serve national objectives of economic growth with equity.

Even for an effective implementation, the government has to take certain necessary steps. First, it has to create the transparent legal and regulatory framework for business to enter and exit a field; invest, expand, borrow and collaborate with others at home and abroad and then operate freely in buying, selling and producing goods and services. Within that framework, one should be able to function without anybody's permission. If a businessman violates the rules following the due process of law, then alone he should be liable to penalty. Otherwise he does not have to go from pillar to post from one office to another, for getting a permission here and business there as has been the practice in the past. There is a little point in deregulation and opening up the market and still require prior permission and clearance to operate in that context.

Another point that need be emphasised is that governments held to those adversely affected by deregulation, may have to expand much beyond supplementing the worker's compensation. In every industrialised country, including the United States, there is a social security system which takes care of the unemployed persons, who have been thrown out from employment because the companies for one reason or the other want to curtail the labour force.

'Liberalisation' and invitation to FDI create a situation where backward regions get more backward and the rich to get richer through earning incomes and commanding mode of goods they would like to consume. We should keep in mind that it is the responsibility of the government to protect human rights of the people. As such, the government will have to provide for new schemes and infrastructure support in the backward regions and further expand its anti-poverty programmes.

In brief, globalisation does presents certain opportunities for economic growth, but India has to move with utmost caution. It is necessary (to paraphrase Mahatma Gandhi's advice given in different context) to keep the windows open; it is equally necessary that we refuse to be blown off our feet.

It is for the economists and the policy-makers to decide on the extent to which it should open its doors for globalisation. In the preceding pages we have given a general survey of pitfalls and opportunities that globalisation implies. What India cannot ignore its responsibilities of promoting and protecting human rights, particularly of the vulnerable segment of the society.

Under market-economy, India is expected to withdraw from economic production, market and distribution. But if the government opts for this kind of economy, consumerism would be the dominant ideology and principle of equity would take a back-seat. While the rich and upper-middle class will reap the benefits, the lower classes, i.e., lower-middle class, peasants, farmers and workers, which represent larger segment of our society could suffer increasing deprivation. Thus, a pure market approach—one that would let the chips (and the workers) fall where they may, would neither be fair nor politically sustainable.

As is emphasised in the preceding chapters, especially chapter 16, International Covenant of Economic, Social and Cultural Rights, Articles 6 to 15 emphasise on right to work, right to just and favourable conditions of work, right to form and join trade unions, right to social security and above all right to adequate standard of living including food and shelter. Similarly, the Constitution of India has spelled out these rights and the directive principles of state policy has directed the state to secure a social order for the promotion and welfare of the people—right to work, public assistance in cases of unemployment,old age citizens, disablement and the duty of the state to raise the level of nutrition, standard of living and public health. The governments both at federal and state level cannot absolve itself of these responsibilities. They cannot absolve themselves of the responsibility of providing primary education as well as to promote higher education. Thus, it is essential that the government should not surrender its economic resources to private entrepreneurs especially the TNCs, which as of now, has no human rights accountability.

While India should not allow TNCs a freer hand, there is no reason why in certain areas it should not encourage Indian private entrepreneurs.

Before India could attempt to be an active actor in competitive global market, it has to acquire a degree of autonomy both in term of economic development and fiscal/monetary resources. India has little scope of competing while its hands are tied under the burden of debt and dependence on international institutions such as IMF and IBRD.

The important thing is that India owes to its people and the posterity to give priority attention to the question of promotion and protection of human rights. Whatever economic system it follows, it has to be geared as a means to that objective.

REFERENCES

1. In 1996, Russia was included in the Group of Seven—Britain, Canada, France, Germany, Italy, Japan and the United States of America.
2. Cited in Noam Choamsky, *Powers and Prospects: Reflection on Human Nature and Social Order*, Indian edition, Delhi: Madhyam Books, 1996, pp. 101-2; also see Alexander L. Tchitcherov, *India: Changing Economic Structure in the Sixteenth to Eighteenth Centuries*, 3rd Rev. Ed., New Delhi: Manohar Publishers, 1998, Chapters III & IV.
3. Choamsky, *Ibid*, p. 101.
4. The term "European" is used here in a civilisational sense and include all European countries, including Russia (erstwhile Soviet Union), Canada, USA, Australia, New Zealand and Japan, which are also referred to as the North.

For an elaboration, see K.P. Saksena, "North-South Conflict and the United Nations", in M.R. Rajan S. Ganguly eds. *Great Power Relations, World Order and the Third World* (New Delhi: Vikas, 1981), pp. 65-83. Also, Willy Brandt, *North-South:A Programme for Survival,* The Report of the Independent Commission..., (Cambridge, Massachusetts, The MIT Press, 1980)

5. Robert L. Rothstein, *The Weak in the World of the Strong: The Developing Countries in the International System* New York: Praeger, 1977.
6. Figures are based on World Development Report (1997). It may be added that the GDP of US is around $7,000 billion while that of Japan it is little more than $5,000 billion.
7. Henk Thomas, ed., Globalisation and Third World Trade Unions, Indian reprint (Delhi: Madhyam Books, 1995).
   This book with the support of six case studies shows the precarious situation in which trade unions find themselves in Asia, Africa and Latin America.
8. Ramesh Diwan, "The New Colonial Threat", *Times of India*, July 24, 1997.
9. This point is well elaborated and forcefully argued in Cheryl Payer, *Lent and Lost: Foreign Credit and Third World Development*, Indian Reprint (Delhi: Madhyam Books, 1996).
10. See in particular, Max Millikan and Walt W. Rostow, *A Proposal: Keys to Effective Foreign Policy (New York: Harper*, 1957), p. 82. Also Max Millikan and Donald Balckmer, eds., *The Emerging Nations: Their Growth and US Policy* (Bostan: Little and Brown, 1961).
11. TA, EPTA Programmes meant: on the request of the developing countries UN would provide Technical Assistance which meant that experts invariably drawn from Western Europe and North America would go to the developing countries, their expert fee would be paid out of UN TA/EPTA funds, raised from "voluntary" contributions from the United States and its allies;local expenses borne by the countries concerned, to study and prepare a blueprint for a development project. Once that was done, the developing countries concerned were left in the lurch to raise investment money for the implementation of the project. Here the World Bank or some developed countries of the West would step in with a loan and a TNC would come in to provide the technical know-how. Thus TA & EPTA helped promote TNCs and dependence of the South on the North.
12. Paris Club is not a club at all but a set of procedures and facilities extended by the French Treasury providing meeting rooms and a secretariat. Its members are major creditor governments such as Belgium, Britain, Canada, France, Germany, Italy, Japan, Netherlands, Switzerland and Sweden, etc.
13. For a trenchant analysis of these developments see, in particular, Payer, Lent and Lost, n.7.
14. "The Global Economy and the Nation State" *Foreign Affairs*, Vol.76, No.5 (Sept.-Oct.1997), pp.3-5.
15. For details, see K.P. Saksena, Reforming the United Nations: The Challenge of Relevance (New Delhi: Sage, 1993), pp. 105-62 and 194-201.

16. General Assembly Resolutions 43/195 of 20 Dec., 1988; 44/169 of 19th Dec., 1989; and 45/199 of 21st Dec., 1990.
17. *Time* Magazine, 1 April, 1991, p. 19.
18. Cited in Choamsky, n.1, p. 94.
19. *New York Times*, "Week in Review", June 2, 1992, cited in *Ibid*. p. 95.—
20. Harold J. Laski, "Towards a Universal Declaration of Human Rights", in UNESCO *Human Rights Comments and Interpretations* (London: Wingate, 1949), reproduced in *Human Rights Teaching* (UNESCO), Vol. IV, 1985, pp.1-11.
21. For details, see K.P. Saksena, "South in Bloc-dominated Economy...", *International Studies*, Vol. 27, No. 4, December 1990, pp. 351-63.
22. Charles J. Hanley, "Losers in a global race to the bottomline", *Times of India*, April 10, 1996.
23. "Globalisation: There may be gales ahead", broadcast on BBC Radio, reproduced in *Times of India*, June 14, 1996.
24. *Foreign Affairs*, May-June 1998, p.12
25. Cited in Vaiju Naravane, "Recovery remains a dream in Europe", *Times of India*, December 26, 1996.

APPENDICES

APPENDIX I

I

Excerpts from the Constitution of India

Preamble

WE, THE PEOPLE OF INDIA, having solemnly resolved to constitute India into a SOVEREIGN, SOCIALIST, SECULAR, DEMOCRATIC, REPUBLIC and to secure to all its citizens:

JUSTICE—social, economic and political;

LIBERTY—of thought, expression, belief, faith and worship;

EQUALITY—of status and of opportunity; and to promote among them all;

FRATERNITY—assuring the dignity of the individual and the unity and integrity of the Nation;

IN OUR CONSTITUENT ASSEMBLY this twenty-sixth day of November, 1949, do HEREBY ADOPT, ENACT AND GIVE TO OURSELVES THIS CONSTITUTION.

FUNDAMENTAL RIGHTS

General

12. Definition—In this Part, unless the context otherwise requires, "the State" includes the Government and Parliament of India and the Government and the Legislature of each of the States and all local or other authorities within the territory of India or under the control of the Government of India.

13. Laws Inconsistent with or in Derogation of the Fundamental Rights

1. All laws in force in the territory of India immediately before the commencement of this Constitution, in so far as they are inconsistent with the provisions of this Part, shall, to the extent of such inconsistency, be void.
2. The State shall not make any law which takes away or abridges the rights conferred by this Part and any law made in contravention of this clause shall, to the extent of the contravention, be void.
3. In this article, unless the context otherwise requires –
   (a) "law" includes any Ordinance, order, bye-law, rule, regulation, notification, custom or usage having in the territory of India, the force of law;
   (b) "laws in force" includes laws passed or made by a Legislature or other competent authority in the territory of India before the commencement of this Constitution and not previously repeated notwithstanding that any such law or any part thereof may not be then in operation either at all or in particular areas.
4. Noting in this article shall apply to any amendment of this constitution made under article 368.

Right to Equality

14. Equality before Law

The State shall not deny to any person equality before the law or the equal protection of the laws within the territory of India.

15. Prohibition of Discrimination on Grounds of Religion, Race, Caste, Sex or Place of Birth

(i) The State shall not discriminate against any citizen on grounds only of religion, race, caste, sex, place of birth or any of them.

(ii) No citizen shall, on grounds only of religion, race, caste, sex, place of birth or any of them, be subject to any disability, liability, restriction or condition with regard to—

(a) access to shops, public restaurants, hotels and places of public entertainment; or

(b) the use of wells, tanks, bathing ghats, roads and places of public resort maintained wholly or partly out of State funds or dedicated to the use of general public.

(iii) Nothing in this article shall prevent the State from making any special provision for women and children.

(iv) Nothing in this article or in clause (2) of article 29 shall prevent the State from making any special provision for the advancement of any socially and educationally backward classes of citizens or for the Scheduled Castes and the Scheduled Tribes.

16. Equality of Opportunity in Matters of Public Employment

(i) There shall be equality of opportunity for all citizens in matters relating to employment or appointment to any office under the State.

(ii) No citizen shall, on grounds only of religion, race, caste, sex, descent, place of birth, residence or any of them, be ineligible for, or discriminated against in respect of, any employment or office under the State.

(iii) Nothing in this article shall prevent Parliament from making any law prescribing, in regard to a class or classes of employment or appointment to an office under the Government of, or any local or other authority within, a State or Union territory, any requirement as to residence within that State or Union territory prior to such employment or appointment.

(iv) Nothing in this article shall prevent the State from making any provision for the reservation of appointments or posts in favour of any backward class of citizens which, in the opinion of the State, is not adequately represented in the services under the State.

(a) Nothing in this article shall prevent the state from making any provision for reservation in matters of promotion to any class or classes of posts in the services under the state in favour of the Scheduled Castes and Scheduled Tribes which in the opinion of the States, are not adequately represented in the services under the State.

(v) Nothing in this article shall affect the operation of any law which provides that the incumbent of an office in connection with the affairs of any religious or denominational institution or any member of the governing body thereof shall be a person professing a particular religion or belonging to a particular denomination.

17. Abolition of Untouchability

"Untouchability" is abolished and its practice in any form is forbidden. The enforcement of any disability arising out of "Untouchability" shall be an offence punishable in accordance with law.

18. Abolition of Titles

(i) No title, not being a military or academic distinction, shall be conferred by the State.

(ii) No citizen of India shall accept any title from any foreign State.

(iii) No person who is not a citizen of India shall, while he holds any office of profit or trust under the State, accept without the consent of the President any title from any foreign State.

(iv) No person holding any office of profit or trust under the State shall, without the consent of the President, accept any present, emolument, or office of any kind from or under any foreign State.

Right to Freedom

19. Protection of Certain Rights Regarding Freedom of Speech, etc.

(i) All citizens shall have the right —

(a) to freedom of speech and expression;

(b) to assemble peaceably and without arms;

(c) to form associations or unions;

(d) to move freely throughout the territory of India;

(e) to reside and settle in any part of the territory of India; and

(f) to practise any profession, or to carry on any occupation, trade or business.

(ii) Nothing in sub-clause (a) of clause (1) shall affect the operation of any existing law, or prevent the State from making any law, in so far as such law imposes reasonable restrictions on the exercise of the right conferred by the said sub-clause in the interests of the sovereignty and integrity of India, the security of the State, friendly relations with foreign States, public order, decency or morality, or in relation to contempt of court, defamation or incitement to an offence.

(iii) Nothing in sub-clause (b) of the said clause shall affect the operation of any existing law in so far as it imposes, or prevent the State from making any law imposing, in the interest of the sovereignty and integrity of India or public order, reasonable restrictions on the exercise of the right conferred by the said sub-clause.

(iv) Nothing in sub-clause (c) of the said clause shall affect the operation of any existing law in so far as it imposes, or prevent the State from making any law imposing, in the interests of the sovereignty and integrity of India or public order or morality, reasonable restrictions on the exercise of the right conferred by the said sub-clause.

(v) Nothing in sub-clause (d) and (e) of the said clause shall affect the operation of any existing law in so far as it imposes, or prevent the State from making any law imposing, reasonable restrictions on the exercise of any of the rights conferred by the said sub-clauses either in the interests of the general public or for the protection of the interests of any Scheduled Tribe.

(vi) Nothing in sub-clause (f) of the said clause shall affect the operation of any existing law in so far as it imposes or prevent the State from making any law imposing, in the interests of the general public, reasonable restrictions on the exercise of the right conferred by the said sub-clause, and, in particular, nothing in the said sub-clause shall affect the operation of any existing law in so far as it relates to, or prevent the State from making any law relating to,—

(a) the professional or technical qualifications necessary for practising any profession or carrying on any occupation, trade or business, or

(b) the carrying on by the State, or by a corporation owned or controlled by the State, of any trade, business, industry or service, whether to the exclusion, complete or partial, of citizens or otherwise.

20. Protection in Respect of Conviction for Offences

(i) No person shall be convicted of any offence except for violation of a law in force at the time of the commission of the act charged as an offence, nor be subjected to a penalty greater than that which might have been inflicted under the law in force at the time of the commission of the offence.

(ii) No person shall be prosecuted and punished for the same offence more than once.

(iii) No person accused of any offence shall be compelled to be a witness against himself.

21. Protection of Life and Personal Liberty

(i) No person shall be deprived of his life or personal liberty except, according to procedure established by law.

22. Protection Against Arrest and Detention in Certain Cases

(i) No person who is arrested shall be detained in custody without being informed, as soon as may be, of the grounds for such arrest nor shall he be denied the right to consult, and to be defended by, a legal practitioner of his choice.

(ii) Every person who is arrested and detained in custody shall be produced before the nearest magistrate within a period of twenty-four hours of such arrest excluding the time necessary for the journey from the place of arrest to court of the magistrate and no such person shall be detained in custody beyond the said period without the authority of a magistrate.

(iii) Nothing in clauses (1) and (2) shall apply–

(a) to any person who for the time being is an enemy alien; or

(b) to any person who is arrested or detained under any law providing for preventive detention.

(iv) No law providing for preventive detention shall authorize the detention of a person for a longer period than three months unless—

(a) an Advisory Board consisting of persons who are, or have been, or are qualified to be appointed as, Judges of a High Court has reported before the expiration of the said period of three months that there is in its opinion sufficient cause for such detention :

Provided that nothing in this sub-clause shall authorize the detention of any person beyond the maximum period prescribed by any law made by Parliament under sub-clause (b) of clause (7); or

(b) such person is detained in accordance with the provisions of any law made by Parliament under sub-clauses (a) and (b) of clause (vii).

(v) When any person is detained in pursuance of an order made under any law providing for preventive detention, the authority making the order shall, as soon as may be, communicate to such person the grounds on which the order has been made and shall afford him the earliest opportunity of making a representation against the order.

(vi) Nothing in clause (v) shall require the authority making any such order as is referred to in that clause to disclose facts which such authority considers to be against the public interest to disclose.

(vii) Parliament may by law prescribe

(a) the circumstances under which, and the class or classes of cases in which, a person may be detained for a period longer than three months under any law providing for preventive detention without obtaining the opinion of an Advisory Board in accordance with the provisions of sub-clause (a) of clause (iv) ;

(b) the maximum period for which any person may in any class or classes of cases be detained under any law providing for preventive detention; and

(c) the procedure to be followed by an Advisory Board in an inquiry under sub-clause (a) of clause (iv).

RIGHT AGAINST EXPLOITATION

23. Prohibition of Traffic in Human Beings and Forced Labour

(i) Traffic in human beings and begar and (other) similar forms of forced labour are prohibited and any contravention of this provision shall be an offence punishable in accordance with law.

(ii) Nothing in this article shall prevent the State from imposing compulsory service for public purposes, and in imposing such service the State shall not make any discrimination on grounds only of religion, race, caste or class or any of them.

24. Prohibition of Employment of Children in Factories, etc.

No child below the age of fourteen years shall be employed to work in any factory or mine or engaged in any other hazardous employment.

Right to Freedom of Religion

25. Freedom of Conscience and free Profession, Practice and Propagation of Religion

(i) Subject to public order, morality and health and to the other provisions of this Part, all persons are equally entitled to freedom of conscience and the right freely to profess, practise and propagate religion.

(ii) Nothing in this article shall affect the operation of any existing law or prevent the State from making any law

(a) regulating or restricting any economic, financial, political or other secular activity which may be associated with religious practice;

(b) providing for social welfare and reform or the throwing open of Hindu religious institutions of a public character to all classes and sections of Hindus.

Explanation I—The wearing and carrying of *kirpans* shall be deemed to be included in the profession of the Sikh religion.

Explanation II—In sub-clause (ii), the reference to Hindus shall be construed as including, a reference to persons professing the Sikh, Jain or Buddhist religion, and the reference to Hindu religious institutions shall be construed accordingly.

26. Freedom to Manage Religious Affairs

(i) Subject to public order, morality and health, every religious denomination or any section thereof shall have the right

(i) to establish and maintain institutions for religious and charitable purpose;

(ii) to manage its own affairs in matters of religion;

(iii) to own and acquire movable and immovable property; and

(iv) to administer such property in accordance with law.

27. Freedom as to Payment of Taxes for Promotion of any Particular Religion

No person shall be compelled to pay any taxes, the proceeds of which are specifically appropriated in payment of expenses for the promotion or maintenance of any particular religion or religious denomination.

28. Freedom as to Attendance at Religious Instruction or Religious Worship in Certain Educational Institutions

(i) No religious instruction shall be provided in any educational institution wholly maintained out of State funds.

(ii) Nothing in clause (i) shall apply to an educational institution which is administered by the State but has been established under any endowment or trust which requires that religious instruction shall be imparted in such institution.

(iii) No person attending any educational institution recognized by the State or receiving aid out of State funds shall be required to take part in any religious instruction that may be imparted in such institution or to attend any religious worship that may be conducted in such institution or in any premises attached thereto unless such person or, if such person is a minor, his guardian has given his consent thereto.

CULTURAL AND EDUCATIONAL RIGHTS

29. Protection of Interests of Minorities

(i) Any section of the citizens residing in the territory of India or any part thereof having a distinct language, script or culture of its own shall have the right to conserve the same.

(ii) No citizen shall be denied admission into any educational institution maintained by the State or receiving aid out of State funds on grounds only of religion, race, caste, language or any of them.

30. Right of Minorities to Establish and Administer Educational Institutions

(i) All minorities, whether based on religion or language, shall have the right to establish and administer educational institutions of their choice.

(i) A In making any law providing for the compulsory acquisition of any property of an educational institution established and administered by a minority, referred to in clause (i), the State shall ensure that the amount fixed by or determined under such law for the acquisition of such property is such as would not restrict or abrogate the right guaranteed under that clause.

(ii) The State shall not, in granting aid to educational institutions, discriminate against any educational institution on the ground that it is under the management of a minority, whether based on religion or language.

31C. **Saving of Laws giving Effect to Certain Directive Principles** Notwithstanding anything contained in article 13, no law giving effect to the policy of the State towards securing all or any of the principles laid down in Part IV shall be deemed to be void on the ground that it is inconsistent with or takes away or abridges any of the rights conferred by article 14 or article 19; and no law containing a declaration that it is for giving effect to such policy shall be called in question in any court on the ground that it does not give effect to such policy.....

RIGHT TO CONSTITUTIONAL REMEDIES

32. Remedies for Enforcement of Rights Conferred by this Part

(i) The right to move the Supreme Court by appropriate proceedings for the enforcement of the rights conferred by this Part is guaranteed.

(ii) The Supreme Court shall have power to issue directions or orders or writs, including writs in the nature of *habeas corpus*, *mandamus*, prohibition, *quo warranto* and *certiorari*, whichever may be appropriate, for the enforcement of any of the rights conferred by this Part.

(iii) Without prejudice to the powers conferred on the Supreme Court by clauses (1) and (2), Parliament may by law empower any other court to exercise within the local limits of its jurisdiction all or any of the powers exercisable by the Supreme Court under clause (2).

(iv) The right guaranteed by this article shall not be suspended except as otherwise provided for by this Constitution.

33. Power of Parliament to Modify the Rights Conferred by this Part in their Application to Forces, etc.

Parliament may, by law, determine to what extent any of the rights conferred by this Part shall in their application to,

(a) the members of the Armed Forces; or

(b) the members of the Forces charged with the maintenance of public order; or

(c) persons employed in any bureau or other organization established by the State for purposes of intelligence or counter intelligence; or

(d) persons employed in, or in connection with, the telecommunication systems set up for the purposes of any Force, bureau or organization referred to in clauses (a) to (c).

be restricted or abrogated so as to ensure the proper discharge of their duties and the maintenance of discipline among them.

34. Restriction on Rights Conferred by this Part while Martial Law is in force in any Area

Notwithstanding anything in the foregoing provisions of this Part, Parliament may by law indemnify any person in the service of the Union or of a State or any other person in respect of any act done by him in connection with the maintenance or restoration of order in any area within the territory of India where martial law was in force or validate any sentence passed, punishment inflicted, forfeiture ordered or other act done under martial law in such area.

III

Part IV

Directive Principles of State Policy

36. Definition

In this Part, unless the context otherwise requires, "the State" has the same meaning as in Part III.

37. Application of the Principles Contained in this Part

The provisions contained in this Part shall not be enforceable by any court, but the principles therein laid down are nevertheless fundamental in the governance of the country and it shall be the duty of the State to apply these principles in making laws.

38. State to Secure a Social Order for the Promotion of Welfare of the People

(i) The State shall strive to promote the welfare of the people by securing and protecting as effectively as it may a social order in which justice, social, economic and political, shall inform all the institutions of the national life.

(ii) The State shall, in particular, strive to minimize the inequalities in income, and endeavour to eliminate inequalities in status, facilities and opportunities, not only amongst individuals but also amongst groups of people residing in different areas or engaged in different vocations.

39. Certain Principles of Policy to be followed by the State

The State shall, in particular, direct its policy towards securing

(a) that the citizen, men and women equally, have the right to an adequate means of livelihood;

(b) that the ownership and control of the material resources of the community are so distributed as best to subserve the common good;

(c) that the operation of the economic system does not result in the concentration of wealth and means of production to the common detriment;

(d) that there is equal pay for equal work for both men and women;

(e) that the health and strength of workers, men and women, and the tender age of children are not abused and that citizens are not forced by economic necessity to enter avocations unsuited to their age or strength;

(f) that children are given opportunities and facilities to develop in a healthy manner and in conditions of freedom and dignity and that childhood and youth are protected against exploitation and against moral and material abandonment.

39A. Equal Justice and Free Legal Aid

The State shall secure that the operation of the legal system promotes justice, on a basis of equal opportunity, and shall, in particular, provide free legal aid, by suitable legislation or schemes or in any other way, to ensure that opportunities for securing justice are not denied to any citizen by reason of economic or other disabilities.

40. Organisation of Village Panchayats

The State shall take steps to organize village panchayats and endow them with such powers and authority as may be necessary to enable them to function as units of self-government.

41. Right to work, to Education and to Public Assistance in Certain Cases

The State shall, within the limits of its economic capacity and development, make effective provision for securing the right to work, to education and to public assistance in cases of unemployment, old age, sickness and disablement, and in other cases of undeserved want.

42. Provision for Just and Humane Conditions of Work and Maternity Relief

The State shall make provision for securing just and humane conditions of work and for maternity relief.

43. Living Wage, etc., for Workers

The State shall endeavour to secure, by suitable legislation or economic organization or in any other way, to all workers agricultural, industrial or otherwise, work, a living wage, conditions of work ensuring a decent standard of life and full enjoyment of leisure and social and cultural opportunities and, in particular, the State shall endeavour to promote cottage industries on an individual or cooperative basis in rural areas.

43A. Participation of Workers in Management of Industries

The State shall take steps, by suitable legislation or in any other way, to secure the participation of workers in the management of undertakings, establishments or other organisations engaged in any industry.

44. Uniform Civil Code for the Citizens

The State shall endeavour to secure for the citizens a uniform civil code throughout the territory of India.

45. Provision for Free and Compulsory Education for Children

The State shall endeavour to provide, within a period of ten years from the commencement of this Constitution, for free and compulsory education for all children until they complete the age of fourteen years.

46. Promotion of Educational and Economic Interests of Scheduled Castes, Scheduled Tribes and other Weaker Sections

The State shall promote with special care the educational and economic interests of the weaker sections of the people, and in particular, of the Scheduled Castes and Scheduled Tribes, and shall protect them from social injustice and all forms of exploitation.

47. Duty of the State to Raise the Level of Nutrition and the Standard of Living and to Improve Public Health

The State shall regard the raising of the level of nutrition and the standard of living of its people and the improvement of public health as among its primary duties and, in particular, the State shall endeavour to bring about prohibition of the consumption except for medicinal purposes of intoxicating drinks and of drugs which are injurious to health.

48. Organization of Agriculture and Animal Husbandry

The State shall endeavour to organize agriculture and animal husbandry on modern and scientific lines and shall, in particular, take steps for preserving and improving the breeds, and prohibiting the slaughter of cows and calves and other milch and draught cattle.

48A. Protection and Improvement of Environment and Safeguarding of Forests and Wildlife

The State shall endeavour to protect and improve the environment and to safeguard the forests and wildlife of the country.

49. Protection of Monuments and Places and Objects of National Importance

It shall be the obligation of the State to protect every monument or place or object of artistic or historic interest, declared by or under law made by Parliament to be of national importance, from spoilation, disfigurement, destruction, removal, disposal or export, as the case may be.

50. Separation of Judiciary from Executive

The State shall take steps to separate the judiciary from the executive in the public services of the State.

51. Promotion of International Peace and Security

The State shall endeavour to—

(a) promote international peace and security;

(b) maintain just and honourable relations between nations;

(c) foster respect for international law and treaty obligations in the dealings of organized people with one another; and

(d) encourage settlement of international disputes by arbitration.

IV

Part IV–A

Fundamental Duties

51A. Fundamental Duties

It shall be the duty of every citizen of India

(a) to abide by the Constitution and respect its ideals and institutions, the National Flag and the National Anthem;

(b) to cherish and follow the noble ideals which inspired our national struggle for freedom;

(c) to uphold and protect the sovereignty, unity and integrity of India;

(d) to defend the country and render national service when called upon to do so;

(e) to promote harmony and the spirit of common brotherhood amongst all the people of India transcending religious, linguistic and regional or sectional diversities; to renounce practices derogatory to the dignity of women;

(f) to value and preserve the rich heritage of our composite culture;

(g) to protect and improve the natural environment including forests, lakes, rivers and wildlife, and to have compassion for living creatures;

(n) to develop the scientific temper, humanism and the spirit of inquiry and reform;

(i) to safeguard public property and to abjure violence;

(j) to strive towards excellence in all spheres of individual and collective activity so that the nation constantly rises to higher levels of endeavour and achievement.

V

Some Other Provisions

Article 226. Power of High Courts to Issue Certain Writs

1. Notwithstanding anything in article 32, every High Court shall have power, throughout the territories in relation to which it exercises jurisdiction, to issue to any person or authority, including in appropriate cases, any Government, within those territories directions, orders or writs, including writs in the nature of *habeas corpus, mandamus,* prohibition, *quo warranto* and *certiorari*, or any of them, for the enforcement of any of the rights conferred by Part III and for any other purpose.
2. The power conferred by clause (1) to issue directions, orders or writs to any Government, authority or person may also be exercised by any High Court exercising jurisdiction in relation to the territories within which the cause of action, wholly or in part, arises for the exercise of such power, notwithstanding that the seat of such Government or authority or the residence of such person is not within those territories.
3. Where any party against whom an interim order, whether by way of injunction or stay or in any other manner, is made on, or in any proceedings relating to, a petition under clause (1), without—

   (a) furnishing to such party copies of such petition and all documents in support of the pleas for such interim order; and

   (b) giving such party an opportunity of being heard, makes an application to the High Court for the vacation of such order and furnishes a copy of such application to the party in whose favour such order has been made or the counsel of such party, the High Court shall dispose of the application within a period of two weeks from the date on which it is received or from the date on which the copy of such application is so furnished, whichever is later, or where the High Court is closed on the last day of that period, before the expiry of the next day afterwards on which the High Court is closed on the last day of that period, before the expiry of the next day afterwards on which the High Court is open; and if the application is not so disposed of, the interim order shall, on the expiry of that period, or, as the case may be, the expiry of the said next day, stand vacated.

4. The power conferred on a High Court by this article shall not be in derogation of the power conferred on the Supreme Court by clause (2) of article 32.

Article 300A. Persons not to be deprived of property save by authority of law

No person shall be deprived of his property save by authority of law.

Article 325. No person to be ineligible for inclusion in, or to claim to be included in a special, electoral roll on grounds of religion, race, caste or sex

There shall be one general electoral roll for every territorial constituency for election to either House of Parliament or to the House or either House of the Legislature of a State and no person shall be ineligible for inclusion in any such roll or claim to be included in any special electoral roll for any such constituency on grounds only of religion, race, caste, sex or any of them.

Article 326. Elections to the House of the People and to the Legislative Assemblies of States to be on the basis of adult suffrage

The elections to the House of the People and to the Legislative Assembly of every State shall be on the basis of adult suffrage; that is to say, every person who is a citizen of India and who is not less than eighteen years of age on such date as may be fixed in that behalf by or under any law made by the appropriate Legislature and is not otherwise disqualified under this Constitution or any law made by the appropriate Legislature on the ground of non-residence, unsoundness of mind, crime or corrupt or illegal practice, shall be entitled to be registered as a voter at any such election.

APPENDIX II

Universal Declaration of Human Rights

Preamble

Whereas recognition of the inherent dignity and of the equal and inalienable rights of all members of the human family is the foundation of freedom, justice and peace in the world,

Whereas disregard and contempt for human rights have resulted in barbarous acts which have outraged the conscience of mankind, and the advent of a world in which human beings shall enjoy freedom of speech and belief and freedom from fear and want has been proclaimed as the highest aspiration of the common people,

Whereas it is essential, if man is not to be compelled to have recourse, as a last resort, to rebellion against tyranny and oppression, that human rights should be protected by the rule of law,

Whereas it is essential to promote the development of friendly relations between nations,

Whereas the peoples of the United Nations have in the Charter reaffirmed their faith in fundamental human rights, in the dignity and worth of the human person and in the equal rights of men and women and have determined to promote social progress and better standards of life in larger freedom,

Whereas Member States have pledged themselves to achieve, in cooperation with the United Nations, the promotion of universal respect for the observance of human rights and fundamental freedoms,

Whereas a common understanding of these rights and freedoms is of the greatest importance for the full realization of this pledge,

Now, therefore,

The General Assembly Proclaims

This Universal Declaration of Human Rights as a common standard of achievement for all peoples and all nations, to the end that every individual and every organ of society, keeping this Declaration constantly in mind, shall strive by teaching and education to promote respect for these rights and freedoms and by progressive measures, national and international, to secure their universal and effective recognition and observance, both among the peoples of Member States themselves and among the peoples of territories under their jurisdiction.

ARTICLE 1

All human beings are born free and equal in dignity and rights. They are endowed with reason and conscience and should act towards one another in a spirit of brotherhood.

ARTICLE 2

Everyone is entitled to all the rights and freedoms set forth in this Declaration, without distinction of any kind, such as race, colour, sex, language, religion, political or other opinion, national or social origin, property, birth or other status.

Furthermore, no distinction shall be made on the basis of the political, jurisdictional or international status of the country or territory to which a person belongs, whether it be independent, trust, non-self-governing or under any other limitation of sovereignty.

ARTICLE 3

Everyone has the right to life, liberty and the security of person.

ARTICLE 4

No one shall be held in slavery or servitude; slavery and the slave trade shall be prohibited in all their forms.

ARTICLE 5

No one shall be subjected to torture or to cruel, inhuman or degrading treatment or punishment.

ARTICLE 6

Everyone has the right to recognition everywhere as a person before the law.

ARTICLE 7

All are equal before the law and are entitled without any discrimination to equal protection of the law. All are entitled to equal protection against any discrimination in violation of this Declaration and against any incitement to such discrimination.

ARTICLE 8

Everyone has the right to an effective remedy by the competent national tribunal for acts violating the fundamental rights granted to him by the Constitution or by law.

ARTICLE 9

No one shall be subjected to arbitrary arrest, detention or exile.

ARTICLE 10

Everyone is entitled in full equality to a fair and public hearing by an independent and impartial tribunal, in the determination of his rights and obligations and of any criminal charge against him.

ARTICLE 11

1. Everyone charged with a penal offence has the right to be presumed innocent until proved guilty according to law in a public trial at which he has had all the guarantees necessary for his defence.

2. No one shall be held guilty of any penal offence on account of any act or omission which did not constitute a penal offence, under national or international law, at the time when it was committed. Nor shall a heavier penalty be imposed than the one that was applicable at the time the penal offence was committed.

ARTICLE 12

No one shall be subjected to arbitrary interference with his privacy, family, home or correspondence, nor to attacks upon his honour and reputation. Everyone has the right to the protection of the law against such interference or attacks.

ARTICLE 13

1. Everyone has the right to freedom of movement and residence within the borders of each State.

2. Everyone has the right to leave any country, including his own, and to return to his country.

ARTICLE 14

1. Everyone has the right to seek and to enjoy in other countries asylum from persecution.

2. This right may not be invoked in the case of prosecutions genuinely arising from non-political crimes or from acts contrary to the purposes and principles of the United Nations.

ARTICLE 15

1. Everyone has the right to a nationality.

2. No one shall be arbitrarily deprived of his nationality nor denied the right to change his nationality.

ARTICLE 16

1. Men and women of full age, without any limitation due to race, nationality or religion, have the right to marry and to found a family. They are entitled to equal rights as to marriage, during marriage and at its dissolution.

2. Marriage shall be entered into only with the free and full consent of the intending spouses.

3. The family is the natural and fundamental group unit of society and is entitled to protection by society and the State.

ARTICLE 17

1. Everyone has the right to own property alone as well as in association with others.

2. No one shall be arbitrarily deprived of his property.

ARTICLE 18

Everyone has the right to freedom of thought, conscience and religion; this right includes freedom to change his religion or belief, and freedom, either alone or in community with others and in public or private, to manifest his religion or belief in teaching, practice, worship and observance.

ARTICLE 19

Everyone has the right to freedom of opinion and expression; this right includes freedom to hold opinions without interference and to seek, receive and impart information and ideas through any media and regardless of frontiers.

ARTICLE 20

1. Everyone has the right to freedom of peaceful assembly and association.

2. No one may be compelled to belong to an association.

ARTICLE 21

1. Everyone has the right to take part in the government of his country, directly or through freely chosen representatives.

2. Everyone has the right of equal access to public service in his country.

3. The will of the people shall be the basis of the authority of government; this will shall be expressed in periodic and genuine elections which shall be by universal and equal suffrage and shall be held by secret vote or by equivalent free voting procedures.

ARTICLE 22

Everyone, as a member of society, has the right to social security and is entitled to realization, through national effort and international cooperation and in accordance with the organization and resources of each State, of the economic, social and cultural rights indispensable for his dignity and the free development of his personality.

ARTICLE 23

1. Everyone has the right to work, to free choice of employment, to just and favourable conditions of work and to protection against unemployment.

2. Everyone, without any discrimination, has the right to equal pay for equal work.

3. Everyone who works has the right to just and favourable remuneration ensuring for himself and his family an existence worthy of human dignity, and supplemented, if necessary, by other means of social protection.

4. Everyone has the right to form and to join trade unions for the protection of his interests.

ARTICLE 24

Everyone has the right to rest and leisure, including reasonable limitation of working hours and periodic holiday with pay.

ARTICLE 25

1. Everyone has the right to a standard of living adequate for the health and well-being of himself and of his family, including food, clothing, housing and medical care and necessary social services, and the right to security in the event of unemployment, sickness, disability, widowhood, old age or other lack or livelihood in circumstances beyond his control.

2. Motherhood and childhood are entitled to special care and assistance. All children, whether born in or out of wedlock, shall enjoy the same social protection.

ARTICLE 26

1. Everyone has the right to education. Education shall be free, at least in the elementary and fundamental stages. Elementary education shall be compulsory. Technical and professional education shall be made generally available and higher education shall be equally accessible to all on the basis of merit.

2. Education shall be directed to the full development of the human personality and to the strengthening of respect for human rights and fundamental freedoms. It shall promote understanding, tolerance and friendship among all nations, racial or religious groups, and shall further the activities of the United Nations for the maintenance of peace.

3. Parents have a prior right to choose the kind of education that shall be given to their children.

ARTICLE 27

1. Everyone has the right to freely participate in the cultural life of the community, to enjoy the arts and to share in scientific advancement and its benefits.

2. Everyone has the right to the protection of the moral and material interests resulting from any scientific, literary or artistic production of which he is the author.

ARTICLE 28

Everyone is entitled to a social and international order in which the rights and freedoms set forth in this Declaration can be fully realized.

ARTICLE 29

1. Everyone has duties to the community in which alone the free and full development of his personality is possible.

2. In the exercise of his rights and freedoms, everyone shall be subject only to such limitations as are determined by law solely for the purpose of securing due recognition and respect for the rights and freedom of others and of meeting the just requirements of morality, public order and the general welfare in a democratic society.

3. These rights and freedoms may in no case be exercised contrary to the purposes and principles of United Nations.

ARTICLE 30

Nothing in this Declaration may be interpreted as implying for any State, group or person any right to engage in any activity or to perform any act aimed at the destruction of any of the rights and freedoms set forth herein.

APPENDIX III

International Covenant on Economic, Social and Cultural Rights

Preamble

THE STATES PARTIES TO THE PRESENT COVENANT,

Considering that, in accordance with the principles proclaimed in the Charter of the United Nations, recognition of the inherent dignity and of the equal and inalienable rights of all members of the human family is the foundation of freedom, justice and peace in the world,

Recognizing that these rights derive from the inherent dignity of the human person,

Recognizing that, in accordance with the Universal Declaration of Human Rights, the ideal of free human beings enjoying freedom from fear and want can only be achieved if conditions are created whereby everyone may enjoy his economic, social and cultural rights, as well as his civil and political rights,

Considering the obligation of States under the Charter of the United Nations to promote universal respect for, and observance of, human rights and freedoms,

Realizing that the individual, having duties to other individuals and to the community to which he belongs, is under a responsibility to strive for the promotion and observance of the rights recognized in the present Covenant,

Agree upon the following articles:

Part I

ARTICLE 1

1. All peoples have the right of self-determination. By virtue of

that right they freely determine their political status and freely pursue their economic, social and cultural development.

2. All peoples may, for their own ends, freely dispose of their natural wealth and resources without prejudice to any obligations arising out of international economic cooperation, based upon the principle of mutual benefit, and international law. In no case may a people be deprived of its own means of subsistence.

3. The States Parties to the present Covenant, including those having responsibility for the administration of Non-Self-Governing and Trust Territories, shall promote the realization of the right of self-determination, and shall respect that right, in conformity with the provisions of the Charter of the United Nations.

Part II

ARTICLE 2

1. Each State Party to the present Covenant undertakes to take steps, individually and through international assistance and co-operation, especially economic and technical, to the maximum of its available resources, with a view to achieving progressively the full realization of the rights recognized in the present Covenant by all appropriate means, including particularly the adoption of legislative measures.

2. The States Parties to the present Covenant undertake to guarantee that the rights enunciated in the present Covenant will be exercised without discrimination of any kind as to race, colour, sex, language, religion, political or other opinion, national or social origin, property, birth or other status.

3. Developing countries, with due regard to human rights and their national economy, may determine to what extent they would guarantee the economic rights recognized in the present Covenant, to non-nationals.

ARTICLE 3

The States Parties to the present Covenant undertake to ensure the equal right of men and women to the enjoyment of all economic, social and cultural rights set forth in the present Covenant.

ARTICLE 4

The States Parties to the present Covenant recognize that, in the enjoyment of those rights provided by the State in conformity with the present Covenant, the State may subject such rights only to such limitations as are determined by law only in so far as this may be compatible with the nature of these rights and solely for the purpose of promoting the general welfare in a democratic society.

ARTICLE 5

1. Nothing in the present Covenant may be interpreted as implying for any State, group or person any right to engage in any activity or to perform any act aimed at the destruction of any of the rights or freedoms recognized herein, or at their limitation to a greater extent than is provided for in the present Covenant.

2. No restriction upon or derogation from any of the fundamental human rights recognized or existing in any country in virtue of law, conventions, regulations or custom shall be admitted on the pretext that the present Covenant does not recognize such rights or that it recognizes them to a lesser extent.

Part III

ARTICLE 6

1. The States Parties to the present Covenant recognize the right to work, which include the right of everyone to the opportunity to gain his living by work which he freely chooses or accepts, and will take appropriate steps to safeguard this right.

2. The steps to be taken by a State Party to the present Covenant to achieve the full realization of this right shall include technical and vocational guidance and training programmes, policies and techniques to achieve steady economic, social and cultural development and full and productive employment under conditions safeguarding fundamental political and economic freedoms to the individual.

ARTICLE 7

The States Parties to the present Covenant recognize the right of everyone to the enjoyment of just and favourable conditions of work which ensure, in particular :

(a) Remuneration which provides all workers, as a minimum, with:

(i) Fair wages and equal remuneration for work of equal value without distinction of any kind, in particular women being guaranteed conditions of work not inferior to those enjoyed by men, with equal pay for equal work;

(ii) A decent living for themselves and their families in accordance with the provisions of the present Covenant;

(b) Safe and healthy working conditions;

(c) Equal opportunity for everyone to be promoted in his employment to an appropriate higher level, subject to no considerations other than those of seniority and competence;

(d) Rest, leisure and reasonable limitation of working hours and periodic holidays with pay, as well as remuneration for public holidays.

ARTICLE 8

1. The States Parties to the present Covenant undertake to ensure:

(a) The right of everyone to form trade unions and join the trade union of his choice, subject only to the rules of the organization concerned, for the promotion and protection of his economic and social interests. No restrictions may be placed on the exercise of this right other than those prescribed by law and which are necessary in a democratic society in the interests of national security or public order or for the protection of the rights and freedoms of others;

(b) The right of trade unions to establish national federations or confederations and the right of the latter to form or join international trade union organizations;

(c) The right of trade unions to function freely subject to no limitations other than those prescribed by law and which are necessary in a democratic society in the interests of national security or public order or for the protection of the rights and freedoms of others;

(d) The right to strike, provided that it is exercised in conformity with the laws of the particular country.

2. This article shall not prevent the imposition of lawful restrictions on the exercise of these rights by members of the armed forces or of the police or of the administration of the State.

3. Nothing in this article shall authorize States Parties to the International Labour Organisation Convention of 1948 concerning Freedom of Association and Protection of the Right to Organise to

take legislative measures which would prejudice, or apply the law in such a manner as would prejudice, the guarantees provided for in that Convention.

ARTICLE 9

The States Parties to the present Covenant recognize the right of everyone to social security, including social insurance.

ARTICLE 10

The States Parties to the present Covenant recognize that:

1. The widest possible protection and assistance should be accorded to the family, which is the natural and fundamental group unit of society, particularly for its establishment and while it is responsible for the care and education of dependent children. Marriage must be entered into with the free consent of the intending spouses.

2. Special protection should be accorded to mothers during a reasonable period before and after childbirth. During such period working mothers should be accorded paid leave or leave with adequate social security benefits.

3. Special measures of protection and assistance should be taken on behalf of all children and young persons without any discrimination for persons of parentage or other conditions. Children and young persons should be protected from economic and social exploitation. Their employment in work harmful to their morals or health or dangerous to life or likely to hamper their normal development should be punishable by law. States should also set age limits below which the paid employment of child labour should be prohibited and punishable by law.

ARTICLE 11

1. The States Parties to the present Covenant recognize the right of everyone to an adequate standard of living for himself and his family, including adequate food, clothing and housing, and to the continuous improvement of living conditions. The States Parties will take appropriate steps to ensure the realization of this right, recognizing to this effect the essential importance of international cooperation based on free consent.

2. The States Parties to the present Covenant, recognizing the fundamental right of everyone to be free from hunger, shall take,

individually and through international cooperation, the measures, including specific programmes, which are needed:

(a) To improve methods of production, conservation and distribution of food by making full use of technical and scientific knowledge, by disseminating knowledge of the principles of nutrition and by developing or reforming agrarian systems in such a way as to achieve the most efficient development and utilization of natural resources;

(b) Taking into account the problems of both food-importing and food-exporting countries, to ensure an equitable distribution of world food supplies in relation to need.

ARTICLE 12

1. The States Parties to the present Covenant recognize the right of everyone to the enjoyment of the highest attainable standard of physical and mental health.

2. The steps to be taken by the States Parties to the present Covenant to achieve the full realization of this right shall include those necessary for :

(a) The provision for the reduction of the stillbirth rate and of infant mortality and for the healthy development of the child;

(b) The improvement of all aspects of environmental and industrial hygiene;

(c) The prevention, treatment and control of epidemic, endemic, occupational and other diseases;

(d) The creation of conditions which would assure to all medical service and medical attention in the event of sickness.

ARTICLE 13

1. The States Parties to the present Covenant recognize the right of everyone to education. They agree that education shall be directed to the full development of the human personality and the sense of its dignity, and shall strengthen the respect for human rights and fundamental freedoms. They further agree that education shall enable all persons to participate effectively in a free society, promote understanding, tolerance and friendship among all nations and all racial, ethnic or religious groups, and further the activities of the United Nations for the maintenance of peace.

2. The States Parties to the present Covenant recognize that, with a view to achieving the full realization of this right:

(a) Primary education shall be compulsory and available free to all;

(b) Secondary education in its different forms, including technical and vocational secondary education, shall be made generally available and accessible to all by every appropriate means, and in particular by the progressive introduction of free education;

(c) Higher education shall be made equally accessible to all, on the basis of capacity, by every appropriate means, and in particular by the progressive introduction of free education;

(d) Fundamental education shall be encouraged or intensified as far as possible for those persons who have not received or completed the whole period of their primary education;

(e) The development of a system of schools at all levels shall be actively pursued, an adequate fellowship system shall be established, and the material conditions of teaching staff shall be continuously improved.

3. The States Parties to the present Covenant undertake to have respect for the liberty of parents and, when applicable, legal guardians to choose for their children schools, other than those established by the public authorities, which conform to such minimum educational standards as may be laid down or approved by the State and to ensure the religious and moral education of their children in conformity with their own convictions.

4. No part of this article shall be construed so as to interfere with the liberty of individuals and bodies to establish and direct educational institutions, subject always to the observance of the principles set forth in paragraph 1 of this article and to the requirement that the education given in such institutions shall conform to such minimum standards as may be laid down by the State.

ARTICLE 14

Each State Party to the present Covenant which, at the time of becoming a Party, has not been able to secure in its metropolitan territory or other territories under jurisdiction compulsory primary education, free of charge, undertakes, within two years, to work out and adopt a detailed plan of action for the progressive implementation, within a reasonable number of years, to be fixed in the plan, of the principle of compulsory education free of charge for all.

ARTICLE 15

1. The States Parties to the present Covenant recognize the right of everyone:

(a) To take part in cultural life;

(b) To enjoy the benefits of scientific progress and its applications;

(c) To benefit from the protection of the moral and material interests resulting from any scientific, literary or artistic production of which he is the author.

2. The steps to be taken by the States Parties to the present Covenant to achieve the full realisation of this right shall include those necessary for the conservation, the development and the diffusion of science and culture.

3. The States Parties to the present Covenant undertake to respect the freedom indispensable for scientific research and creative activity.

4. The States Parties to the present Covenant recognize the benefits to be derived from the encouragement and development of international contacts and cooperation in the scientific and cultural fields.

Part IV

ARTICLE 16

1. The States Parties to the present Covenant undertake to submit in conformity with this part of the Covenant reports on the measures which they have adopted and the progress made in achieving the observance of the rights recognized herein.

2. (a) All reports shall be submitted to the Secretary-General of the United Nations, who shall transmit copies to the Economic and Social Council for consideration in accordance with the provisions of the present Covenant;

(b) The Secretary-General of the United Nations shall also transmit to the specialized agencies copies of the reports, or any relevant parts therefrom, from States Parties to the present Covenant which are also members of these specialized agencies in so far as these reports, or parts therefrom, relate to any matters which fall within the responsibilities of the said agencies in accordance with their constitutional instruments.

ARTICLE 17

1. The States Parties to the present Covenant shall furnish their reports in stages, in accordance with a programme to be established by the Economic and Social Council within one year of the entry into force of the present Covenant after consultation with the States Parties and the specialized agencies concerned.

2. Reports may indicate factors and difficulties affecting the degree of fulfilment of obligations under the present Covenant.

3. Where relevant information has previously been furnished to the United Nations or to any specialized agency by any State Party to the present Covenant, it will not be necessary to reproduce that information, but a precise reference to the information so furnished will suffice.

ARTICLE 18

Pursuant to its responsibilities under the Charter of the United Nations in the field of human rights and fundamental freedoms, the Economic and Social Council may make arrangements with the specialized agencies in respect of their reporting to it on the progress made in achieving the observance of the provisions of the present Covenant falling within the scope of their activities. These reports may include particulars of decisions and recommendations on such implementation adopted by their competent organs.

ARTICLE 19

The Economic and Social Council may transmit to the Commission on Human Rights for study and general recommendation or, as appropriate, for information the reports concerning human rights submitted by States in accordance with articles 16 and 17, and those concerning human rights submitted by the specialized agencies in accordance with article 18.

ARTICLE 20

The States Parties to the present Covenant and the specialised agencies concerned may submit comments to the Economic and Social Council on any general recommendation under article 19 or reference to such general recommendation in any report of the Commission on Human Rights or any documentation referred to therein.

ARTICLE 21

The Economic and Social Council may submit from time to time to the General Assembly reports with recommendations of a general nature and a summary of the information received from the States Parties to the present Covenant and the specialized agencies on the measures taken and the progress made in achieving general observance of the rights recognized in the present Covenant.

ARTICLE 22

The Economic and Social Council may bring to the attention of other organs of the United Nations, their subsidiary organs and specialized agencies concerned with furnishing technical assistance any matters arising out of the reports referred to in this part of the present Covenant which may assist such bodies in deciding, each within its field of competence, on the advisability of international measures likely to contribute to the effective progressive implementation of the present Covenant.

ARTICLE 23

The States Parties to the present Covenant agree that international action for the achievement of the rights recognized in the present Covenant includes such methods as the conclusion of conventions, the adoption of recommendations, the furnishing of technical assistance and the holding of regional meetings and technical meetings for the purpose of consultation and study organized in conjunction with the Governments concerned.

ARTICLE 24

Nothing in the present Covenant shall be interpreted as impairing the provisions of the Charter of the United Nations and of the constitutions of the specialized agencies which define the respective responsibilities of the various organs of the United Nations and of the specialized agencies in regard to the matters dealt with in the present Covenant.

ARTICLE 25

Nothing in the present Covenant shall be interpreted as impairing the inherent right of all peoples to enjoy and utilize fully and freely their natural wealth and resources.

Part V

ARTICLE 26

1. The present Covenant is open for signature by any State Member of the United Nations or member of any of its specialized agencies, by any State Party to the Statute of the International Court of Justice and by any other State which has been invited by the General Assembly of the United Nations to become a party to the present Covenant.

2. The present Covenant is subject to ratification. Instruments of ratification shall be deposited with the Secretary-General of the United Nations.

3. The present Covenant shall be open to accession by any State referred to in paragraph 1 of this article.

4. Accession shall be effected by the deposit of an instrument of accession with the Secretary-General of the United Nations.

5. The Secretary-General of the United Nations shall inform all States which have signed the present Covenant or acceded to it of the deposit of each instrument of ratification or accession.

ARTICLE 27

1. The present Covenant shall enter into force three months after the date of the deposit with the Secretary-General of the United Nations of the thirty-fifth instrument of ratification or instrument of accession.

2. For each State ratifying the present Covenant or acceding to it after the deposit of the thirty-fifth instrument of ratification or instrument of accession, the present Covenant shall enter into force three months after the date of the deposit of its own instrument of ratification or instrument of accession.

ARTICLE 28

The provisions of the present Covenant shall extend to all parts of federal States without any limitations or exceptions.

ARTICLE 29

1. Any State Party to the present Covenant may propose an amendment and file it with the Secretary-General of the United Nations. The Secretary-General shall thereupon communicate any

proposed amendments to the States Parties to the present Convenant with a request that they notify him whether they favour a conference of States Parties for the purpose of considering and voting upon the proposals. In the event that at least one–third of the States Parties favours such a conference, the Secretary-General shall convene the conference under the auspices of the United Nations. Any amendment adopted by a majority of the States Parties present and voting at the conference shall be submitted to the General Assembly of the United Nations for approval.

2. Amendments shall come into force when they have been approved by the General Assembly of the United Nations and accepted by a two-thirds majority of the States Parties to the present Covenant in accordance with their respective constitutional processes.

3. When amendments come into force they shall be binding on those States Parties which have accepted them, other States Parties still being bound by the provisions of the present Covenant and any earlier amendment which they have accepted.

ARTICLE 30

Irrespective of the notifications made under article 26, paragraph 5, the Secretary-General of the United Nations shall inform all States referred to in paragraph 1 of the same article of the following particulars:

(a) Signatures, ratifications and accessions under article 26;

(b) The date of the entry into force of the present Covenant under article 27 and the date of the entry into force of any amendments under article 29.

ARTICLE 31

1. The present Covenant, of which the Chinese, English, French, Russian and Spanish texts are equally authentic, shall be deposited in the archives of the United Nations.

2. The Secretary-General of the United Nations shall transmit certified copies of the present Covenant to all States referred to in article 26.

APPENDIX III

International Covenant on Economic, Social and Cultural Rights

Preamble

THE STATES PARTIES TO THE PRESENT COVENANT,

Considering that, in accordance with the principles proclaimed in the Charter of the United Nations, recognition of the inherent dignity and of the equal and inalienable rights of all members of the human family is the foundation of freedom, justice and peace in the world,

Recognizing that these rights derive from the inherent dignity of the human person,

Recognizing that, in accordance with the Universal Declaration of Human Rights, the ideal of free human beings enjoying freedom from fear and want can only be achieved if conditions are created whereby everyone may enjoy his economic, social and cultural rights, as well as his civil and political rights,

Considering the obligation of States under the Charter of the United Nations to promote universal respect for, and observance of, human rights and freedoms,

Realizing that the individual, having duties to other individuals and to the community to which he belongs, is under a responsibility to strive for the promotion and observance of the rights recognized in the present Covenant,

Agree upon the following articles:

Part I

ARTICLE 1

1. All peoples have the right of self-determination. By virtue of

having responsibility for the administration of Non-Self Governing and Trust Territories, shall promote the realization of the right of self-determination, and shall respect that right, in conformity with the provisions of the Charter of the United Nations.

Part II

ARTICLE 2

1. Each State Party to the present Covenant undertakes to respect and to ensure to all individuals within its territory and subject to its jurisdiction the rights recognized in the present Covenant, without distinction of any kind, such as race, colour, sex, language, religion, political or other opinion, national or social origin, property, birth or other status.

2. Where not already provided for by existing legislative or other measures, each State Party to the present Covenant undertakes to take the necessary steps, in accordance with its constitutional processes and with the provisions of the present Covenant, to adopt such legislative or other measures as may be necessary to give effect to the rights recognized in the present Covenant.

3. Each State Party to the present Covenant undertakes:

(a) To ensure that any person whose rights or freedoms as herein recognized are violated shall have an effective remedy, notwithstanding that the violation has been committed by persons acting in an official capacity;

(b) To ensure that any person claiming such a remedy shall have his right thereto determined by competent judicial, administrative or legislative authorities, or by any other competent authority provided for by the legal system of the State, and to develop the possibilities of judicial remedy;

(c) To ensure that the competent authorities shall enforce such remedies when granted.

ARTICLE 3

The States Parties to the present Covenant undertake to ensure the equal right of men and women to the enjoyment of all civil and political rights set forth in the present Covenant.

ARTICLE 4

1. In time of public emergency which threatens the life of the

nation and the existence of which is officially proclaimed, the States Parties to the present Covenant may take measures derogating from their obligations under the present Covenant to the extent strictly required by the exigencies of the situation, provided that such measures are not inconsistent with their other obligations under international law and do not involve discrimination solely on the ground of race, colour, sex, language, religion or social origin.

2. No derogation from articles 6, 7, 8 (paragraphs 1 and 2), 11, 15, 16 and 18 may be made under this provision.

3. Any State Party to the present Covenant availing itself of the right of derogation shall immediately inform the other States Parties to the present Covenant, through the intermediary of the Secretary-General of the United Nations, of the provisions from which it has derogated and of the reasons by which it was actuated. A further communication shall be made, through the same intermediary, on the date on which it terminates such derogation.

ARTICLE 5

1. Nothing in the present Covenant may be interpreted as implying for any State, group or person any right to engage in any activity or perform any act aimed at the destruction of any of the rights and freedoms recognized herein or at their limitation to a greater extent than is provided for in the present Covenant.

2. There shall be no restriction upon or derogation from any of the fundamental human rights recognized or existing in any State Party to the present Covenant pursuant to law, conventions, regulations or custom on the pretext that the present Covenant does not recognize such rights or that it recognizes them to a lesser extent.

Part III

ARTICLE 6

1. Every human being has the inherent right to life. This right shall be protected by law. No one shall be arbitrarily deprived of his life.

2. In countries which have not abolished the death penalty, sentence of death may be imposed only for the most serious crimes in accordance with the law in force at the time of the commission of the crime and not contrary to the provisions of the present Covenant and to the Convention on the Prevention and Punishment of the Crime of

Genocide. This penalty can only be carried out pursuant to a final judgement rendered by a competent court.

3. When deprivation of life constitutes the crime of genocide, it is understood that nothing in this article shall authorize any State Party to the present Covenant to derogate in any way from any obligation and Punishment of the Crime of Genocide.

4. Anyone sentenced to death shall have the right to seek pardon or commutation of the sentence. Amnesty, pardon or commutation of the sentence of death may be granted in all cases.

5. Sentence of death shall not be imposed for crimes committed by persons below eighteen years of age and shall not be carried out on pregnant women.

6. Nothing in this article shall be invoked to delay or to prevent the abolition of capital punishment by any State Party to the present Covenant.

ARTICLE 7

No one shall be subjected to torture or to cruel, inhuman or degrading treatment or punishment. In particular, no one shall be subjected without his free consent to medical or scientific experimentation.

ARTICLE 8

1. No one shall be held in slavery; slavery and the slave-trade in all their forms shall be prohibited.

2. No one shall be held in servitude.

3. (a) No one shall be required to perform forced or compulsory labour;

(b) Paragraph 3(a) shall not be held to preclude, in countries where imprisonment with hard labour may be imposed as a punishment for a crime, the performance of hard labour in pursuance of a sentence to such punishment by a competent court;

(c) For the purpose of this paragraph the term "forced or compulsory labour" shall not include:

(i) Any work or service, not referred to in subparagraph

(b) normally required of a person who is under detention in consequence of a lawful order of a court, or of a person during conditional release from such detention;

(ii) Any service of a military character and, in countries where conscientious objection is recognized, any national service required by law of conscientious objectors;

(iii) Any service exacted in cases of emergency or calamity threatening the life or well being of the community;

(iv) Any work or service which forms part of normal civil obligations.

ARTICLE 9

1. Everyone has the right to liberty and security of person. No one shall be subjected to arbitrary arrest or detention. No one shall be deprived of his liberty except on such grounds and in accordance with such procedure as are established by law.

2. Anyone who is arrested shall be informed, at the time of arrest, of the reasons for his arrest and shall be promptly informed of any charges against him.

3. Any one arrested or detained on a criminal charge shall be brought promptly before a judge or other officer authorized by law to exercise judicial power and shall be entitled to trial within a reasonable time or to release. It shall not be the general rule that persons awaiting trial shall be detained in custody, but release may be subject to guarantees to appear for trial, at any other stage of the judicial proceedings, and, should occasion arise, for execution of the judgement.

4. Anyone who is deprived of his liberty by arrest or detention shall be entitled to take proceedings before a court, in order that court may decide without delay on the lawfulness of his detention and order his release if the detention is not lawful.

5. Anyone who has been the victim of unlawful arrest or detention shall have an enforceable right to compensation.

ARTICLE 10

1. All persons deprived of their liberty shall be treated with humanity and with respect for the inherent dignity of the human person.

2. (a) Accused persons shall, save in exceptional circumstances, be segregated from convicted persons and shall be subject to separate treatment appropriate to their status as unconvicted persons;

(b) Accused juvenile persons shall be separated from adults and brought as speedily as possible for adjudication.

3. The penitentiary system shall comprise treatment of prisoners the essential aim of which shall be their reformation and social rehabilitation. Juvenile offenders shall be segregated from adults and be accorded treatment appropriate to their age and legal status.

ARTICLE 11

No one shall be imprisoned merely on the ground of inability to fulfill a contractual obligation.

ARTICLE 12

1. Everyone lawfully within the territory of a State shall, within that territory, have the right to liberty of movement and freedom to choose his residence.

2. Everyone shall be free to leave any country, including his own.

3. The above–mentioned rights shall not be subject to any restrictions except those which are provided by law, are necessary to protect national security, public order (*ordre public*), public health or morals or the rights and freedoms of others, and are consistent with the other rights recognized in the present Covenant.

4. No one shall be arbitrarily deprived of the right to enter his own country.

ARTICLE 13

An alien lawfully in the territory of a State Party to the present Covenant may be expelled therefrom only in pursuance of a decision reached in accordance with law and shall, except where compelling reasons of national security otherwise require, be allowed to submit the reasons against his expulsion and to have his case reviewed by, and be represented for the purpose before, the competent authority or a person or persons especially designated by the competent authority.

ARTICLE 14

1. All persons shall be equal before the courts and tribunals. In the determination of any criminal charge against him, or of his rights and obligations in a suit at law, everyone shall be entitled to a fair and public hearing by a competent, independent and impartial tribunal established by law. The Press and the public may be excluded from all or part of a trial for reasons, morals, public order (*ordre public*) or national security in a democratic society, or when the interest of the

private lives of the parties so requires, or to the extent strictly necessary in the opinion of the court in special circumstances where publicity would prejudice the interests of justice; but any judgement rendered in a criminal case or in a suit at law shall be made public except where the interest of juvenile persons otherwise requires or the proceedings concern matrimonial disputes or the guardianship of children.

2. Everyone charged with a criminal offence shall have the right to be presumed innocent until proved guilty according to law.

3. In the determination of any criminal charge against him, everyone shall be entitled to the following minimum guarantees, in full equality:

(a) To be informed promptly and in detail in a language which he understands of the nature and cause of the charge against him;

(b) To have adequate time and facilities for the preparation of his defence and to communicate with counsel of his own choosing;

(c) To be tried without undue delay;

(d) To be tried in his presence, and to defend himself in person or through legal assistance of his own choosing; to be informed, if he does not have legal assistance, of this right; and to have legal assistance assigned to him, in any case where the interests of justice so require, and without payment by him in any such case if he does not have sufficient means to pay for it;

(e) To examine, or have examined, the witnesses against him and to obtain the attendance and examination of witnesses on his behalf under the same conditions as witnesses against him;

(f) To have the free assistance of an interpreter if he cannot understand or speak the language used in court;

(g) Not to be compelled to testify against himself or to confess guilt.

4. In the case of juvenile persons, the procedure shall be such as will take account of their age and the desirability of promoting their rehabilitation.

5. Everyone convicted of a crime shall have the right to his conviction and sentence being reviewed by a higher tribunal according to law.

6. When a person has by a final decision been convicted of a

criminal offence and when subsequently his conviction has been reversed or he has been pardoned on the ground that a new or newly discovered fact shows conclusively that there has been a miscarriage of justice, the person who has suffered punishment as a result of such conviction shall be compensated according to law, unless it is proved that the non-disclosure of the unknown fact in time is wholly or partly attributable to him.

7. No one shall be liable to be tried or punished again for an offence for which he has already been finally convicted or acquitted in accordance with the law and penal procedure of each country.

ARTICLE 15

1. No one shall be held guilty of any criminal offence on account of any act or omission which did not constitute a criminal offence, under national or international law, at the time when it was committed. Nor shall a heavier penalty be imposed than the one that was applicable at the time when the criminal offence was committed. If subsequent to the commission of the offence, provision is made by law for the imposition of a lighter penalty, the offender shall benefit thereby.

2. Nothing in this article shall prejudice the trial and punishment of any person for any act or omission which, at the time when it was committed, was criminal according to the general principles of law recognised by the community of nations.

ARTICLE 16

Everyone shall have the right to recognition everywhere as a person before the law.

ARTICLE 17

1. No one shall be subjected to arbitrary or unlawful interference with his privacy, family, home or correspondence, nor to unlawful attacks on his honour and reputation.

2. Everyone has the right to the protection of the law against such interference or attacks.

ARTICLE 18

1. Everyone shall have the right to freedom of thought, conscience and religion. This right shall include freedom to have or to adopt a religion or belief of his choice, and freedom, either individually or in

community with others and in public or private, to manifest his religion or belief in worship, observance, practice and teaching.

2. No one shall be subject to coercion which would impair his freedom to have or to adopt a religion or belief of his choice.

3. Freedom to manifest one's religion or beliefs may be subject only to such limitations as are prescribed by law and are necessary to protect public safety order, health, or morals or the fundamental rights and freedoms of others.

4. The State Parties to the present Covenant undertake to have respect for the liberty of parents and, when applicable, legal guardians to ensure the religious and moral education of their children in conformity with their own convictions.

ARTICLE 19

1. Everyone shall have the right to hold opinions without interference.

2. Everyone shall have the right to freedom of expression; this right shall include freedom to seek, receive and impart information and ideas of all kinds, regardless of frontiers, either orally, in writing or in print, in the form of art, or through any other media of his choice.

3. The exercise of the rights provided for in paragraph 2 of this article carries with it special duties and responsibilities. It may therefore be subject to certain restrictions, but these shall only be such as are provided by law and are necessary:

(a) For respect of the rights or reputations of others;

(b) For the protection of national security or of public order (*ordre public*) or of public health or morals.

ARTICLE 20

1. Any propaganda for war shall be prohibited by law.

2. Any advocacy of national, racial or religious hatred that constitutes incitement to discrimination, hostility or violence shall be prohibited by law.

ARTICLE 21

The right of peaceful assembly shall be recognized. No restrictions may be placed on the exercise of this right other than those imposed in conformity with the law and which are necessary in a democratic society in the interests of national security or public safety, public order (*ordre public*), the protection of public health or morals or the protection of the rights and freedom of others.

ARTICLE 22

1. Everyone shall have the right to freedom of association with others, including the right to form and join trade unions for the protection of his interests.

2. No restrictions may be placed on the exercise of this right other than those which are prescribed by law and which are necessary in a democratic society in the interests of national security or public safety, public order (*ordre public*), the protection of public health or morals or the protection of the rights and freedoms of others. This article shall not prevent the imposition of lawful restrictions on members of the armed forces and of the police in their exercise of this right.

3. Nothing in this article shall authorize States Parties to the International Labour Organisation Convention of 1948 concerning Freedom of Association and Protection of the Right to Organise to take legislative measures which would prejudice, or to apply the law in such a manner as to prejudice, the guarantees provided for in that Convention.

ARTICLE 23

1. The family is the natural and fundamental group unit of society and is entitled to protection by society and the State.

2. The right of men and women of marriageable age to marry and to found a family shall be recognized.

3. No marriage shall be entered into without the free and full consent of the intending spouses.

4. States Parties to the present Covenant shall take appropriate steps to ensure equality of rights and responsibilities of spouses as to marriage, during marriage and at its dissolution. In the case of dissolution, provision shall be made for the necessary protection of any children.

ARTICLE 24

1. Every child shall have, without any discrimination as to race, colour, sex, language, religion, national or social origin, property or birth, the right to such measures of protection as are required by his status as a minor, on the part of his family, society and the State.

2. Every child shall be registered immediately after birth and shall have a name.

3. Every child has the right to acquire a nationality.

ARTICLE 25

Every citizen shall have the right and the opportunity, without any of the distinctions mentioned in article 2 and without unreasonable restrictions:

(a) To take part in the conduct of public affairs, directly or through freely chosen representatives;

(b) To vote and to be elected at genuine periodic elections which shall be by universal and equal suffrage and shall be held by secret ballot, guaranteeing the free expression of the will of the electors;

(c) To have access, on general terms of equality, to public service in his country.

ARTICLE 26

All persons are equal before the law and are entitled without any discrimination to the equal protection of the law. In this respect, the law shall prohibit any discrimination and guarantee to all persons equal and effective protection against discrimination on any ground such as race, colour, sex, language, religion, political or other opinion, national or social origin, property, birth or other status.

ARTICLE 27

In those States in which ethnic, religious or linguistic minorities exist, persons belonging to such minorities shall not be denied the right, in community with the other members of their group, to enjoy their own culture, to profess and practise their own religion, or to use their own language.

Part IV

ARTICLE 28

1. There shall be established a Human Rights Committee (hereafter referred to in the present Covenant as the Committee). It shall consist of eighteen members and shall carry out the functions hereinafter provided.

2. The Committee shall be composed of nationals of the States Parties to the present Covenant who shall be persons of high moral

character and recognized competence in the field of human rights, consideration being given to the usefulness of the participation of some persons having legal experience.

3. The members of the Committee shall be elected and shall serve in their personal capacity.

ARTICLE 29

1. The members of the Committee shall be elected by secret ballot from a list of persons possessing the qualifications prescribed in article 28 and nominated for the purpose by the States Parties to the present Covenant.

2. Each State Party to the present Covenant may nominate not more than two persons. These persons shall be nationals of the nominating State.

3. A person shall be eligible for renomination.

ARTICLE 30

1. The initial election shall be held no later than six months after the date of the entry into force of the present Covenant.

2. At least four months before the date of each election to the Committee, other than an election to fill a vacancy declared in accordance with article 34, the Secretary-General of the United Nations shall address a written invitation to the States Parties to the present Covenant to submit their nominations for membership of the Committee within three months.

3. The Secretary-General of the United Nations shall prepare a list in alphabetical order of all the persons thus nominated, with an indication of the States Parties which have nominated them, and shall submit it to the States Parties to the present Covenant no later than one month before the date of each election.

4. Elections of the members of the Committee shall be held at a meeting of the States Parties to the present Covenant convened by the Secretary–General of the United Nations at the Headquarters of the United Nations. At that meeting, for which two–thirds of the States Parties to the present Covenant shall constitute a quorum, the persons elected to the Committee shall be those nominees who obtain the largest number of votes and an absolute majority of the votes of the representatives of States Parties present and voting.

ARTICLE 31

1. The Committee may not include more than one national of the same State.

2. In the election of the Committee, consideration shall be given to equitable geographical distribution of membership and to the representation of the different forms of civilization and of the principal legal systems.

ARTICLE 32

1. The members of the Committee shall be elected for a term of four years. They shall be eligible for re-election if renominated. However, the terms of nine of the members elected at the first election shall expire at the end of two years; immediately after the first election, the names of these nine members shall be chosen by lot by the Chairman of the meeting referred to in article 30, paragraph 4.

2. Elections at the expiry of office shall be held in accordance with the preceding articles of this part of the present Covenant.

ARTICLE 33

1. If, in the unanimous opinion of the other members, a member of the Committee has ceased to carry out his functions for any cause other than absence of a temporary character, the Chairman of the Committee shall notify the Secretary–General of the United Nations, who shall then declare the seat of that member to be vacant.

2. In the event of the death or the resignation of a member of the Committee, the Chairman shall immediately notify the Secretary-General of the United Nations, who shall declare the seat vacant from the date of death or the date on which the resignation takes effect.

ARTICLE 34

1. When a vacancy is declared in accordance with article 33 and if the term of office of the member to be replaced does not expire within six months of the declaration of the vacancy, the Secretary-General of the United Nations shall notify each of the States Parties to the present Covenant, which may within two months submit nominations in accordance with article 29 for the purpose of filling the vacancy.

2. The Secretary-General of the United Nations shall prepare a list

in alphabetical order of the persons thus nominated and shall submit it to the States Parties to the present Covenant. The election to fill the vacancy shall then take place in accordance with the relevant provisions of this part of the present Covenant.

3. A member of the Committee elected to fill a vacancy declared in accordance with article 33 shall hold office for the remainder of the term of the member who vacated the seat on the Committee under the provisions of that article.

ARTICLE 35

The members of the Committee shall, with the approval of the General Assembly of the United Nations, receive emoluments from United Nations resources on such terms and conditions as the General Assembly may decide, having regard to the importance of the Committee's responsibilities.

ARTICLE 36

The Secretary-General of the United Nations shall provide the necessary staff and facilities for the effective performance of the functions of the Committee under the present Covenant.

ARTICLE 37

1. The Secretary-General of the United Nations shall convene the initial meeting of the Committee at the Headquarters of the United Nations.

2. After its initial meeting, the Committee shall meet at such times as shall be provided in its rules of procedure.

3. The Committee shall normally meet at the Headquarters of the United Nations or at the United Nations Office at Geneva.

ARTICLE 38

Every member of the Committee shall, before taking up his duties, make a solemn declaration in open committee that he will perform his functions impartially and conscientiously.

ARTICLE 39

1. The Committee shall elect its officers for a term of two years. They may be reelected.

2. The Committee shall establish its own rules of procedure, but these rules shall provide, inter alia, that:

(a) Twelve members shall constitute a quorum;

(b) Decisions of the Committee shall be made by a majority vote of the members present.

ARTICLE 40

1. The States Parties to the present Covenant undertake to submit reports on the measures they have adopted which give effect to the rights recognized herein and on the progress made in the enjoyment of those rights:

(a) Within one year of the entry into force of the present Covenant for the States Parties concerned;

(b) Thereafter whenever the Committee so requests.

2. All reports shall be submitted to the Secretary–General of the United Nations, who shall transmit them to the Committee for consideration. Reports shall indicate the factors and difficulties, if any, affecting the implementation of the present Covenant.

3. The Secretary–General of the United Nations may, after consultation with the Committee, transmit to the specialized agencies concerned copies of such parts of the reports as may fall within their field of competence.

4. The Committee shall study the reports submitted by the States Parties to the present Covenant. It shall transmit its reports, and such general comments as it may consider appropriate, to the States Parties. The Committee may also transmit to the Economic and Social Council these comments along with the copies of the reports it has received from States Parties to the present Covenant.

5. The States Parties to the present Covenant may submit to the Committee observations on any comments that may be made in accordance with paragraph 4 of this article.

ARTICLE 41

1. A State Party to the present Covenant may at any time declare under this article that it recognizes the competence of the Committee to receive and consider communications to the effect that a State Party claims that another State Party is not fulfilling its obligations under the present Covenant. Communications under this article may be received and considered only if submitted by a State Party which has made a declaration recognizing in regard to itself the competence of

the Committee. No communication shall be received by the Committee if it concerns a State Party which has not made such a declaration. Communications received under this article shall be dealt with in accordance with the following procedure:

(a) If a State Party to the present Covenant considers that another State Party is not giving effect to the provisions of the present Covenant, it may, by written communication, bring the matter to the attention of that State Party. Within three months after the receipt of the communication, the receiving State shall afford the State which sent the communication an explanation or any other statement in writing clarifying the matter, which should include, to the extent possible and pertinent, reference to domestic procedures and remedies taken, pending, or available in the matter.

(b) If the matter is not adjusted to the satisfaction of both States Parties concerned within six months after the receipt by the receiving State of the initial communication, either State shall have the right to refer the matter to the Committee, by notice given to the Committee and to the other State.

(c) The Committee shall deal with a matter referred to it only after it has ascertained that all available domestic remedies have been invoked and exhausted in the matter, in conformity with the generally recognized principles of international law. This shall not be the rule where the application of the remedies is unreasonably prolonged.

(d) The Committee shall hold closed meetings when examining communications under this article.

(e) Subject to the provisions of subparagraph (c), the Committee shall make available its good offices to the States Parties concerned with a view to a friendly solution of the matter on the basis of respect for human rights and fundamental freedoms as recognized in the present Covenant.

(f) In any matter referred to it, the Committee may call upon the States Parties concerned, referred to in subparagraph (b), to supply any relevant information.

(g) The States Parties concerned, referred to in subparagraph (b), shall have the right to be represented when the matter is being considered in the Committee and to make submissions orally and/or in writing.

(h) The Committee shall, within twelve months after the date of receipt of notice under subparagraph (b), submit a report:

(i) If a solution within the terms of subparagraph (e) is reached, the Committee shall confine its report to a brief statement of the facts and of the solution reached;

(ii) If a solution within the terms of subparagraph (e) is not reached, the Committee shall confine its report to a brief statement of the facts; the written submissions and record of the oral submissions made by the States Parties concerned shall be attached to the report.

In every matter, the report shall be communicated to the States Parties concerned.

2. The provisions of this articles shall come into force when ten States Parties to the present Covenant have made declarations under paragraph 1 of this article. Such declarations shall be deposited by the States Parties with the Secretary-General of the United Nations, who shall transmit copies thereof to the other States Parties. A declaration may be withdrawn at any time by notification to the Secretary-General. Such a withdrawal shall not prejudice the consideration of any matter which is the subject of a communication already transmitted under this article; no further communication by any State Party shall be received after the notification of withdrawal of the declaration has been received by the Secretary-General, unless the State Party concerned has made a new declaration.

ARTICLE 42

1. (a) If a matter referred to the Committee in accordance with article 41 is not resolved in the satisfaction of the States Parties concerned, the Committee may, with the prior consent of the States Parties concerned, appoint an *ad* hoc Conciliation Commission (hereinafter referred to as the Commission). The good offices of the Commission shall be made available to the States Parties concerned with a view to an amicable solution of the matter on the basis of respect for the present Covenant;

(b) The Commission shall consist of five persons acceptable to the States Parties concerned. If the States Parties concerned fail to reach agreement within three months on all or part of the composition of the Commission, the members of the Commission concerning whom no agreement has been reached shall be elected by secret ballot by a two-thirds majority vote of the Committee from among its members.

2. The members of the Commission shall serve in their personal capacity. They shall not be nationals of the States Parties concerned, or of a State not party to the present Covenant, or of a State Party which has not made a declaration under article 41.

3. The Commission shall elect its own Chairman and adopt its own rules of procedure.

4. The meetings of the Commission shall normally be held at the Headquarters of the United Nations or at the United Nations Office at Geneva. However, they may be held at such other convenient places as the Commission may determine in consultation with the Secretary-General of the United Nations and the States Parties concerned.

5. The secretariat provided in accordance with article 36 shall also service the commissions appointed under this article.

6. The information received and collected by the Committe shall be made available to the Commission and the Commission may call upon the States Parties concerned to supply any other relevant information.

7. When the Commission has fully considered the matter, but in any event no later than twelve months after having been seized of the matter, it shall submit to the Chairman of the Committee a report for communication to the States Parties concerned:

(a) If the Commission is unable to complete its consideration of the matter within twelve months, it shall confine its report to a brief statement of the status of its consideration of the matter;

(b) If an amicable solution to the matter on the basis of respect for human rights as recognized in the present Covenant is reached, the Commission shall confine its report to a brief statement of the facts and of the solution reached;

(c) If a solution within the terms of subparagraph (b) is not reached, the Commission's report shall embody its findings on all questions of fact relevant to the issues between the States Parties concerned, and its views on the possibilities of an amicable solution of the matter. This report shall also contain the written submissions and a record of the oral submissions made by the States Parties concerned;

(d) If the Commission's report is submitted under subparagraph (c), the States Parties concerned shall, within three months of the receipt of the report, notify the Chairman of the Committee whether or not they accept the contents of the report of the Commission.

8. The provisions of this article are without prejudice to the responsibilities of the Committee under article 41.

9. The States Parties concerned shall share equally all the expenses of the members of the Commission in accordance with estimates to be provided by the Secretary-General of the United Nations.

10. The Secretary-General of the United Nations shall be empowered to pay the expenses of the members of the Commission, if necessary, before reimbursement by the States Parties concerned, in accordance with paragraph 9 of this article.

ARTICLE 43

The members of the Committee, and of the *ad hoc* conciliation commissions which may be appointed under article 42, shall be entitled to the facilities, privileges and immunities of experts on mission for the United Nations as laid down in the relevant sections of the Convention on the Privileges and Immunities of the United Nations.

ARTICLE 44

The provisions for the implementation of the present Covenant shall apply without prejudice to the procedures prescribed in the field of human rights by or under the constituent instruments and the conventions of the United Nations and of the specialized agencies and shall not present the States Parties to the present Covenant from having recourse to other procedures for settling a dispute in accordance with general or special international agreements in force between them.

ARTICLE 45

The Committee shall submit to the General Assembly of the United Nations, through the Economic and Social Council, an annual report on its activities.

Part V

ARTICLE 46

Nothing in the present Covenant shall be interpreted as impairing the provisions of the Charter of the United Nations and of the constitutions of the specialized agencies which define the respective responsibilities of the various organs of the United Nations and of the specialized agencies in regard to the matters dealt with in the present Covenant.

ARTICLE 47

Nothing in the present Covenant shall be interpreted as impairing the inherent right of all peoples to enjoy and utilize fully and freely their natural wealth and resources.

Part VI

ARTICLE 48

1. The present Covenant is open for signature by any State Member of the United Nations or member of any of its specialized agencies, by any State Party to the Statute of the International Court of Justice, and by any other State which has been invited by the General Assembly of the United Nations to become a party to the present Covenant.

2. The present Covenant is subject to ratification. Instruments of ratification shall be deposited with the Secretary-General of the United Nations.

3. The present Covenant shall be open to accession by any State referred to in paragraph 1 of this article.

4. Accession shall be effected by the deposit of an instrument of accession with the Secretary-General of the United Nations.

5. The Secretary-General of the United Nations shall inform all States which have signed this Covenant or acceded to it of the deposit of each instrument of ratification or accession.

ARTICLE 49

1. The present Covenant shall enter into force three months after the date of the deposit with the Secretary-General of the United Nations of the thirty-fifth instrument of ratification or instrument of accession.

2. For each State ratifying the present Covenant or acceding to it after the deposit of the thirty-fifth instrument of ratification or instrument of accession, the present Covenant shall enter into force three months after the date of the deposit of its own instrument of ratification or instrument of accession.

ARTICLE 50

The provisions of the present Covenant shall extend to all parts of federal States without any limitations or exceptions.

ARTICLE 51

1. Any State Party to the present Covenant may propose an amendment and file it with the Secretary-General of the United Nations. The Secretary-General of the United Nations shall thereupon communicate any proposed amendments to the States Parties to the present Covenant with a request that they notify him whether they favour a conference of States Parties for the purpose of considering and voting upon the proposals. In the event that at least one–third of the States Parties favours such a conference, the Secretary-General shall convene the conference under the auspices of the United Nations. Any amendment adopted by a majority of the States Parties present and voting at the conference shall be submitted to the General Assembly of the United Nations for approval.

2. Amendments shall come into force when they have been approved by the General Assembly of the United Nations and accepted by a two–thirds majority of the States Parties to the present Covenant in accordance with their respective constitutional processes.

3. When amendments come into force, they shall be binding on those States Parties which have accepted them, other States Parties still being bound by the provisions of the present Covenant and any earlier amendment which they have accepted.

ARTICLE 52

Irrespective of the notifications made under article 48, paragraph 5, the Secretary-General of the United Nations shall inform all States referred to in paragraph 1 of the same article of the following particulars:

(a) Signatures, ratifications and accessions under article 48;

(b) The date of the entry into force of the present Covenant under article 49 and the date of the entry into force of any amendments under article 51.

ARTICLE 53

1. The present Covenant, of which the Chinese, English, French, Russian and Spanish texts are equally authentic, shall be deposited in the archives of the United Nations.

2. The Secretary-General of the United Nations shall transmit certified copies of the present Covenant to all States referred to in article 48.

APPENDIX IV

Convention on the Rights of the Child

Reproduced below are parts of this **Convention** which was adopted by the General Assembly of the United Nations on 20th November, 1989 and came in force on 2nd September, 1990.

Preamble

The States Parties to the Present Convention

Considering that, in accordance with the principles proclaimed in the Charter of the United Nations, recognition of the inherent dignity and of the equal and inalienable rights of all members of the human family is the foundation of freedom, justice and peace in the world,

Bearing in mind that the peoples of the United Nations have, in the Charter, reaffirmed their faith in fundamental human rights and in the dignity and worth of the human person, and have determined to promote social progress and better standards of life in larger freedom,

Recognizing that the United Nations has, in the Universal Declaration of Human Rights and in the International Covenants on Human Rights, proclaimed and agreed that everyone is entitled to all the rights and freedoms set forth therein, without distinction of any kind, such as race, colour, sex, language, religion, political or other opinion, national or social origin, property, birth or other status,

Recalling that, in the Universal Declaration of Human Rights, the United Nations has proclaimed that childhood is entitled to special care and assistance.

Convinced that the family, as the fundamental group of society and the natural environment for the growth and well–being of all its members and particularly children, should be afforded the necessary protection and assistance so that it can fully assume its responsibilities within the community,

Recognizing that the child, for the full and harmonious development of his or her personality, should grow up in a family environment, in an atmosphere of happiness, love and understanding.

Considering that the child should be fully prepared to live an individual life in society, and brought up in the spirit of the ideals proclaimed in the Charter of the United Nations, and in particular in the spirit of peace, dignity, tolerance, freedom, equality and solidarity,

Bearing in mind that the need to extend particular care to the child has been stated in the Geneva Declaration of the Rights of the Child of 1924 and in the Declaration of the Rights of the Child adopted by the General Assembly on 20th November, 1959 and recognized in the Universal Declaration of Human Rights, in the International Covenant on Civil and Political Rights (in particular in Articles 23 and 24), in the International Covenant on Economic, Social and Cultural Rights (in particular in Article 10) and in the statutes and relevant instruments of specialized agencies and international organizations concerned with the welfare of children.

Bearing in mind that, as indicated in the Declaration of the Rights of the Child, "the child, by reason of his physical and mental immaturity, needs special safeguards and care, including appropriate legal protection, before as well as after birth",

Recalling the provisions of the Declaration on Social and Legal Principles relating to the Protection and Welfare of Children, with Special Reference to Foster Placement and Adoption Nationally and Internationally, the United Nations Standard Minimum Rules for the Administration of Juvenile Justice (The Beijing Rules); and the Declaration on the Protection of Women and Children in Emergency and Armed Conflict.

Recognizing that, in all countries in the world, there are children living in exceptionally difficult conditions, and that such children need special consideration.

Taking due account of the importance of the traditions and cultural values of each people for the protection and harmonious development of the child.

Recognizing the importance of International Cooperation for improving the living conditions of children in every country, in particular in the developing countries.

Have agreed as follows:

Part I

ARTICLE 1

For the purposes of the present Convention, a child means every human being below the age of eighteen years unless, under the law applicable to the child, majority is attained earlier.

ARTICLE 2

1. States Parties shall respect and ensure the rights set forth in the present Convention to each child within their jurisdiction without discrimination of any kind, irrespective of the child's or his or her parent's or legal guardian's race, colour, sex, language, religion, political or other opinion, national, ethnic or social origin, property, disability, birth or other status.
2. States Parties shall take all appropriate measures to ensure that the child is protected against all forms of discrimination or punishment on the basis of the status, activities, expressed opinions, or beliefs of the child's parents, legal guardians, or family members.

ARTICLE 3

1. In all actions concerning children, whether undertaken by public or private social welfare institutions, courts of law, administrative authorities or legislative bodies, the best interests of the child shall be a primary consideration.
2. States Parties undertake to ensure the child such protection and care as is necessary for his or her well-being, taking into account the rights and duties of his or her parents, legal guardians, or other

individuals legally responsible for him or her, and, to this end, shall take all appropriate legislative and administrative measures.

ARTICLE 5

States Parties shall respect the responsibilities, rights and duties of parents or, where applicable, the members of the extended family or community as provided for by local custom, legal guardians or other persons legally responsible for the child, to provide, in a manner consistent with the evolving capacities of the child, appropriate direction and guidance in the exercise by the child of the rights recognized in the present Convention.

ARTICLE 6

1. States Parties recognize that every child has the inherent right to life.
2. States Parties shall ensure to the maximum extent possible the survival and development of the child.

ARTICLE 7

1. The child shall be registered immediately after birth and shall have the right from birth to a name, the right to acquire a nationality and, as far as possible, the right to know and be cared for by his or her parents.

ARTICLE 9

1. States Parties shall ensure that a child shall not be separated from his or her parents against their will, except when competent authorities subject to judicial review determine, in accordance with applicable law and procedures, that such separation is necessary for the best interests of the child. Such determination may be necessary in a particular case such as one involving abuse or neglect of the child by the parents, or one where the parents are living separately and a decision must be made as to the child's place of residence.

ARTICLE 11

1. States Parties shall take measures to combat the illicit transfer and non-return of children abroad.

2. To this end, States Parties shall promote the conclusion of bilateral or multilateral agreements or accession to existing agreements.

ARTICLE 12

1. States Parties shall assure to the child who is capable of forming his or her own views the right to express those views freely in all matters affecting the child, the views of the child being given due weight in accordance with the age and maturity of the child.

ARTICLE 13

1. The child shall have the right to freedom of expression; this right shall include freedom to seek, receive and impart information and ideas of all kinds, regardless of frontiers, either orally, in writing or in print, in the form of art, or through any other media of the child's choice.

ARTICLE 14

1. States Parties shall respect the right of the child to freedom of thought, conscience and religion.
2. States Parties shall respect the rights and duties of the parents and, when applicable, legal guardians, to provide direction to the child in the exercise of his or her right in a manner consistent with the evolving capacities of the child.
3. Freedom to manifest ones religion or beliefs may be subject only to such limitations as are prescribed by law and are necessary to protect public safety, order, health or morals, or the fundamental rights and freedoms of others.

ARTICLE 15

1. States Parties recognize the rights of the child to freedom of association and to freedom of peaceful assembly.
2. No restrictions may be placed on the exercise of these rights other than those imposed in conformity with the law and which are necessary in a democratic society in the interests of national security or public safety, public order (*ordre public*), the protection of public health or morals or the protection of the rights and freedoms of others.

ARTICLE 16

1. No child shall be subjected to arbitrary or unlawful interference with his or her privacy, family, home or correspondence, nor to unlawful attacks on his or her honour and reputation.
2. The child has the right to the protection of the law against such interference or attacks.

ARTICLE 17

States Parties recognize the important function performed by the mass media and shall ensure that the child has access to information and material from a diversity of national and international sources, especially those aimed at the promotion of his or her social, spiritual and moral well-being and physical and mental health. To this end, States Parties shall:

(a) encourage the mass media to disseminate information and material of social and cultural benefit to the child and in accordance with the spirit of Article 29;

(b) encourage international cooperation in the production, exchange and dissemination of such information and material from a diversity of cultural, national and international sources;

(c) encourage the production and dissemination of children's books;

(d) encourage the mass media to have particular regard to the linguistic needs of the child who belongs to a minority group or who is indigenous;

(e) encourage the development of appropriate guidelines for the protection of the child from information and material injurious to his or her well-being, bearing in mind the provisions of Articles 13 and 18.

ARTICLE 18

1. States Parties shall use their best efforts to ensure recognition of the principle that both parents have common responsibilities for the upbringing and development of the child. Parents or, as the case may be, legal guardians, have the primary responsibility for the upbringing and development of the child. The best interests of the child will be their basic concern.

2. For the purpose of guaranteeing and promoting the rights set forth in the present Convention, States Parties shall render appropriate assistance to parents and legal guardians in the performance of their child-rearing responsibilities and shall ensure the development of institutions, facilities and services for the care of children.
3. States Parties shall take all appropriate measures to ensure that children of working parents have the right to benefit from child–care services and facilities for which they are eligible.

ARTICLE 19

1. States Parties shall take all appropriate legislative, administrative, social and educational measures to protect the child from all forms of physical or mental violence, injury or abuse, neglect or negligent treatment, maltreatment or exploitation, including sexual abuse, while in the care of parent(s), legal guardian(s) or any other person who has the care of the child.

ARTICLE 20

1. A child temporarily or permanently deprived of his or her family environment, or in whose own best interest cannot be allowed to remain in that environment, shall be entitled to special protection and assistance provided by the State.

ARTICLE 21

1. States Parties that recognize and/or permit the system of adoption shall ensure that the best interests of the child shall be the paramount consideration ......

ARTICLE 23

1. States Parties recognize that a mentally or physically disabled child should enjoy a full and decent life, in conditions which ensure dignity, promote self-reliance and facilitate the child's active participation in the community.
2. States Parties recognize the right of the disabled child to special care and shall encourage and ensure the extension, subject to available resources, to the eligible child and those responsible for his or her care, of assistance for which application is made and

which is appropriate to the child's condition and to the circumstances of the parents or others caring for the child.

3. Recognizing the special needs of a disabled child, assistance extended in accordance with paragraph 2 of the present Article shall be provided free of charge, whenever possible, taking into account the financial resources of the parents or others caring for the child, and shall be designed to ensure that the disabled child has effective access to and receives education, training, health care services, rehabilitation services, preparation for employment and recreation opportunities in a manner conducive to the child's achieving the fullest possible social integration and individual development, including his or her cultural and spiritual development.

4. States Parties shall promote, in the spirit of international cooperation, the exchange of appropriate information in the field of preventive health care and of medical, psychological and functional treatment of disabled children, including dissemination of and access to information concerning methods of rehabilitation, education and vocational services, with the aim of enabling States Parties to improve their capabilities and skills and to widen their experience in these areas. In this regard, particular account shall be taken of the needs of developing countries.

ARTICLE 24

1. States Parties recognize the right of the child to the enjoyment of the highest attainable standard of health and to facilities for the treatment of illness and rehabilitation of health. States Parties shall strive to ensure that no child is deprived of his or her right of access to such health care services.

2. States Parties shall pursue full implementation of this right and, in particular, shall take appropriate measures:

   (a) to diminish infant and child mortality;

   (b) to ensure the provision of necessary medical assistance and health care to all children with emphasis on the development of primary health care;

   (c) to combat disease and malnutrition, including within the

(c) the development of respect for the child's parents, his or her own cultural identity, language and values, for the national values of the country in which the child is living, the country from which he or she may originate, and for civilizations different from his or her own;

(d) the preparation of the child for responsible life in a free society, in the spirit of understanding, peace, tolerance, equality of sexes, and friendship among all peoples, ethnic, national and religious groups and persons of indigenous origin;

(e) the development of respect for the natural environment.

2. No part of the present Article or Article 28 shall be construed so as to interfere with the liberty of individuals and bodies to establish and direct educational institutions, subject always to the observance of the principles set forth in paragraph 1 of the present Article and to the requirements that the education given in such institutions shall conform to such minimum standards as may be laid down by the State.

ARTICLE 30

1. In those States in which ethnic, religious or linguistic minorities or persons of tridigenous origin exist, a child belonging to such a minority or who is indigenous shall not be denied the right, in community with other members of his or her group, to enjoy his or her own culture, to profess and practise his or her own religion, or to use his or her own language.

ARTICLE 31

1. States Parties recognize the right of the child to rest and leisure, to engage in play and recreational activities appropriate to the age of the child and to participate freely in cultural life and the arts.

2. States Parties shall respect and promote the right of the child to participate fully in cultural and artistic life and shall encourage the provision of appropriate and equal opportunities for cultural, artistic, recreational and leisure activity.

ARTICLE 32

1. States Parties recognize the right of the child to be protected from economic exploitation and from performing any work that is likely to be hazardous or to interfere with the child's education, or to be harmful to the child's health or physical, mental, spiritual, moral or social development.

2. States Parties shall take legislative, administrative, social and educational measures to ensure the implementation of the present Article. To this end, and having regard to the relevant provisions of other international instruments. States Parties shall in particular:

   (a) provide for a minimum age or minimum ages for admission to employment;

   (b) provide for appropriate regulations of the hours and conditions of employment;

   (c) provide for appropriate penalties or other sanctions to ensure the effective enforcement of the present Article.

ARTICLE 33

States Parties shall take all appropriate measures, including legislative, administrative, social and educational measures, to protect children from the illicit use of narcotic drugs and psychotropic substances as defined in the relevant international treaties, and to prevent the use of children in the illicit production and trafficking of such substances.

ARTICLE 34

States Parties undertake to protect the child from all forms of sexual exploitation and sexual abuse. For these purposes, States Parties shall in particular take all appropriate national, bilateral and multilateral measures to prevent:

(a) the inducement or coercion of a child to engage in any unlawful sexual activity;

(b) the exploitative use of children in prostitution or other unlawful sexual practices;

(c) the exploitative use of children in pornographic performances and materials.

ARTICLE 35

States Parties shall take all appropriate national, bilateral and multilateral measures to prevent the abduction of, the sale of or traffic in children for any purpose or in any form.

ARTICLE 36

States Parties shall protect the child against all other forms of exploitation prejudicial to any aspects of the child's welfare.

ARTICLE 37

States Parties shall ensure that:

(a) no child shall be subjected to torture or other cruel, inhuman or degrading treatment or punishment Neither capital punishment nor life imprisonment without possibility of release shall be imposed for offenses committed by persons below eighteen years of age;

(b) no child shall be deprived of his or her liberty unlawfully or arbitrarily. The arrest, detention or imprisonment of a child shall be in conformity with the law and shall be used only as a measure of last resort and for the shortest appropriate period of time;

(c) every child deprived of liberty shall be treated with humanity and respect for the inherent dignity of the human person, and in a manner which takes into account the needs of persons of his or her age. In particular, every child deprived of liberty shall be separated from adults unless it is considered in the child's best interest not to do so and shall have the right to maintain contract with his or her family through correspondence and visits, save in exceptional circumstances;

(d) every child deprived of his or her liberty shall have the right to prompt access to legal and other appropriate assistance, as well as the right to challenge the legality of the deprivation of his or her liberty before a court or other competent, independent and impartial authority, and to a prompt decision on any such action.

ARTICLE 38

1. States Parties undertake to respect and to ensure respect for rules of international humanitarian law applicable to them in armed conflicts which are relevant to the child.
2. States Parties shall take all feasible measures to ensure that persons who have not attained the age of fifteen years do not take a direct part in hostilities.
3. States Parties shall refrain from recruiting any person who has not attained the age of fifteen years into their armed forces...
4. In accordance with their obligations under international humanitarian law to protect the civilian population in armed conflicts, States Parties shall take all feasible measures to ensure protection and care of children who are affected by an armed conflict.

ARTICLE 39

1. States Parties shall take all appropriate measures to promote physical and psychological recovery and social reintegration of a child victim of : any form of neglect, exploitation, or abuse; torture or any other form of cruel, inhuman or degrading treatment or punishment; or armed conflicts. Such recovery and reintegration shall take place in an environment which fosters the health, self-respect and dignity of the child.

Part 2

ARTICLE 42

1. States Parties undertake to make the principles and provisions of the Convention widely known, by appropriate and active means, to adults and children alike.

APPENDIX V

Status of International Instruments Relating to Human Rights (As on 31st December, 1997)

International Instruments (Date of Entry into Force)	*Total No. of States Parties*	*Total No. of Asian States*	*Ratification Accession Notification of Succession Acceptance etc. by Asian States*
1. International Covenant on Economic, Social and Cultural Rights (3rd January, 1976)	137	22	Afghanistan, Azerbaijan, Cambodia, India, Iran, Iraq, Japan, Jordan, Democratic People's Republic of Korea (North) Kuwait, Kyrgyzstan, Lebanon, Mongolia, Nepal, Sri Lanka, Philippines, Republic of Korea (South), Syria, Turkmenistan, Uzbekistan, Vietnam, Yemen.
2. International Covenant on Civil and Political Rights (23rd March, 1976)*	140	22	Afghanistan, Azerbaijan, Cambodia, India, Iran, Iraq, Japan, Jordan, Democratic People's Republic or Korea (North), Kuwait, Kyrgyzstan, Lebanon, Mongolia, Nepal, Sri Lanka, Philippines, Republic of Korea (South), Syria, Thailand, Uzbekistan, Vietnam, Yemen.
3. Optional Protocol to International Covenant on Civil and Political Rights (23rd March, 1976)	93	7	Kyrgzstan, Republic ofKorea (South), Mongolia, Nepal, Philippines, Thailand, Uzbekistan.

* Following 40 State-parties have so far made declarations recognising the competence of Human Rights Committee under Article 41 of the Covenant : Algeria, Argentina, Austria, Australia, Belarus, Belgium, Canada, Chile, Congo, Denmark, Ecuador, Finland, The Gambia, Germany, Guyana, Hungary, Iceland, Italy, Luxembourg, Malta, The Netherlands, New Zealand, Norway, Peru, The Philippines, Poland, Republic of Korea, Senegal, Slavenia, Spain, Sri Lanka, Sweden, Switzerland, Tunisia, Ukraine, USA, UK and Zambia, Bosnia-Herzegovina.

International Instruments (Date of Entry into Force)	*Total No. of States Parties*	*Total No. of Asian States*	*Ratification Accession Notification of Succession Acceptance etc. by Asian States*
4. Second Optional Protocol to the International Co-venant on Civil and Political Rights aiming at the aboli-tion of the death penalty	31	Nil	
5. Convention on the Prevention and Punishment of the Crime of Genocide (12th January, 1951)	124	30	Afghanistan, Azerbaijan, China, Cambodia, Democratic People's Republic of Korea (North), Fiji, India, Iran, Iraq, Israel, Jordan, Kyrgzstan, Laos, Lebanon, Maldives, Mongolia, Malaysia, Myanmar, Nepal, Pakistan, Papua New Guinea, Republic of Korea (South) Singapore, South Vietnam, Philippines, Saudi Arabia, Sri Lanka, Syria, Vietnam.
6. Convention on the Non-Availability of Statutory Limitations to War Crimes and Crimes Against Humanity (11th November, 1970)	43	10	Afghanistan, Azerbaijan, India, Laos, Mongolia, Philippines, Democratic People's Republic of Korea (North), Kuwait, Vietnam, Yemen.
7. International Convention on the Elimination of All Form of Racial Discriminations (4th January, 1969)*	150	31	Afghanistan, Azerbaijan, Bangladesh, China, Cambodia, Fiji, India, Iran, Iraq, Israel, Japan, Jordan, Kuwait, Laos, Lebanon, Maldives, Mongolia, Nepal, Pakistan, Papua New Guinea, Philippines, Qatar, Republic of Korea, Sri Lanka, Syria, Tajikistan, Turkministan, United Arab Emirates, Uzbekistan, Vietnam.

* Following 19 State-parties have so far made declarations recognising the competence of the Committee on the Elimination of Racial Discrimination under Article 14 of the Convention : Algeria, Australia, Bulgaria, Costa Rica, Denmark, Ecuador, France, Hungary, Iceland, Italy, Netherlands, Norway, Peru, Russian Federation, Senegal, Sweden, Ukrain and Uruguay, Cyprus.

International Instruments (Date of Entry into Force)	*Total No. of States Parties*	*Total No. of Asian States*	*Ratification Accession Notification of Succession Acceptance etc. by Asian States*
8. Convention Relating to the Status of Refugees (22nd April, 1954)	131	13	Azerbaijan, China, Cambodia, Fiji, Iran, Israel, Japan, Kyrgzstan, Philippines, Papua New Guinea, RepublicofKorea, Singapore, Yemen.
9. Protocol Relating to the Status of Refugees (4th October, 1967)	130	13	Azerbaijan, Cambodia, Fiji, Iran, Israel, Japan, Kyrgyzstan, Papua New Guinea, Philippines, Republic of Korea (South), Tajikistan, Yemen.
10. Convention Relating to the Status of Stateless Persons (6th June, 1960)	44	4	Azerbaijan, Fiji, Israel, Republic of Korea (South).
11. Convention on the Reduction of Statelessness (13th December, 1975)	19	1	Azerbaijan
12. Convention on the Political Rights of Women (7th July, 1954)	110	17	Afghanistan, Azerbaijan, Fiji, India, Indonesia, Israel, Japan, Jordan, Republic of Korea (South). Kuwait, Kyrgyzstan, Laos, Lebanon, Mongolia, Nepal, Pakistan, Philippines, Papua New Guinea, Thailand, Uzbekistan, Yemen.
13. Convention on the Nationality of Married Women (11th August, 1958)	66	7	Azerbaijan, Fiji, Israel, Jordan, Malaysia, Singapore, Sri Lanka.
14. Convention on the Consent to Marriage, Minimum Age for Marriage and Registration of Marriages (9th December, 1954)	47	6	Azerbaijan, Fiji, Jordan, Mongolia, Philippines, Yemen.
15. Slavery Convention of 1926	35	11	Afghanistan, Azerbaijan, Bangladesh, Fiji, India, Iraq, Israel, Lebanon, Myanmar, Nepal, Syria.

International Instruments (Date of Entry into Force)	*Total No. of States Parties*	*Total No. of Asian States*	*Ratification Accession Notification of Succession Acceptance etc. by Asian States*
16. Protocol Amending the Slavery Convention (7th December, 1953)	59	9	Afghanistan, Azerbaijan, Bangladesh, Fiji, India, Iraq, Israel, Myanmar, Syria.
17. Slavery Convention of 1926 as amended in 1953 (7th July, 1955)	94	18	Afghanistan, Bangladesh, Fiji, India, Iraq, Israel, Jordan, Kuwait, Mongolia, Myanmar, Nepal, Philippines, Papua New Guinea, Pakistan, Saudi Arabia, Sri Lanka, Syria, Yemen.
18. Supplementary Convention on the Abolition of Slavery, the Slave Trade and Institutions and Practices similar to Slavery (30th April, 1957)	117	21	Afghanistan, Azerbaijan, Bangladesh, Cambodia, Fiji, India, Iran, Iraq, Israel, Jordan, Kuwait, Laos, Malaysia, Mongolia, Nepal, Pakistan, Philippines, Saudi Arabia, Singapore, Sri Lanka, Syria.
19. Convention for the Suppression of the Traffic in Persons and of the Exploitation of the Prostitution of Others (25th July, 1951)	72	17	Afghanistan, Azerbaijan, Bangladesh, India, Iraq, Israel, Japan, Jordan, Kuwait, Laos, Pakistan, Republic of Korea (South), Philippines, Singapore, Sri Lanka, Syria, Yemen.
20. International Convention on the Suppression and Punishment of the Crime of Apartheid (18th July, 1976)	101	22	Afghanistan, Azerbaijan, Bangladesh, Cambodia, China, India, Iran, Iraq, Jordan, Kuwait, Laos, UAE, Maldives, Mongolia, Pakistan, Nepal, Philippines, Qatar, Sri Lanka, Syria, Vietnam, Yemen.
21. Convention on the Elimination of All Forms of Discrimination Against Women (3rd September, 1981)	161	28	Azerbaijan, Bangladesh, Bhutan, China, Cambodia, Fiji, India, Indonesia, Iraq, Israel, Japan, Jordan, Kyrgyzstan, Laos, Malaysia, Maldives, Mongolia, Nepal, Pakistan, Philippines, Republic of Korea (South), Singapore, Sri Lanka, Tajikistan, Thailand, Uzbekistan, Vietnam.

International Instruments (Date of Entry into Force)	*Total No. of States Parties*	*Total No. of Asian States*	*Ratification Accession Notification of Succession Acceptance etc. by Asian States*
22. Convention Against Torture and Other Cruel, Inhuman or Degrading Treat-ment or Punish-ment (26th June, 1987)*	104	15	Afghanistan, Azerbaijan, Cambodia, China, Israel, Jordan, Republic of Korea (South), Kuwait, Myanmar, Nepal, Philippines, Qatar, Sri Lanka, Uzbekistan, Yemen.
23. International Convention Against Apartheid in Sports (3rd April, 1988)	57	10	India, Indonesia, Iran, Iraq, Jordan, Mongolia, Nepal, Philippines, Qatar, Syria.
24. Convention on the Rights of the Child (2nd September, 1990)	191	39	Afghanistan, Azerbaijan, Bangladesh, Bhutan, Cambodia, China, Democratic People's Republic of Korea (North), Fiji, India, Indonesia, Iran, Iraq, Israel, Japan, Jordan, Kazakstan, Republic of Korea (South), Kuwait, Kyrgyzstan, Laos, Lebanon, Malaysia, Maldives, Mongolia, Myanmar, Nepal, Pakistan, Papua New Guinea, The Philippines, Saudi Arabia, Singapore, Sri Lanka, Syria, Turkmenistan, UAE, Uzbekistan, Vietnam, Yemen.

* Following 36 State-parties have so far made declarations recognising the competence of the Committee Against Torture under Articles 21 and 22 of the Convention : Algeria, Argentina, Austria, Australia, Bulgaria, Canada, Croatia, Cyprus, Denmark, Ecuador, Finland, France, Germany, Greece, Hungary, Italy, Leichtenstein, Luxembourg, Malta, Monaco, Netherlands, New Zealand, Norway, Portugal, Poland, Russian Federation, Spain, Sweden, Switzerland, Slovenia, Togo, Tunisia, Turkey, UK, Uruguay, Yugoslavia.

INDEX